CORPORATE CULTURE AND ORGANIZATIONAL EFFECTIVENESS

Corporate Culture and Organizational Effectiveness

Daniel R. Denison

WILEY

JOHN WILEY & SONS

New York • Chichester • Brisbane • Toronto • Singapore

This publication is designed to provide accurate and
authoritative information in regard to the subject
matter covered. It is sold with the understanding that
the publisher is not engaged in rendering legal, accounting,
or other professional service. If legal advice or other
expert assistance is required, the services of a competent
professional person should be sought. *From a Declaration
of Principles jointly adopted by a Committee of the
American Bar Association and a Committee of Publishers.*

Library of Congress Cataloging-in-Publication Data

Denison, Daniel R.
  Corporate culture and organizational effectiveness / Daniel R.
Denison.
    p.   cm. — (Wiley series on organizational assessment and
change)
  Includes bibliographical references.
  ISBN 0-471-80021-X
  1. Corporate culture.   2. Organizational effectiveness.
I. Title.   II. Series.
HD58.7.D46   1990
302.3'5—dc20
                                                        89-27938
                                                            CIP

Printed and bound in the United States of America

10 9 8 7 6 5 4

For Graciela and Roland

Series Preface

The ORGANIZATIONAL ASSESSMENT AND CHANGE SERIES is concerned with informing and furthering contemporary debate on the effectiveness of work organizations and the quality of life they provide for their members. Of particular relevance is the adaptation of work organizations to changing social aspirations and economic constraints. There has been a phenomenal growth of interest in employee involvement and organizational effectiveness in recent years. Issues that not long ago were the quiet concern of a few academics and a few leaders in unions and management have become issues of broader public interest. They have intruded upon broadcast media prime time, lead newspaper and magazine columns, the houses of Congress, and the board rooms of both firms and unions.

A thorough discussion of what organizations should be like and how they can be improved must comprehend many issues. Some are concerned with basic moral and ethical questions—What is the responsibility of an organization to its employees?—What, after all, is a "good job"?—How should it be decided that some might benefit from and others pay for gains in the quality of work life?—Should there be a public policy on the matter? Yet others are concerned with the strategies and tactics of bringing about changes in organizational life, the advocates of alternative approaches being numerous, vocal, and controversial; and still others are concerned with the task of measurement and assessment on grounds that the choices to be made by leaders, the assessment of consequences, and the bargaining of equities must be informed by reliable, comprehensive, and relevant information of kinds not now readily available.

The WILEY SERIES ON ORGANIZATIONAL ASSESSMENT AND CHANGE is concerned with all aspects of the debate on how organizations should be managed, changed, and controlled. It includes books that are concerned with organizational effectiveness, and the study of organizational changes that represent new approaches to organization design and management. The volumes in the series have in common a concern with work organizations, a focus on change and the dynamics of change, an assumption that diverse social and personal interests need to be taken into account in discussions of organizational effectiveness, and a view that concrete cases and quantitative data are essential ingredients in a lucid debate. As such, these books consider a broad but integrated set of issues and ideas. They are intended to be read by managers, union officials, researchers, consultants, policy makers, students, and others seriously concerned with organizational assessment and change.

The present volume reports on an important study that uses innovative research to analyze the relationship between corporate culture and organizational performance. It presents new data showing that corporate culture does make a difference in organizational performance. For the first time, solid, empirical data indicate that employee involvement approaches to management yield better financial performance across a wide range of corporations. The book not only reports overall correlations between culture and performance but also demonstrates through case studies of five companies how culture affects performance. Overall this book makes solid contributions to research, theory, and practice and thus adds a great deal to our knowledge of organizational effectiveness and organizational change.

EDWARD E. LAWLER, III
STANLEY E. SEASHORE

Los Angeles, California

Preface

Mergers, declining productivity, and global competition all have focused attention on the cultures of organizations and the impact that they have on adaptation and effectiveness. Despite a decade of attention to this topic, we still do not know very much about it. On one hand, the academic and research literature has examined the unique aspects of organizational cultures, but has resisted the temptation to generalize about topics so broad as culture and effectivenss. On the other hand, the popular business literature has raised awareness about the cultural aspects of business, but has yet to present convincing evidence to support their assertions and recommendations.

This book asks the question, ''What are the ways in which the culture of an organization can influence its effectiveness?'' The answer provided in this book comes in the form of a new way of thinking about culture and effectiveness, backed up by research evidence. The culture and effectiveness model presented here is rooted in the organizational literature, and is supported by both a quantitative and a qualitative study. Even though the emphasis in this volume is on the development of the conceptual model and the presentation of evidence about the relationship between culture and effectiveness, the book is written for a broad audience that includes academic colleagues, researchers and consultants, and managers and executives.

Chapter 1 introduces the culture and effectiveness model and discusses its implications for managing human resources. This chapter also sets the stage for the quantitative and qualitative studies presented later in the book. Chapter 2 begins by reviewing some past attempts at studying culture and effectiveness, arguing that there is a substantive similarity but a methodological difference with earlier research on organizational climate. The chapter attempts to synthesize the research on climate with the research on culture, and points out the advantages offered by each research paradigm.

Chapter 3 follows with a detailed description of the data and research design used for the qualitative study: the behavioral data, the financial data, the sample of companies, and the analysis plan. Chapter 4 presents the quantitative results of the study. Primary attention is given to various components of involvement and adaptability such as decision making, work organization, and leadership, as well as other areas such as job design. This chapter also examines the relationship between the unit of analysis in the survey (system, leader, or work group) and the lag time over which performance can be predicted. In addition, this chapter examines the impact of two other cultural features: the consistency of the culture in each of the organizations and the ideal visions of leadership that the members of each organization hold.

Chapter 5 begins the case study section of the book and serves as both a challenge and a complement to the quantitative findings presented in Chapter 4. The chapter begins with a critique of the quantitative approach taken in Chapter 4 and a rationale for combining case studies and comparative research. This chapter also presents the logic by which five firms were selected for case studies which would analyze the organization's culture from a historical and evolutionary perspective.

Chapter 6 presents the first case study, Medtronic, Inc., which is the leading producer of cardiovascular pacemakers. This chapter introduces the basic format by which each of the case studies will be presented: an analysis of the history and background, a discussion of the current culture and management practices, and an analysis of the effectiveness of the organization. The Medtronic case study, like each of the others, ends with an analysis of the organization from the perspective of the culture and effectiveness model and a discussion of the lessons about culture offered by the case.

The case study in Chapter 7 examines People Express Airlines. This organization presents an excellent example of the creation of a new organization, and the creation of a distinctive culture by a charismatic leader. The People Express case also provides a glimpse of a very innovative organization that applied many progressive approaches to human resource management.

Detroit Edison, the third case study, is an electric utility in southeastern Michigan. This case, in Chapter 8, provides an example of the evolution of a culture over a period of decades and of the inertia that a traditional culture acquires. Chapter 9 follows with a case study of Procter & Gamble, the premier consumer goods company in Cincinnati, Ohio. Procter & Gamble also has a history measured in decades and a culture that has evolved over many years. The organization has been highly successful, and many of those interviewed attributed this success directly to the organization's culture.

In Chapter 10, the final case study focuses on Texas Commerce Banc-shares, a large bank holding company in Houston. Texas Commerce also has a long history, a compelling and charismatic leader, and an excellent record of performance that has been threatened only recently by the crisis in the Texas economy.

The final chapter summarizes what has been learned from this research. The original theory is revisited and discussed in light of both the comparative data and the case studies, and conclusions are drawn in terms of a set of recommendations about studying culture and effectiveness. Finally, the book ends by discussing the implications that these ideas have for managers and executives.

DANIEL R. DENISON

Ann Arbor, Michigan
November 1989

Acknowledgments

The idea to write this book began near the end of the oral examination for my doctoral dissertation. As the conversation turned to the ways in which the research might be published, my advisor Stanley Seashore paused, puffed his pipe, and in his inimitable *basso profundo* suggested that it be published "intact." Now realizing how much work it would take to do that right, I was elated.

My original plan was to prepare a brief revision of the dissertation and publish the book in a few months. Fortunately, this plan was interrupted by J. Richard Hackman. He made the simple yet powerful suggestion that I pick some organizations that fit the pattern of high involvement and high performance, which the dissertation had identified, and compare them to some organizations that did not fit the pattern. By doing clinical case studies, I could find out what actually happened and broaden my theory of organizational culture and effectiveness. So my plans changed, and I began to visualize a book that was 80 percent based on my dissertation with 20 percent revision.

Presenting this work to academic and business colleagues always generated spirited discussion about the theoretical model I was using to study culture and effectiveness. Mike Beer and Bob Quinn, in particular, made comments that led me to rethink and revise the culture and effectiveness model several times, which improved it significantly. These changes, coupled with the realization that the case studies were more complicated and more interesting than I had anticipated, altered my plans again. Instead of 80 percent dissertation and 20 percent revision, I was now closer to 20 percent dissertation and 80 percent revision!

At various points along the way, many other colleagues guided my revisions. Series editors Ed Lawler and Stan Seashore provided valuable comments on several drafts, and combined patience and encouragement along with some helpful prodding. Stewart Black, Bob Dvorin, Goran Ekvall, Stuart Hart, Doug Henderson, Susan Jackson, Michael O'Driscoll, Robert Quinn, and Karl Weick read all or part of the manuscript at

xiii

critical points and gave me useful direction and encouragement. Bill McCaughrin and other students in a Contemporary Organizational Theory seminar I taught in 1987 also gave me useful reactions and insights.

Many managers and executives contributed generously of their time and insight. Several hundred were interviewed for the five case studies in this book, and a number of them have read and commented on the manuscript. Ben Love, chairman of Texas Commerce Bancshares, and Don Burr, past chairman of People Express Airlines, made detailed comments on the sections I wrote about their companies. Their efforts improved my knowledge and portrayal of their companies and sometimes my writing style as well.

Many other colleagues also supported my efforts with patience and encouragement. In particular, Dave Bowers, Bob Kahn, and Noel Tichy, members of my original dissertation committee, helped see this project through to completion. I am also grateful for the financial support provided during the summer of 1988 by the University of Michigan Business School, which enabled me to finish this book. Aneil Mishra helped proofread and critique and searched for hours to make certain references were correct. Sher Foutch, Mary Hardy, and Christi Bemister of the Business School did outstanding work on wordprocessing, and Dave Fischer did beautiful work on the graphics. Finally, to my family and friends go my sincere thanks and appreciation for all the support you have offered. I am grateful to you all.

The strengths of this book can be attributed to this highly valued collection of colleagues and friends. For the flaws, however, I alone must claim responsibility.

D.R.D.

Contents

CORPORATE CULTURE
AND
ORGANIZATIONAL
EFFECTIVENESS

CHAPTER ONE

Corporate Culture and Organizational Effectiveness

The 1980s witnessed an unprecedented event in the field of organizational studies and management. Summaries of the field have become best-sellers and have made a significant mark on management practices and the general public. This trend began with two books that examined the challenges that Japan posed for American industry, *Theory Z* (Ouchi 1981) and *The Art of Japanese Management* (Pascale and Athos 1981). The trend continued with two books that focused more closely on American industry itself, *Corporate Cultures* (Deal and Kennedy 1982) and *The Change Masters* (Kanter 1983), and reached an early peak with the book that perhaps best exemplifies this trend, *In Search of Excellence* (Peters and Waterman 1982). Both popular and academic authors have continued to produce a string of books that focus on management and have captured our attention throughout the decade.

These books present a different picture of management from that usually offered by the strategists, financiers, and marketers who have traditionally run American corporations. Rather than assume, as many have, that large corporations are simply "black boxes" that respond to external markets and regulatory forces and can be run solely on financial criteria, these authors have concentrated on what might be called the "behavioral side" of management and organization. They have argued that the difference between successful and not-so-successful organizations rests with the values and principles that underlie their internal organization. This group of authors has emphasized a set of elusive, "soft" variables that are usually regarded as important, but are often seen as having little direct and predictable impact on the fate of an organization.

Organizational culture is the term that has come to comprise this set of behavioral variables that have drawn so much attention. "Culture" refers to the underlying values, beliefs, and principles that serve as a foundation for an organization's management system as well as the set of management practices and behaviors that both exemplify and reinforce those basic principles. These principles and practices endure because they have meaning for the members of an organization. They represent strategies for survival that have worked well in the past and that the members believe will work again in the future. Thus, a cultural theory of organizational effectiveness must take as its starting point the observation that the values, beliefs, and meanings that underlie a social system are the primary source of motivated and coordinated activity.

The authors who address this topic represent a curious mix of academics and consultants, and the research they do has usually involved close collaboration with the managers and organizations they studied. Each of these works is rooted, to some degree, within the academic discipline of organizational behavior and organizational theory, although the research could not, strictly speaking, be called academic. The "evidence" most often consists of stories and anecdotes that are entertaining but not always convincing. Each book seems to rise and fall based on the author's insight, intuitive ability to integrate and simplify, and talent at turning a phrase. Very few data have been presented to support their contentions.

None of these studies, for example, have followed a pattern of first formulating a set of criteria that would capture their "theory" of what makes organizations tick, and then going out to gather some information to see if they were right or wrong. This disregard for the criteria of "normal science" represents both a strength and a weakness of these studies. Unencumbered by research designs, instruments, and procedures, they breathe life into the organizations that they study in a laudable fashion that is nearly unprecedented for those who write about management and organizations. Nonetheless, without some basis for comparing organizations at arm's length, it is difficult, if not impossible, for a reader to decide if he or she is convinced by the author's evidence or the author's arguments. A position of advocacy, rather than inquiry, further clouds the issue.

This problem is heightened because only "exemplary" organizations were included in most of the studies listed above. None of these authors studied firms that failed or did poorly, and none used a framework that contrasted failures and successes. Presumably, if a ''theory'' is correct, the factors that contribute to success should also serve to separate successful and unsuccessful firms. Several critics of *In Search of Excellence* have pointed out these shortcomings (Carroll 1983) and documented the many cases in which companies with the characteristics of ''excellence'' did not, in fact, perform well over time (Who's Excellent Now?   1984). Without a systematic test of the relationship between culture and effectiveness, the answer will continue to remain unclear.

The theory and research presented in this book address this problem of ''no evidence'' by taking both a qualitative and a quantitative approach to studying the impact that organizational culture can have on performance and effectiveness over time. The research is presented in two parts. The first part takes a quantitative approach and relies on a research design, standardized instrumentation, and a set of research procedures, applied in a comparable fashion to a set of 34 organizations. The results are presented as a set of statistical generalizations about the impact of various aspects of an organization's culture on performance over time. The second part examines 5 of these 34 organizations in considerable detail through a series of case studies that focus on the history and background of each corporation, and the firm's culture, management practices, and effectiveness. The quantitative and qualitative approaches are used both to build and to test a general theory of organizational culture and effectiveness.

The study shows that organizational culture has a close relationship to the effectiveness of these companies. The quantitative results show that behavioral measures gathered through survey research can be strong predictors of the future financial performance of these organizations. The case studies, in contrast, trace the roots of each organization's current culture through the firm's historical development and then analyze both the constraints and the competitive advantage that the culture appears to offer. The combination of these two approaches helps to provide both quantitative evidence and qualitative understanding about the relationship between culture and effectiveness.

This study shows that a comparative framework can be used successfully to study the impact of corporate culture on performance and effectiveness, and that the case method and comparative method are quite compatible when applied jointly to develop and test a useful theory. This approach also suggests that any of the authors noted above could have used a comparative approach to generate evidence that would support (or perhaps disconfirm) their ideas.

This approach also seems to hold the promise of addressing both the problems of theory and the problems of application. In order to apply theories of organizational behavior, current and future managers and executives need evidence that the ideas work, as well as qualitative understanding of how and why they do. In order to develop the best theories, researchers need to have their theories continually tested in the real world on a broad scale. The best research should attempt to combine rationality and intuition in a way that makes the strongest case for both theory and action.

The most important point raised by this book, however, is not one of method, or approach, or the quality of evidence. These issues are important, but they should not detract from the subject at hand—the close relationship between the culture of an organization, its management practices, and its future performance and effectiveness. The book begins with a simple theory that serves as a framework for the presentation and discussion of the results.

A Theory of Organizational Culture and Effectiveness

Much of the published research on organizational culture has emphasized the central importance of the values and beliefs that lie at the core of an organization's social system. The most frequent topics of interest have been the ways in which organizations develop and maintain these central values and the behaviors that accompany them, or the manner in which these values and behaviors are transmitted to new members of an organization (Sathe 1983; Schein 1985; Louis 1980). Two of the most prominent management journals have helped develop a consensus regarding the concept by presenting special issues on organizational culture. These have helped to define the meaning of the term, the relevant issues it raises, and the emerging research style and agenda (Jelinek, Smircicw, and Hirsch 1983; Organizational Dynamics 1983). Few publications, however, have explored the interrelations of an organization's culture, its management practices, and its performance and effectiveness. The few exceptions (Wilkins and Ouchi 1983; Martin, Sitkin, and Boehm 1985; Denison 1984; Gordon 1985) represent a small minority of published studies.

Linking management practices with underlying assumptions and beliefs is an important but often neglected step in the study of organizational culture and effectiveness. The values and beliefs of an organization give rise to a set of management practices—concrete activities that are usually rooted in the values of the organization. These activities stem from and reinforce the dominant values and beliefs of the organization. Concrete policies and practices are often difficult to separate from the core values and beliefs and the system of shared meaning that supports them. This is part of the reason why organizational culture often seems to be both mystical and practical at the same time.[1]

Furthermore, most of the implicit ideas about the relationship between culture and effectiveness presented to date have attributed the success of organizations to some combination of values and beliefs, policies and practices, and the relationship between the two. These ideas suggest a general framework such as the one presented in Figure 1.1. Within this general framework, there are several ways that the relationship between culture and effectiveness might be viewed.

Effectiveness (or lack of it) is a function of the values and beliefs held by the members of an organization. Specific values, or agreement on specific values, influence effectiveness. This idea is perhaps the most mystical ex-

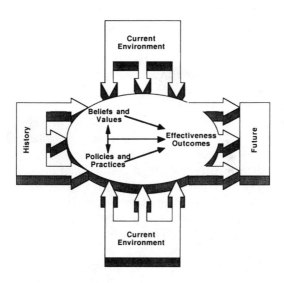

Figure 1.1 A framework for studying organizational culture and effectiveness

---

[1]Cambridge sociologist Anthony Giddens (1979), for example, has studied the relationship between social structure and meaning and has argued that structure cannot be said to exist without taking into account the meaning that the structure has for the individuals who are conscious of the structure and affected by it. A similar argument can be made with regard to organizational culture—core beliefs and values and concrete policies and practices are often two sides of the same coin.

planation of why an organization's culture should affect its perform-ance. Nonetheless, strongly held beliefs, a sense of mission, or the consistency that comes from a set of shared values and beliefs do pro-vide a fundamental basis for coordinated action within an organization.

Effectiveness is a function of the policies and practices used by an organiza-tion. Specific practices, particularly as they pertain to the management of human resources and the internal environment of a firm, influence performance and effectiveness. Certain ways of resolving conflict, plan-ning a strategy, designing work, or making decisions will result in better performance in the short or long run.

Effectiveness is a function of translating the core values and beliefs into poli-cies and practices in a consistent manner. The "vision" of a leader must be operationalized through action. Building a "strong culture" implies that values and actions are highly consistent. This form of consistency often has been mentioned as a source of organizational strength and as a way of improving performance and effectiveness.

Effectiveness is a function of the interrelation of core values and beliefs, orga-nizational policies and practices, and the business environment of the organiza-tion. Thus, no generalizations can be made about culture and effective-ness that do not incorporate the relation of the culture to the business environment. Particular environments may, over time, create a particu-lar type of culture, or may require a particular type of culture for an organization to survive. Rather than propose hypotheses about the spe-cific concepts in Figure 1.1 or about the specific relationships among these concepts, this book focuses on four integrative principles that ad-dress the interrelationships proposed by the diagram. Drawing on both the popular and the academic literature, the principles describe a proc-ess by which an organization's culture influences its effectiveness. For the purposes of this discussion, I have labeled them "hypotheses"—the *involvement* hypothesis, the *consistency* hypothesis, the *adaptability* hy-pothesis, and the *mission* hypothesis. Each is discussed below, and a summary combines them into a single framework describing the rela-tionship between organizational culture and effectiveness.

The Involvement Hypothesis

Involvement appears as a key factor in the cultures of each of the cases presented in this book. People Express Airlines probably provides the best example of a high-involvement culture: All of the employees were considered managers, charged with managing the assets of the firm. "Self-management" implied that all individuals were responsible for managing themselves. Stock ownership and profit sharing were an integral part of the compensation system. The structure relied on an informal rather than a formal control system. In addition, a number of the leadership roles in the organization were *elected*. The case, presented in Chapter 7, explores in detail the role of the culture in the growth and decline of the airline.

The involvement hypothesis about the relationship between organizational culture and effectiveness is not really a new idea. It has many precedents in the organizational behavior literature and has gone by many names other than organizational culture. The central idea—that organizational effectiveness is a function of the level of involvement and participation of an organization's members—stems most directly from human relations theory.

The hypothesis argues that high levels of involvement and participation create a sense of ownership and responsibility. Out of this ownership grows a greater commitment to an organization and a lesser need for an overt control system. Voluntary and implicit normative systems ensure the coordination of behavior, rather than explicit bureaucratic control systems.

This hypothesis is grounded in many of the classics of organizational behavior. Chris Argyris's early work *Integrating the Individual and the Organization* (1964), Rensis Likert's *New Patterns of Management* (1961), and Douglas McGregor's *The Human Side of Enterprise* (1960) all emphasize the principles of involvement, participation, and integration. Many of the same themes sounded in these early works have echoed loudly in the 1980s.

More recent work on high-involvement organizations by Walton (1977, 1986) and Lawler (1977, 1986) also present a similar line of argument: involvement can be both a management strategy for effective performance and a worker strategy for a better work environment. These authors also focus more on the actual structures and strategies for forming and sustaining a high-involvement system. The high-involvement organizations hold a great deal of promise, but also run the risk of failure when those conditions are not met. The "chain" of involvement is only as strong as its weakest link.

Ouchi (1981) described high-involvement organizations as having the characteristics of a "clan" rather than a formal bureaucracy. He also discussed the clan concept of organization with reference to the economist Williamson's distinction between markets and hierarchies (Williamson 1975; Williamson & Ouchi 1981). Williamson initially contrasted markets, where transactions are governed solely by the laws of supply and demand, with hierarchies (his term for a bureaucracy) in an effort to develop a rational theory of organization boundaries. Formal organizations develop, he argued, whenever the transaction costs associated with a particular exchange surpass the benefits associated with the efficiencies of a market.[2]

Ouchi (1980) also argued that in a clan organization transactions are governed primarily by values, beliefs, norms, and traditions. Organizations with high levels of inclusion, involvement, and participation could thus rely on a management system that capitalized on emergent consensus. Transaction costs can be minimized when each member of an organization acts from an intuitive value consensus rather than from a set of bureaucratic rules and regulations. The familiar contrast between the litigious nature of American pluralism and the consensual efficiency of Japanese society serves to underscore this principle.

For all the attention that the different forms of the involvement hypothesis have received, it has relatively little supporting evidence. Recent reviews of the participation literature (Locke and Schweiger 1979; Miller and Monge 1986) in fact concluded that there was, in most cases, only a modest relationship between participation and performance. Nonetheless, the hypothesis is a compelling one and persists as a central element in this theory of organizational culture and effectiveness.

The Consistency Hypothesis

A consistency theory about the relationship between organizational culture and effectiveness presents a somewhat different perspective. This explanation, in its popular version, emphasizes the positive impact that a "strong culture" can have on effectiveness and argues that a shared system of beliefs, values, and symbols, widely understood by an organization's members, has a positive impact on their ability to reach consensus and carry out coordinated actions. The fundamental concept is that implicit control systems, based on internalized values, are a more effective means of achieving coordination than external control systems that rely on explicit rules and regulations (Weick 1985, 1987).

Procter & Gamble and Texas Commerce Bancshares both provide excellent examples of highly consistent cultures. The description of these companies, presented in Chapters 9 and 10, shows that they have

---

[2]To illustrate this principle, consider two examples: When purchasing key raw materials, most organizations accept the costs of negotiating transactions with external suppliers in return for the efficiencies of market competition, and decide to buy from the "outside." In contrast, long-term employment contracts recognize that negotiating all work interactions with a network of "free agents" would be highly inefficient, and thus construct an organization (hierarchy or bureaucracy in Williamson's terms) favoring minimized transaction costs rather than the efficiency and flexibility of a market.

highly committed employees, key central values, a distinctive method of doing business, a tendency to promote from within, and a clear set of "do's and don'ts." These characteristics help create a strong culture that is well understood by the members of the organization. Employees interviewed in both of these organizations saw a close relationship among their strong culture, a methodical approach to doing business, and the successes and setbacks their organizations have experienced.

A number of authors (Frost, Moore, Louis, Lundberg & Martin 1985; Martin and Siehl 1983; Peters and Waterman 1982; Deal and Kennedy 1982) have stressed this theme and emphasized the importance of shared beliefs and values to organizational effectiveness. Very few, however, have made a clear distinction between a theory of consistency and the theory of involvement noted above. It would appear, nonetheless, that an approach emphasizing consistency raises a number of points not mentioned by those who have emphasized involvement, inclusion, and participation.

First, consistency theories have argued that shared meaning has a positive impact because an organization's members all work from a common framework of values and beliefs that forms the basis through which they communicate. Because communication is fundamentally a process of manipulating symbols, then a high level of agreement about the meaning of each symbol greatly enhances the encoding-decoding process necessary for communication (Berger and Luckmann 1967; Mead 1934). A strong culture thus has a much greater potential for implicit coordination and control of behavior. A strong culture, with well-socialized members, improves effectiveness because it facilitates the exchange of information and coordination of behavior.

Consistency theories also have many precedents in the organizational literature. Several authors (Seashore 1954; Moch and Seashore 1981; Cameron 1989; Georgopoulos 1986) have emphasized the role that normative integration plays in organizational effectiveness. Normative integration, which is in many ways the behavioral analogue to shared meaning, refers to the existence of a strong system of norms and expectations that is widely agreed with and serves to regulate behavior in a way that rules, bureaucracy, and formal structures cannot. The power of this means of control is particularly apparent when organizational members encounter unfamiliar situations. Emphasis on a few general, value-based principles, on which actions can be grounded, enables individuals to better react in a predictable way to an unpredictable environment.

One of the earliest pieces of research to examine the question of normative integration and effectiveness reports a finding that may well be reflected in future empirical work on cultural consistency and effectiveness. Seashore (1954) found that a high level of consistency and integration in support of performance norms was a good predictor of a high level of effectiveness, but that high integration around a set of norms that did not contribute to performance resulted in lower than normal performance. Thus, consistency may well be the classic double-edged sword—it can work in favor of or against performance depending on the nature of the norms and expectations. This finding is perhaps reflected in the more popular literature by the acknowledgment that a strong culture not well suited to an organization's current business environment is a significant liability and generates a tremendous amount of inertia, making change and adaptability difficult (Pascale 1985).

A consistency explanation of organizational effectiveness also suggests that the beliefs and values central to an organization must be closely aligned with actual policies and practices if the management system is to obtain a high degree of integration and coordination. Inconsistencies between espoused values and actual practice tend to undermine the shared meaning, normative integration, and consistency that the theory implies are related to organizational effectiveness. The "strong culture" hypothesis argues that there must be consistency between principles and behavior and a conformity to valued organizational practices. This conformity element of consistency theory also has its antecedents in the organizational literature, starting as early as Whyte's *The Organization Man* (1951).

Despite several similarities between the involvement and consistency hypotheses, they make different predictions about the conditions under which organizations will be most effective. Most popular authors have tended to lump these two theories together based on their emphasis on the psychology of inclusion. On closer examination, however, the involvement hypothesis asserts that the inclusion and participation of members in the processes of the organization will outweigh the dissension, inconsistency, and nonconformity associated with a more democratic internal process. Employees will have the opportunity to contribute their knowledge and skill, and decisions will reflect multiple viewpoints, be perceived legitimate, and have a higher likelihood of implementation. This process, given the time to work, will result in "better" decisions and responses from an organization. Over time, better decisions should be associated with better performance.

Consistency theory, in contrast, would make the prediction that low levels of involvement and participation can be outweighed by high levels of consistency, conformity, and consensus. A high degree of normative integration, shared meaning, and a common frame of reference can increase an organization's capacity for coordinated action and promote a more rapid decision process. A coordinated response, with a common meaning for an organization's members, allows an organization to react to its environment and to preserve the system of meaning held by its members.

Effective organizations seem to combine both principles in a continual cycle. Involvement is used to generate potential ideas and solutions, which are then refined into a more precise set of principles. As White (1988) describes, continuous improvement in manufacturing systems requires that ideas generated through involvement are used to create the next higher level of standardization in a production process.

The Adaptability Hypothesis

The first two components of the culture and effectiveness theory focus almost exclusively on the internal dynamics of an organization. They say little about the external environment of organizations or the way in which a culture relates to the adaptation process. Much has been written about the relation between organizations and their environments (Lawrence and Lorsch 1967; Katz and Kahn 1978; Pfeffer and Salancik 1978; Aldrich 1979), but very little of this work has approached the problem from a cultural perspective.

Schein (1985) discusses the relationship between adaptation and culture, and emphasizes that a culture usually consists of the collective behavioral responses that have proven to be adaptive in the past for a particular social organization. When confronted with a new situation, an organization first "tries" the learned collective responses that are already a part of its repertoire. In addition, these responses are meaningful ones for the organization's members because they also represent individuals' strategies for successfully adapting to the organization itself over time.

Schein's discussion explains quite clearly how it is that the process of adaptation contributes to the culture of a social system, but does little to help explain how the culture of a social system contributes to adaptation. Without examining both halves of the question, it is impossible to go beyond a reactive theory to formulate a more proactive theory of organizational culture.

To formulate a proactive, cultural theory of organizational adaptation, one needs to describe a system of norms and beliefs that can support the capacity of an organization to receive, interpret, and translate signals from its environment into internal behavioral changes that increase its chances for survival, growth, and development. Theorists such as William Starbuck (1971) and Walter Buckley (1968), for example, using the language of general systems theory, have discussed the concept of morphogenesis, or the capacity of a system to acquire an increasingly complex adaptative structure. Such concepts can readily be used to describe the means by which an organization continually alters its internal structure and processes in a manner that increases its chances for survival. The system of norms and beliefs that supports this capacity can help to define a theory of the way in which culture can influence the adaptation process.

In practical terms, the absence of adaptive morphogenesis is well known and easy to identify; it is rigid bureaucratization, which derives from and inevitably supports a system of values and beliefs oriented toward stability. In *The Change Masters* (1983), Kanter discusses the issue of the capacity to restructure and its relationship to adaptation, and emphasizes that managers with the capacity for integration and the ability to "see the big picture" are most likely to be successful at introducing change. Balkanized organizational structures are often impossible to change because of the low likelihood of finding a common direction in which all elements can pull at the same time.

Thus, three aspects of adaptability are likely to have an impact on an organization's effectiveness. First is the ability to perceive and respond to the external environment. As Abegglen & Stalk (1986) have pointed out, one of the distinguishing characteristics of successful Japanese organizations is that they are *obsessed* with their customers and their competitors. Peters & Austin (1985) describe a similar orientation among American companies. Second is the ability to respond to internal customers. Insularity with respect to other departments, divisions, or districts within the same corporation exemplifies a lack of adaptability and has direct impacts on effective performance. Third, reacting to either internal or external customers requires the capacity to restructure and reinstitutionalize a set of behaviors and processes that allow the organization to adapt (Zald & Ash 1966). Without this ability to implement an adaptive response, an organization cannot be effective.

Each of these three aspects of adaptability are supported (or not supported) by an organization's culture. They go beyond mere departmental functions or programs to the core of an organization's value system. As such they need to be addressed as an outgrowth of the basic assumptions, values, and norms that provide structure and direction for an organization.

One of the best examples of the critical importance of these aspects of adaptability comes from the Detroit Edison case study in Chapter 8. As a public utility in an industrial region, the company operated under conditions of stable, predictable growth for most of this century. The 1970s brought fundamental change in nearly all of the organization's key external environments: the energy crisis, nuclear power, affirmative action, and the end of growth in demand all occurred at the same time.

These forces required the organization to change from a technical focus, concerned primarily with adding new capacity to meet increasing demand, to a political focus, primarily concerned with linking itself to a diverse set of constituents. The inertia of the old culture, which was well adapted to the stable environment of the past, has meant that the organization is still adapting to the fundamental changes of the past, while at the same time it is trying to prepare for a future that may include significant deregulation of the industry.

The Mission Hypothesis

Chapter 6 describes Medtronic, an organization that in its early years was a prime example of a culture driven by a clear mission. This company, the premier manufacturer of cardiac pacemakers, was founded with a pro-health, technical mission designed to ''contribute to human welfare by application of biomedical engineering.'' Economic goals were easily met and were secondary considerations; several of the members of the company described it as a ''scientific-technical club.'' Others said that, in the early days, Medtronic did not *have* a mission, it *was* a mission. Changes in competition, government regulation, and health care funding have required substantial changes over the years, but the organization remains closely bound to its original mission.

This last component of the culture and effectiveness model stresses a fourth implicit theme in the literature on organizational culture—the importance of a mission, or a shared definition of the function and purpose of an organization and its members. Although few authors have written directly on the topic, most have agreed that a sense of mission provides two major influences on an organization's functioning. First, a mission provides purpose and meaning, as well as a host of noneconomic reasons why the work of an organization is important. Second, a sense of mission provides clear direction and goals that serve to define the appropriate course of action for the organization and its members. Both of these factors grow out of and support the key values of the organization.

A mission provides purpose and meaning by defining a social role and external goals for an institution and defining individual roles with respect to the institutional role. Through this process, behavior is given intrinsic, or even spiritual, meaning that transcends functionally defined bureaucratic roles. This process of internalization and identification contributes to short- and long-term commitment and leads to effective performance.

The second major influence that a strong sense of mission has on an organization is to provide clarity and direction. On an individual level, there is convincing evidence that success is more likely when individuals are goal-directed (Locke 1968). On an organizational level, despite the fact that organizational "goals" may often be post hoc reconstructions, a related process seems to take place. The impact at the organizational level may stem from the coordination that results from defining a *common* goal as well as the definition of objective, external criteria. Both factors seemed to have a positive effect on performance.

A sense of mission also requires that organizations apply *future perfect* thinking (Weick 1979; Davis 1987). Using this mode of thought has an impact on behavior (Weick 1979) and allows an organization to shape current behavior by envisioning a desired future state. (Example: by June 30 of next year our exports *will have* doubled). Such a mission presents a set of goals that reach far beyond the short-term planning of most corporations. Particularly in successful corporations, whose age is measured in decades rather than years, a shared sense of the broad long-term goals of the firm is implicit and helps to structure behavior (Torbert 1987).

Mission is an elusive feature of an organization, and little attempt has been made to measure mission in the quantitative part of this study or to relate a quantitative measure of mission to each organization's performance. The case study section of this book, however, clearly shows the historical development and definition of a mission and its critical role in an organization's success.

Integrating the Four Hypotheses

Taken separately, each of the hypotheses presented above represents a central idea about the cultural determinants of performance and effectiveness. Through these four principles, most of the implicit or explicit ideas about culture and effectiveness that have appeared in the literature have been represented. The task now is to integrate these four ideas into a single framework and then specify the interrelationships among them.

The first element of the integrative framework concerns the focus of the four concepts. As noted earlier, involvement and consistency primarily address the internal dynamics of an organization, but do not address the interaction of the organization with the external environment. Adaptability and mission, in contrast, take as their focus the relationship between the organization and its external environment. Thus, on the dimension of internal versus external focus, the four concepts can be divided into two pairs, one pair with internal focus and one pair with external focus.

The four elements in this framework can also be divided in another way. Involvement and adaptability form one pair, emphasizing the organization's capacity for flexibility and change. Consistency and mission, in contrast, are oriented toward stability. A system oriented toward adaptability and involvement will introduce more variety, more input, and more possible solutions to a given situation than a system oriented toward a high level of consistency and a strong sense of mission. In contrast, a bias toward consistency and mission is more likely to reduce variety and place a higher emphasis on control and stability. As noted by contingency theorists, this orientation toward control and stability probably best serves a situation in which an organization has established a limited but appropriate response set that is well suited to a stable environment. These four concepts are integrated in the framework presented in Figure 1.2.

Although each of the four concepts in this framework represents a separate "path" by which an organization's culture might have a positive impact on effectiveness, some of the concepts are in part contradictory—a rigid, highly consistent system may be the antithesis of a high-involvement or high-flexibility system. Instead of arguing, however, that the classification of an organization's culture must be an either/or type of decision, this framework assumes that an effective culture must provide all of these elements. By implication, a culture that is at the same time adaptive, yet highly consistent, or responsive to individual involvement, but within the context of a strong shared mission, will be most effective. Thus, the reconciliation of conflicting demands is the essence of an effective organizational culture.

As such, this framework is similar to other authors who have recently

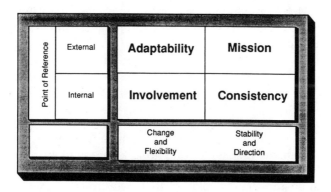

Figure 1.2 The culture and effectiveness model

argued for the importance of understanding the paradoxes and contradictions that are an integral part of organizational life (Mitroff 1984; Quinn and Cameron 1988; Quinn 1988). As Quinn has noted in his competing values model of organizational effectiveness, it is the *balancing* of competing demands that distinguishes excellent managers and organizations from their more mediocre counterparts. Many theories of management have ignored this dynamic tension by promoting "one best way" to manage and organize.

This framework is used throughout the book as a "set of lenses" for viewing organizational culture and for understanding both the quantitative and qualitative results. Although the framework can be used to make a number of predictions about the expected relationship between culture and effectiveness, it would be misleading to present this book as an exercise in "hypothesis testing." Rather this book is an attempt to look at several different forms of evidence and, within the general bounds of the framework outlined above, attempt to better understand and predict the impacts that an organization's culture will have on effectiveness.

Organizational Culture and Human Resource Management

The issues raised by the topic of organizational culture all point to the idea that an organization's normative system—its system of values and management practices—can be one of an organization's most important assets or most destructive liabilities. This perspective is continually presented in studies that have compared American and Japanese industry or have discussed American international competitiveness in general (Abernathy and Hayes 1980; Reich 1982; Thurow 1980; Abegglen & Stalk 1986). All of these studies attribute a consistent 20 to 30 percent of the cost differential between American and Japanese automobiles to an elusive quality called the "management system," or the capacity of an organization to coordinate itself with lower administrative expense.

Conventional systems of management and accounting do little to acknowledge the impact that the effective management of human assets has on performance. People are treated as expenses rather than assets, and are thus managed with an eye to reducing costs rather than increasing return on assets. At a time when public education in the United States does an inadequate job of preparing future workers and employees, many large corporations have been forced to develop major training programs to ensure that the skill of their workforce is adequate to remain competitive. In addition, the consequences of managing human resources as expenses rather than investments is made particularly clear by the recent wave of mergers and acquisitions. The problems associated with integration of firms often lead to a lower level of postmerger performance (Mirvis and Marks 1985, 1986; Marks and Mirvis 1985; 1986; Pritchett 1987). "Synergy," as a manager in one conglomerate put it, "is strictly a pre-merger concept."

Each of these problems requires a better understanding both of organizations as cultures and social systems and of the relationship between the characteristics of the cultures and their effective performance as businesses. This requires evidence regarding the relationship between culture and effectiveness that has yet to be produced by organizational researchers. Most thus far have been content to discuss the issues associated with organizational culture primarily in academic terms and have not yet dealt in terms of the business organizations they are studying.

There is some tradition of addressing human resource issues from this perspective, and a few authors have attempted to express themselves in the financial language common to organizations. Early attempts in personnel and organizational behavior (Brogden and Taylor 1950) and economics (Becker 1964; Katona 1975) have led to a number of different approaches to this problem. A brief review and critique of this literature will help frame the research presented in this book from the perspective of those who have focused on the impact that behavior can have on individual and organizational effectiveness.

Perhaps the most generic approach to this problem, human capital theory (Becker 1964), was developed to explain how investment in human skills had payoffs beyond the accounting period in which the original investment was made. This economic theory primarily emphasizes the value added to a person's worth in the labor market (and presumably to an organization) through two types of investments: education and experience. Both of these contributions require an initial outlay and presumably increase an individual's value to an organization or value in the labor market at large. In this sense, investment in individuals may be equated with capital investment in other areas. It is worth noting, however, that value is attributed only to individuals and not to the behavior of groups of individuals, organizations of individuals, or the management systems designed to integrate their activities.

Within the field of organizational behavior, one of the earliest attempts to draw the connection between behaviors and financial outcomes came from Brogden and Taylor's (1950) suggestion that personnel studies ought to apply cost-accounting concepts to the construction of their measures of criteria. It is interesting to note that most of the work that has followed in this tradition has some of the same shortcomings as the human capital perspective described above—value is attributed exclusively to individuals' behaviors, and the criteria studied are, with few exceptions, individual rather than organizational outcomes.

This criticism is also true of studies in human resource accounting (Brummet, Flamholtz, and Pyle 1968), which have generally attempted to value human assets by assigning a value to an individual rather than to his or her behavior. Suggested ways to establish this were usually based on an individual's salary (Myers and Flowers 1974) or replacement cost (Flamholtz 1974). Alternatively, several authors have focused on either costly behaviors themselves (turnover, absenteeism, quality of performance, and the like) or the attitudes that seem to be related to those costly employee behaviors (Mirvis and Macy 1976; Macy and Mirvis 1976; Mirvis and Lawler 1977). More recently, Cascio (1982, 1987) and Flamholtz (1985) have presented further work establishing cost-accounting procedures for a wide range of employee behaviors.

A third approach to valuing human resources has emphasized the relationship between employee behaviors and the costs and performance of business units (Likert 1967, 1973; Likert and Bowers 1969, 1973; Likert, Bowers, and Norman 1969). This approach has primarily relied on correlating survey measures of perceived behavior with cost data and then using this observed relationship to predict future cost savings based on changes in perceived behavior. Later research in this tradition has focused on predicting the performance of cost centers based on survey measures of behavior (Pecorella, Bowers, Davenport, and LaPointe 1978). Aside from these studies, there has been very little empirical research on employee behaviors and unit performance.

More recently, Ouchi (1983), in an interesting variation on the human resource theme, has argued that a firm's performance can be predicted by the level of "human asset specificity"—the degree to which organizations develop human assets that are unique to a particular organization. His argument is that human assets or skills that have a broad market and applicability in many settings will always be compensated at near market value. Thus, only by cultivating skills that are unique to a particular setting can an organization gain an advantage over its competitors, since generalizable skills will always reflect market value. This argument translates Ouchi's notion of the "clan" as a system of organization into strategic and economic terms, with some interesting implications. Clearly, local knowledge is attributed value in this model, but it is difficult to tell, for example, how to determine which forms of knowledge are local and which are general, and which of those constitute assets.

It is important to note that nearly all of these examples have involved attributing value to the salaries or replacement costs associated with individuals or to discrete behaviors such as absenteeism, turnover, or motivation. Few of these approaches have attempted to characterize the value of a human system. Only Likert and Ouchi begin to address the relationship between the internal set of norms that govern behavior in an organization and the performance of that organization. Even Ouchi addresses this rather indirectly by concentrating on the degree to which an individual's skills represent assets that are unique to a particular organization. This perspective implies that integration represents an asset to an organization, but Ouchi addresses it with reference to the relationship between an individual and an organization, rather than as a characteristic of the organization itself.

Trying to assess the value of an organization's human resources by adding up the value associated with each individual only captures one part of the picture. It is a little like trying to establish a differential in-flight value to the vital engine parts of a single engine aircraft. Until the plane lands, the parts have no real value; value is created by the ability of the parts to function together as a whole. Without that, none of the individual parts has any value at all until the plane reaches the ground safely. Once the plane lands, the market value of a particular part again becomes a relevant measure of worth, just as an individual's salary or replacement cost may be a relevant measure of a person's worth once he or she leaves an organization. Some may wish to argue that this metaphor does not apply to their organization because it is more analogous to a grounded aircraft rather than to one in flight. They may be right!

This metaphor nonetheless brings us back to the central topic of this book—the relationship between corporate culture and organizational effectiveness. Only by placing value on the interactive characteristics of organizations—the system of norms, beliefs, and patterns of behavior that forms the core of an organization's culture—can the true contribution of human resources to an organization's ultimate effectiveness be determined. The research presented in this book moves toward that goal.

Summary

This chapter began with a brief critique of the popular and academic literature on organizational culture and effectiveness. Following was the presentation of a model that combined many of the implicit ideas in the literature into an explicit theory and set of concepts intended to address both the internal dynamics of organizations and the dynamics of organizations as cultural systems in interaction with their environment. The chapter ended with a discussion of the close relationship between human resource management and organizational effectiveness, and reviewed some of the issues and problems that research in this area has encountered. The chapters that follow present the results of a large-scale research project that has tried to address the issues raised in this first chapter. The research is presented in two parts. The first part compares behavioral data and financial performance data from 34 large corporations in an attempt to predict future performance from information about each company's current culture and management system. The second part presents detailed case studies on five of these companies, and traces the development of the organization's culture and its impact on effectiveness.

The final chapter summarizes what has been learned from this research, focusing specifically on cultural change, and the implications of these findings for both organizational researchers and managers.

CHAPTER TWO

Studying Culture
and Effectiveness

This chapter plunges into the academic literature and examines its treatment of three topics that are central to this book: organizational culture, organizational climate, and organizational effectiveness. The purpose is both to ground the discussion in the key issues that have been a source of inspiration and controversy in the literature and to achieve some degree of integration between the culture and climate perspectives. The academic reader may find this chapter to be among the book's most interesting, but the manager or professional may prefer to skim this and Chapter 3 and go directly to the quantitative results in Chapter 4 and the case studies in Chapters 5 through 10.

Developing a historical perspective on the study of organizational culture and effectiveness is somewhat difficult. On the surface, the field appears to have sprung fully grown, with unknown ancestry, sometime during the year 1980. Then, within two years, the concept had taken the business and academic world by storm, and created a small industry in the process (Uttal 1983). Understanding the dynamics that underlie this phenomenon is crucial for two reasons: first, to evaluate the many contributions that the "culture revolution" has made to organizational theory and management practices; and second, to avoid the faddish "rise and fall" that is sometimes typical of new ideas in both the business world and academia. Understanding the dynamics is necessary if the "culture revolution" is to be translated effectively into new research, new theory, and new management practices that have staying power.

In one of the first actual review articles to deal with organizational culture, Schneider (1985) comments that writers on culture have, with few exceptions, ignored past work on related topics such as organizational climate. Despite the existence of specific attempts to deny the connection (Schwartz and Davis 1981), Schneider chose to emphasize the similarity and treated the two topics jointly. This chapter expands on that assumption of similarity and briefly reviews past research on the topics of organizational climate, organizational culture, and organizational effectiveness. This review has its roots in the 1950s, and summarizes the relevant research from that period forward in an effort to establish a new sense of continuity.

The Culture-Climate Debate

The debate over organizational culture and climate is in many ways a classic example of methodological (and epistemological) differences obscuring a basic substantive similarity. The argument is not so much about *what* to study as *how* to study it. Climate researchers, bearing questionnaires, sought to characterize specific organizational settings with respect to universal dimensions and principles. Almost all were capable psychometricians who saw progress as consisting of incremental improvements within the context of this basic approach. In contrast, culture researchers, with copious field notes, tried to understand the basic values and assumptions that individual members of organizations attached to the social system they were a part of, and the importance that *meaning* had for organizational functioning. Nearly all favored qualitative research, and felt that progress comprised both changing attitudes about the way in which research should be done and understanding the development of meaning systems in organizations and their impact on individual behavior and management practices.

With this radical difference of opinion over the way to do research, and the differences in the particular topics of immediate interest, it is not surprising that the underlying similarity of the subject at hand was often ignored. The point is, however, that if an agreement can be reached on the similarity of the substance, then the differences in style can be complementary and productive. Without such an agreement, however, climate and culture research are likely to remain two unrelated activities.

This situation is not unlike that in many other fields of study. For example, several authors have made the point that the concept of an organization's culture has many parallels to the concept of an individual's personality. Furthermore, methods for diagnosing and interpreting an individual's personality reflect the same dichotomy as culture and climate research. Psychological tests, such as the Minnesota Multiphasic Personality Inventory (MMPI), take a quantitative, rational approach to understanding an individual's personality, whereas a psychoanalyst or clinician applies methods that are qualitative and focus on the individual's history, subconscious, underlying assumptions, and developmental processes. Debate over the appropriate method is spirited, and the simultaneous application of these disparate techniques is quite common. A similar argument could be made for other psychological concepts such as intelligence.

Several examples are also apparent from the field of business and economics. Attributing value to an individual corporation is always an interesting combination of technical financial analyses and subjective judgments about "future potential." Effective managers appear to combine rationality and intuition in their reasoning process, and excessive reliance on one approach or the other can be a significant liability (Pondy 1983; Quinn 1988). Finally, the debate over the use of case studies as opposed to comparative studies to understand and teach about organizations also calls into question whether one learns more from the specific example or from the more abstract generalization. Each of these examples raises the same underlying issues as the culture-climate debate.

The position taken in this book and elsewhere (see, for example, Black and Stephens 1988) argues that the method and approach should be of *secondary importance to the underlying phenomenon*. Thus, an integration of the research on culture and climate is necessary if we are to combine both rational and intuitive approaches to the understanding of organizations as social systems.

The argument for the similarity of organizational culture and organizational climate seems to stand on three basic points. These are presented below to provide a framework for the discussion of climate and culture research that follows, and then are discussed again later in this chapter in an attempt to integrate the two perspectives.

First, both concepts focus on *organization-level behavioral characteristics*, and implicitly argue that organizational units are a viable level for the analysis of behavior. This assumes some degree of consistency and behavioral integration within an organizational system, and also assumes that the foundations of that consistency (assumptions, meaning, beliefs, patterns of behavior) are a useful way to understand the actions taken by organizations and by the individuals within them.

Second, both concepts cover a very *wide range of phenomena*. Topics range from the deeply held assumptions that form the basis of a culture to the actual practices and patterns of behavior that are rooted in those assumptions. Although culture researchers have paid more attention to the former and climate researchers the latter, the overlap between the two has been considerable. More important, the relationship between these two extremes (underlying assumptions and actual behaviors) is perhaps the most interesting aspect of the phenomenon to study.

Third, both concepts share a *similar problem*. They must explain the way in which the behavioral characteristics of a system affect the behavior of individuals, while at the same time explain the way in which the behavior of individuals, over time, creates the characteristics of an organizational system. This problem is further complicated because the "existence" of either concept, culture or climate, depends on intersubjectivity—agreement among organizational members or researchers. Although the two research traditions take quite different approaches to solving this problem, they do in fact address the same problem.

Past Attempts: The Organizational Climate Literature

The scholarly literature on organizational climate, is, in a word, *inclusive*. The first edition of the widely used text *Organizations* (Gibson, Ivancevich, and Donnelly 1973) listed at least 60 subheadings under organizational climate in the index, but the second edition lists only five—perhaps strong evidence of what Mohr (1982) has called a "labelling tide." Criteria for inclusion as an element in the "climate" domain are vague, and must be understood in terms of the orientation of a particular theorist, rather than a set of criteria for inclusion that are common across theorists.

The term *climate* also has two distinctly different meanings in the literature, which helps to add to the impression that organizational climate "includes everything." The first widely used definition argues that climate refers to a *common perception*, or a common reaction of individuals to a situation. Thus there may be a climate of satisfaction, resistance, involvement, or, as Studs Terkel (1970) put it, "salubrity." Given this definition, the only limit on sampling the climate domain is one's ability to evoke relevant attitudinal adjectives and demonstrate some degree of concurrence among organizational members.

A second, quite distinct definition argues that the term *climate* should be used to refer to a *set of conditions* that exist and have an impact on individuals' behavior. Although the existence of these "conditions" can often only be determined by perceptual data, they are nonetheless taken to be an "objective" characteristic of a social system, as well as a set of consistent reactions to that characteristic of the system. Examples might include coordination between different units within an organization, the social distance required by status differences, or the involvement of individuals in decision making. In this case, the only limit on the climate domain is the range of potential processes, practices, and conditions that affect the way in which organizations function.

These competing definitions are compatible in the situation where a set of objective conditions leads to a common individual perception. In situations where this is not the case, a researcher or manager is stuck with two definitions, one arguing that climate is an individual psychological state like satisfaction, and the other arguing that climate is an objective set of circumstances like organizational structure.

The roots of the climate concept are Lewinian. Lewin's concept of behavior as the product of individuals acting in context has provided the basic metaphor and conceptual framework for climate research. Use of the term *organizational climate,* and elaboration of this principle in organizational research began during the 1960s. Halpin and Croft (1962), Litwin and Stringer (1968), The Forum Corporation (1974), Forehand (1968), Likert (1961, 1967), Campbell, Dunnette, Lawler and Weick (1970), and Tagiuri and Litwin (1968) all presented formulations that specified a number of dimensions of organizational climate. Tagiuri and Litwin's (1968) collection of essays is possibly the most widely cited, and presents the range of perspectives extending from climate as an objective set of system characteristics (Evan 1968) to climate as the interaction of system and individual characteristics (Forehand 1968). Tagiuri and Litwin offered the following conceptual definition:

> Organizational climate is a relatively enduring quality of the internal environment of an organization that (a) is experienced by its members, (b) influences their behavior, and (c) can be described in terms of the values of a particular set of characteristics (or attitudes) of the organization. (p. 27)

There is an active attempt in the literature to differentiate organizational climate with respect to two other constructs: satisfaction and organizational structure. It seems to make most sense to regard climate, particularly with respect to unit of analysis, as lying somewhere "between" the two. The problem of differentiating climate from satisfaction has drawn the attention of several authors (Lafollette and Sims 1975; Johanneson 1976; Schneider and Snyder 1975; Payne, Fineman, and Wall 1976; Guion 1973), and arises when one takes a subjective "common perception" perspective on climate. If, as several authors have argued, "climate" refers to a shared reaction to a set of largely unspecified conditions, at what point does "climate" converge with other more individual level domains such as satisfaction? What differentiates the two?

In contrast, if one adopts the more system-level "set of organizational conditions" perspective on climate, the concept eventually becomes indistinguishable, in some ways, from organizational structure. Payne and Pugh (1976), as well as Lawler, Hall, and Oldham (1974) have addressed this issue. Interestingly enough, the issue of response homogeneity (Drexler 1977; James 1982a, 1982b), frequently discussed as a validity criterion for climate measures, is also a well-established empirical criterion for demonstrating the existence of structural, as opposed to individual, effects when using perceptual data (Blau 1957, 1960; Davis, Spaeth, and Huson 1961). Although some structural characteristics (i.e., size, lines of authority, span of control, and so forth) refer more directly to configurations and are quite distinct from climate, others such as decentralization or distribution of control are less distinct.

Continued attempts to integrate the multiple perspectives on climate research are reflected in the work of Schneider (1972, 1975) and in several review articles, which appeared in the mid-1970s (James and Jones 1974; Hellriegel and Slocum 1974; Payne and Pugh 1976). Perhaps the most widely cited, the James and Jones review identifies three approaches to conceptualization and measurement within climate research: the perceptual measurement of individual attributes; the perceptual measurement of organizational attributes; and the multiple measurement of organizational attributes (combining both perceptual and more objective measures).

These three perspectives reflect the same distinctions drawn earlier in this chapter. Perceptual measurement of individual attributes corresponds to the "common perception" approach to climate, and the "set of conditions" approach corresponds to both the perceptual and multiple measurement of organizational attributes.

Despite a number of years of research, the concept of organizational climate still retains a questionable status (Woodman and King 1978), even though the measures used have shown some demonstrated relationship to performance (Pritchard and Karasick 1973; Lawler, Hall, and Oldham 1974; Frederickson 1966; Pecorella, et al. 1978) and some new issues of interest (Pennings 1982) have developed. On the whole, however, it must be concluded that there are still substantial problems with research in this domain.

First, the specific content of the climate domain is chosen by individual theorists, and there are few criteria of inclusion that are widely held. There is substantial overlap in the sense that most approaches are sociopsychological in perspective, but beyond that there is only limited agreement.

Second, there is still debate about the nature of the domain. The system-attribute versus individual-attribute issue still confuses the use of the term. In addition, there is relatively little empirical evidence that distinguishes organizational attributes from more individual-level attributes.

Third, the basic assumption, comparative in nature, that "variables" or "dimensions" are universally meaningful is still largely undemonstrated, although some applicability across multiple settings has been shown.

Fourth, there is little evidence of the impact of system attributes on system outcomes. Tests of the climate-performance relationship have concentrated on individual, group, or subunit performance.

In one of the clearer comments and critiques in the climate literature, Robert Guion (1973) framed the climate problem in a way that outlines the rationale for the priorities selected for the research presented in this book. Guion argues that conceptually a measure of organizational climate is much like the windchill index, which is the subjective perception of the joint effects of two objective characteristics—temperature and wind speed. If a climate measure, or the concept itself, is to remain distinct from an individual attribute such as satisfaction, he argues, it must in some way address the objective character of the organizational attribute. Using this conceptualization of climate helps to move toward the goal of this book: examining the relationship between the behavioral attributes of organizational systems and their impact on performance and effectiveness.

Organizational Culture: Theory and Research

A more recent literature emphasizing the importance of the behavioral characteristics of organizational systems is that of organizational culture. This literature, though in some ways addressing a similar phenomenon to the organizational climate literature, has a different emphasis and flavor, and has addressed a number of aspects of organizational behavior that have been neglected by those who have chosen the climate approach to the study of behavior in organizations.

The culture perspective has focused on the basic values, beliefs, and assumptions that are present in organizations, the patterns of behavior that result from these shared meanings, and the symbols that express the links between assumptions, values, and behavior to an organization's members. The focus on organizational culture has, in contrast to climate research, been more qualitative and idiographic in approach, and has employed methods that have been predominantly clinical, ethnographic, and anthropological.

Although culture research has been portrayed as a "new" perspective on organizations, there are, in fact, many precedents. Elliot Jaques, for example, gave this definition of the culture of a factory in 1951:

> The culture of the factory is its customary and traditional way of thinking and of doing things, which is shared to a greater or lesser degree by all its members, and which new members must learn, and at least partially accept, in order to be accepted into service in the firm. Culture in this sense covers a wide range of behavior: the methods of production; job skills and technical knowledge; attitudes towards discipline and punishment; the customs and habits of managerial behavior; the objectives of the concern; its way of doing business; the methods of payment; the values placed on different types of work; beliefs in democratic living and joint consultation; and the less conscious conventions and taboos. Culture is part of second nature to those who have been with the firm for some time. Ignorance of culture marks out the newcomers, while maladjusted members are recognized as those who reject or are otherwise unable to use the culture of the firm. In short, the making of relationships requires the taking up of roles within a social structure; the quality of these relationships is governed by the extent to which the individuals concerned have each absorbed the culture of the organization so as to be able to operate within the same general code. The culture of the factory consists of the means or techniques which lie at the disposal of the individual for handling his relationships, and on which he depends for making his way among, and with, other members and groups. (p. 251)

The roots of culture research in organizations include both the symbolic interactionist perspective (Mead 1934; Cooley 1922; Blumer 1969) and a social-anthropological approach (Kluckhorn 1951; Levi-Strauss 1963). Cultural reality is perceived to be socially constructed (Berger and Luckmann 1966) and social interaction takes place through the exchange of symbols that have a shared meaning for a set of social actors. Coming to recognize and use these symbols entails the development of a "self" defined in terms of culturally specified symbols. From this perspective, myths (Eliade 1959), archetypes (Mitroff 1984), and stories and ideologies (Starbuck 1982) are often as useful in explaining the behavior of individuals as the more objective features of organizations because they embody and articulate the identity of organizational members.

Several specific topics have been addressed frequently within the academic culture literature. One of the most popular has been socialization, or the process by which a new member comes to understand and manipulate the symbols of an organization's culture. This topic has been examined from a cultural or symbolic interactionist perspective by Van Maanen (1977), Siehl and Martin (1981), Sathe (1983), Trice and Beyer (1984), and Schein (1985). Stories, as a means of conveying culturally based values and assumptions have been a particular interest of Joanne Martin and Alan Wilkins (Martin 1982b; Martin and Powers 1983; Wilkins 1978).

Other topics often addressed in the literature on organizational culture are the issues of managing culture and the relationship between business strategy and the culture of an organization. Work on these topics (Schwartz and Davis 1981; Phillips and Kennedy 1980; O'Toole 1985; Ouchi 1981; Starbuck 1982; Deal and Kennedy 1982; Siehl and Martin 1982; Peters and Waterman 1982; Tichy 1983; Schein 1985) is usually rooted in the assumption that a culture has inertia—that is, once values, shared meanings, and patterns of behavior are established, they continue until some force is exerted to change them. This implies an important role for cultural theories in planned organizational changes designed to implement or accommodate a new business strategy within an existing human organization. These perspectives have also usually taken a contingency view of organizational structure (Lawrence and Lorsch 1967) and argued that different environmental conditions give rise to, and are consistent with, different patterns of behavior and cultures within organizations.

Finally, the literature on organizational culture has directed a great deal of attention to epistemology and methodology. Typically, this has taken the form of a critique of the nomothetic, survey-based methodologies so often used in organizational research (Martin 1981, 1982a, 1982b; Geertz 1973; Pettigrew 1979; Argyris 1980; Knorr-Cetina and Cicourel 1981; Louis 1981), and usually advocates an idiographic, ethnographic, clinical, or anthropological approach to studying behavior (Garfinkel 1967; White 1949; Jones 1988).

Two notions that appear in the literature on organizational culture are in many ways unique and have had a direct influence on the research to be presented in this book. The first of these is the idea that a "strong" culture is often a characteristic of a successful organization. Several authors have argued that some organizations have "more" culture than others, and this helps socialize members, direct their actions, and define and reinforce goals. Ouchi (1981), Deal and Kennedy (1982), and Peters and Waterman (1982) have each emphasized this point, as have many others. The second point, and in some ways related to the first, is the idea that ideologies, symbols, and shared beliefs have an important impact on organizations, quite apart from their objective, material, or structural characteristics. These two principles will, where possible, be operationalized and examined as to their impact on performance and effectiveness.

The cultural perspective on organizations has made several important contributions to those who manage and research them. This section of the chapter ends by reviewing some of these contributions—highlighting what has been gained and noting some of the areas where culture research has fallen short.

Perhaps the most positive impact of the cultural perspective is that it has represented a return to inductive thinking about the behavioral characteristics of organizations. As such, it has opened up the issue of the appropriate content and topics of interest for organization and management studies to a discipline, in some ways exemplified by climate research, which had for some time been preoccupied with psychometric tests of a priori conceptual structures. This has helped to return the focus of research to organizational life, rather than abstracted quantitative analysis.

The culture perspective has also drawn attention to the symbolic nature of organizational life and to the importance of meaning systems in organizations. The perspective has presented the idea that basic assumptions, internalized over time as they prove themselves to be meaningful, adaptive strategies, give rise to structures that both reflect and support the basic assumptions. These two ideas imply that effective management requires the recognition of this long chain of events and the necessity of integrating basic assumptions, the symbolic functions of management, and day-to-day activities. This has, in part, given rise to a new model of leadership (Tichy 1987; Bennis and Nanus 1985) that emphasizes the symbolic as well as the purely functional and technical aspects of leadership.

Perhaps the major shortcoming of the culture perspective concerns the lack of evidence that scholars and researchers have presented in defense of their positions. Kanter (1983) notes this problem and presents a brief attempt to test the idea that corporations possessing the characteristics proposed by her ideal model have in fact any better performance record than those that do not. As mentioned in the first chapter, Peters and Waterman (1982) have also received pointed criticism for their neglect of this issue (Carroll 1983; ''Who's Excellent Now?'' 1984).

This problem appears even more serious when it becomes apparent that academic researchers have largely neglected the functional aspects of organizational culture. Although the study of socialization (Sathe 1983; Van Maanen 1977; Schein 1985) is one exception to this criticism, it is nonetheless clear that the functional aspects of organizational culture have been addressed by the more popular literature, and academics and researchers have primarily been concerned with the social constructionist dimensions of the concept (Barley, Meyer, & Gash 1988). The popular literature, however, has almost without exception taken a position of advocacy and left the empirical question to the academics and researchers. Thus, the issue of evidence has fallen, for the most part, between the cracks.

An Attempt at Synthesis

Any attempt to integrate and synthesize the culture and climate perspectives in organizational studies requires at least three separate components: an argument for the underlying conceptual similarity; a plan for reconciling some of the basic methodological and epistemological differences; and a proposal for ways in which future research might take advantage of the potential offered by both perspectives. This section outlines these three components, concluding with a set of research strategies that can help move toward synthesis.

Conceptual Similarity. The core argument for conceptual similarity presented in this chapter is that both concepts refer to what might be called the perceived nature and logic of the internal social environment of a human organization. As noted earlier in this chapter, several other similarities also help to lay the groundwork for integration: (1) the focus on organizational systems as a meaningful level for behavioral analysis; (2) the attempt to deal with the connections between basic beliefs and assumptions on the one hand and actual behaviors and practices on the other; (3) the difficulty in explaining both the impact that a system has on individuals and the impact that individuals have on a system; and (4) the problems associated with trying to characterize the "objective" features of an organization's character when the only real criteria of existence is intersubjectivity. This range of common orientations and problems would seem to present a strong argument for similarity, even with the clear differences in methods and style.

Methodological and Epistemological Differences. Devising a plan to reconcile the methodological differences between these two perspectives is no small task. The differences go far deeper than simply using different research techniques; they are long-standing differences in theoretical orientation and epistemological tradition. Organizational climate, as noted earlier, is a Lewinian concept that emphasizes the impact of a social context on an actor. The concept developed in response to a neglect in the organizational behavior literature of the situational and contextual factors that influence individual behavior. Nonetheless, Lewin's well-known equation $B = f(p,e)$ (behavior is a function of the person and the environment) assumes the existence of discrete B's, P's, and E's in a way that has drawn consistent criticism from phenomenologists and social constructionists from George Herbert Mead (1934) to Berger and Luckmann (1966) to Anthony Giddens (1979). Mead, for example, argued that the social environment is a symbolic one, the integrity of which depends on the shared meaning that individuals attribute to it. Thus, without society there could be no identity—"person" and "environment" cease to exist when separated. This is a similar argument to that made by Anthony Giddens (1979): structured properties of social systems can be said to exist only in the sense that they have meaning to the actors in that system. Structure has no meaning outside an individual's understanding of it.

The culture researcher faces an entirely different set of problems and pitfalls. After making an initial set of assumptions that emphasize local knowledge, uniqueness, and the limitations on generalization, the culture researcher inevitably faces problems of representativeness. Can culture be managed? Is culture related to effectiveness? Questions such as these are often seen as either unfair or unanswerable by the "cultural purists," because the logic necessary to answer them is often incompatible with the initial assumptions of predominantly local applicability and meaning necessary to understand the "special" case. Like climate researchers, they eventually fall prey to the limitations of their own assumptions.

One strategy for resolving this dilemma is to examine the range of topics addressed by culture researchers in order to begin to outline a contingency model. The goal of such a contingency model would be to distinguish topics for which a set of nomothetic assumptions, similar to those underlying the climate metaphor, might be appropriate, and to contrast those with a set of topics for which the idiographic assumptions characteristic of culture research would be most appropriate. Lundberg (1985), following on from the work of Schein (1981, 1985) and Dyer (1982), provides a useful description of the range of topics that culture researchers have typically addressed. This description presents the idea that there are four levels of culture that, taken together, are a beginning step in operationalizing the concept.

1. *Artifacts.* The tangible aspects of culture shared by members of an organization. The verbal, behavioral, and physical artifacts are the surface manifestations of organizational culture. Language, stories, and myths are examples of verbal artifacts and are represented in rituals and ceremonies. The technology and art exhibited by members are where physical artifacts are found.

2. *Perspectives.* The socially shared rules and norms applicable to a given context. Perspectives may be viewed as the solutions to common problems encountered by organizational members; they involve how members define and interpret situations of organizational life and prescribe the bounds of acceptable behavior.

Perspectives are relatively concrete, and members are usually aware of them.

3. *Values.* The evaluational base that organizational members use for judging situations, acts, objects, and people. Values reflect the real goals, ideals, and standards, as well as the sins of an organization, and represent members' preferred means of resolving life's problems. Values are more abstract than perspectives, although experienced members sometimes articulate them more or less in statements of organizational "philosophy" and "mission."

4. *Assumptions.* The tacit beliefs that members hold about themselves and others, their relationships to other persons, and the nature of the organization in which they live. Assumptions are the nonconscious underpinnings of the first three levels—that is, the implicit, abstract axioms that determine the more explicit system of meanings.

These four separate levels of culture are arranged in order of abstractness, with verbal, behavioral, and physical artifacts as the most readily apparent surface manifestations of culture. This typology reflects a range of abstraction quite similar to that presented by this author. Denison (1982) divided the culture and climate domain into three separate levels: (1) the values and beliefs that underlie actions; (2) the patterns of behavior that reflect and reinforce those values; and (3) the set of conditions, created by these patterns of behavior, within which organizational members must function. The primary difference between this typology and the Lundberg typology is that Lundberg places more emphasis on the unconscious and abstract elements of culture, while my earlier typology focuses more on the concrete actions, conditions, and practices that are rooted in an organization's value system. A view of culture that includes both implicit assumptions and concrete managerial action is also common in much of the popular literature.

The solution suggested by this abstract-concrete distinction is that the nomological assumptions required in order to do comparative research on organizational culture may often be more warranted when the "level" of culture being addressed is more concrete. Artifacts, behavioral patterns, and more objective conditions may be more amenable to comparative research than are the more abstract elements of culture. The danger of this form of comparison, of course, is that it implies that a similar set of behavioral artifacts have a comparable meaning in different situations. When this condition is not met, the set of assumptions necessary to do comparative research on organizational culture begins to break down.

In contrast, most of the topics at the more abstract end of Lundberg's continuum may only be pursued through a set of idiographic assumptions that emphasize the predominantly local meaning of values, beliefs, artifacts, and assumptions, and the unique nature of each culture. This contingency approach to studying different levels of culture may point to areas where a comparative approach to the study of culture would be possible. This research would make use of some of the comparative assumptions more commonly associated with climate research, but would also take into account the emphasis on the importance of symbolic meaning associated with the culture paradigm.

A good example of how research from both traditions can address a highly similar topic is provided by a comparison of the work of Martin, Sitkin, and Boehm (1985) and Joyce and Slocum (1982, 1984). Both studies deal with the more concrete aspects of culture and both address the question of shared meaning. Martin, Sitkin, and Boehm show that the meaning of a set of stories is widely shared and that differences in shared meaning can be used to test for "groupings"—the different meanings can be used to distinguish the "old guard" from the "new guard," as well as to distinguish organizational members by function and hierarchical level. Joyce and Slocum demonstrate a similar point by cluster-analyzing questionnaire responses to find groupings of individuals who share perceptions and meanings. These clusters also revealed "meaning clusters" that often reproduced known groupings such as function or job type. Martin, Sitkin, and Boehm's work gives the reader a greater understanding of the organization researched, but both techniques seem to give an adequate measure of the degree to which meaning is shared, and the ability to define networks, cliques, and groupings by analyzing shared meaning and perception.

This illustration, along with the discussion of the implications of idiographic and nomothetic assumptions, suggests some useful trade-offs that may be made depending on the purpose of the research (Weick 1979). Generalizability must often be traded for detail, and vice versa. A comparative research design, drawn from nomothetic assumptions, places heavy weight on generalizability and takes a risk on the level of detail. A more idiographic design places much higher emphasis on detail and inductive processes and takes risks with respect to generalizability.

Taking Advantage of the Differences. There are several ways in which research might take advantage of the naturally occurring differences between the two research perspectives (Black and Stephens 1988). One way would be to use hybrid designs in which an inductive and qualitative method suggests ideas that a quantitative method (or a later study) eventually tests. There is often great compatibility—and an important payoff—when hybrid designs are used to study a single topic. If such strategies were commonly used, it would be possible to embrace eclecticism and reward boundary-spanning rather than epistemological orthodoxy. This would provide a second way to take advantage of the differences in the two perspectives.

A third way to take advantage of the differences in perspective is to do research with someone who disagrees with you about method but shares a common interest in a particular phenomenon. The resolution of the disagreement is likely to expand your understanding of the phenomenon. A final suggestion might be that the different perspectives may be appropriate at different points in the research process. Good research might, for example, begin by listening to stories and end by telling them. In between, however, much work is required to be certain that you are telling a representative story—one that is worth generalizing. The different perspectives may also be appropriate for explaining different aspects of the same phenomenon—a Lewinian climate metaphor might be most appropriate for explaining the short-term impact of an organizational setting on an individual, while the long-term creation of that setting might better be understood through a culture metaphor.

Organizational Effectiveness: The Criterion

Understanding organizational culture, as the discussion has shown, requires a high tolerance for complexity and ambiguity. Unfortunately, the literature on criteria measures of organizational effectiveness is equally complex. Organizations inevitably have an array of stakeholders, and any particular measure of performance often tends to pit one against the other. Shareholders like dividends, but managers regard dividends as costs and usually prefer profits, growth, and potential. Improved technology and cost-cutting may improve productivity but may also cost employees their jobs. Concerns over quarterly performance may compromise long-term investment. Customers may not be given new products because they are still happily buying the old. This inevitable set of trade-offs has led several authors to argue that effectiveness is an inherent paradox (Cameron 1986b; Quinn 1988; Quinn and Rohrbaugh 1983).

Because the study presented in this book is basically effectiveness research with culture and climate as the "causes" and financial performance as the "effects," it is important to set this work in context by briefly discussing some of the main issues in the effectiveness literature. This final section reviews several of the major perspectives on effectiveness and then discusses the approach taken in this book with respect to them. The intent in reviewing this research is not to reformulate or synthesize the effectiveness literature but to help frame the perspective taken on effectiveness in this book.

Probably the basic question in any formulation of effectiveness is "effectiveness for whom?" (Van de Ven and Ferry 1980). Conceptually, this fundamental question implies a set of stakeholders or constituents (Ross 1980) who have interests that may be overlapping, compatible, opposed, or mutually exclusive. Constituents may include suppliers, customers, employees, stockholders, financial institutions, regulatory agencies, or the general public. If an intraorganizational perspective is taken on this constituent model, then the coalitions within an organization may also be regarded as stakeholders who serve to define differing forms of organizational effectiveness (Pfeffer 1982).

The *stakeholder model* helps to underscore the diversity of interests among relevant parties. Although these differing interests are often in inherent conflict and cannot be reconciled, a number of authors have studied the problem of the functional characteristics of organizational systems that are successful in integrating diverse interests (Parsons 1951; Parsons, Bales, and Shils 1953; Katz and Kahn 1978; Georgopoulos 1972).

Several conceptual frameworks for organizational effectiveness have also been proposed and have summarized the literature with respect to three or four basic models (Goodman, Pennings, & Associates 1977; Scott 1977; Cameron and Whetten 1983; Seashore 1983). The first of these, the *natural systems model*, expands on the biological metaphor of an organism with an internally differentiated and integrated structure, which is interdependent with its environment for information and energy (Miller 1978; Katz and Kahn 1966, 1978). As Miller points out, this implies that organizations do not have simple "goals," and instead must be evaluated with respect to the equilibrium and elaboration of the system itself. Given this perspective, the outcomes of primary interest become system characteristics such as growth, stability, or decline.

A second approach, the *goal attainment model* (sometimes called the rational systems model) equates effectiveness with the attainment of specific organizational objectives. "Goals" may be a set of narrow economic objectives defined by owners, or they may be the set of institutional goals defined by the organization's constituents. In either case, organizations are perceived as contrived, instrumental, and purposeful. This perspective is attractive because it accounts for the sense of purpose that is apparent in many organizations, but is often criticized because goals change quickly, and may often be constructed after the fact to explain what has occurred rather than what is being planned (Weick 1979). Goals may also be internally inconsistent or even contradictory. All of these problems are difficult to resolve within the bounds of the rational goal attainment model of effectiveness.

A third model mentioned by most theorists is the *decision process model*. The central image in this model is that organizations are primarily information-processing and decision-making entities, and that the characteristics of this process will be the foremost determinants and indicators of effectiveness. This model would encompass the work of theorists ranging from March and Simon (1958) to Likert (1961, 1967) and to Vroom and Yetton (1973), all of whom argued that the nature of an organization's decision processes was a prime indicator of effectiveness.

Several authors have criticized these theories of organizational effectiveness, arguing that they all overemphasize the importance of the internal characteristics of organizations or the proactive efforts of individual members of organizations as determinants of effectiveness (Pfeffer and Salancik 1978; Pfeffer 1982). Instead, they argue, what is needed is a set of theories that conceive of effectiveness as a reactive rather than a proactive process (Van de Ven and Astley 1981). The two most prevalent theories that take this perspective are the *resource dependence* perspective of Pfeffer and Salancik (1978) and the *population ecology* perspective (Hannan and Freeman 1977; McKelvey 1979). The resource dependence model argues that the prime determinants of the behavior of organizations are their attempts to control their external environment so as to secure those resources that are most critical to the organization's survival and growth. These behaviors are, of course, enacted by organizational members, but the primary source of motivation comes not from the maintenance or development of the organization's internal system but from the organization's reactions to the external environment.

An even more "reactive" theory of organizational effectiveness comes from the population ecology perspective. The central principle is that the environment determines which types of organizations will survive and which will not, and that the actions of individuals and organizations are relatively weak determinants of effectiveness. Certain "species" of organizations will grow to fill a particular "niche" and will decline accordingly when the demand for that particular type of organization diminishes. This theoretical perspective helps to set a context within which the effectiveness of a particular firm might be analyzed, but does little to explain the fate of a particular firm within a given niche.

This brief overview of the organizational effectiveness literature should make the paradox and complexity of this topic readily apparent to the reader. Many volumes have addressed the resolution of these issues, and an original theoretical contribution in the area of effectiveness is clearly beyond the intent of this book. This background does, however, help to frame the perspective on effectiveness taken in this book.

Summary

This chapter has attempted to review research from a wide variety of areas, all of which are necessary to understand before undertaking comparative research on the relationship between organizational culture and organizational effectiveness. It has set the groundwork for the remaining chapters in this book, which will describe two related studies of organizational culture and effectiveness. The first of these studies relies on a large quantitative data base that matches survey data with financial performance data over time, and then begins to examine the predictive relations. The outline of this first study is presented in Chapter 3 and the results are presented in Chapter 4.

CHAPTER THREE

The Comparative
Research Design

To address the ideas presented and discussed in the first two chapters, the rest of this book presents evidence intended to support, contradict, or elaborate the basic framework. The attention is less explicitly directed to the definition and measurement of the culture concept per se and more explicitly targeted at a specific question: What can the cultural characteristics of an organization tell us about its effectiveness? In addition, what do these findings tell us about our theories of organizational behavior and effectiveness?

The research is divided into two parts. The first part is a comparative study of culture, climate, and effectiveness that uses a standard set of measures applied in comparable fashion to a sample of 34 organizations. The results are presented in quantitative form, with particular attention to predicting performance over time. The second part of the research is a set of five case studies of firms that were drawn from the sample of 34 organizations, but were chosen because they represented different patterns of culture and performance. The evidence presented in this second part is qualitative, and the approach is explicitly historical. Coupling these two methods is intended to draw on the strengths of each in an eclectic fashion that allows for the insights of both clinical and comparative methods.

Chapter 3 presents the research design for the comparative and quantitative part of the study. It describes the behavioral data, the performance data, the sample of firms, and the design for analyzing the data.

Chapter 4 then follows with the basic results of the comparative part of the study: the relationship between the survey data for each firm and performance over a five-year period. Chapters 5 through 10 present the qualitative part of the study, and the concluding chapter is a discussion of the results of the research taken as a whole.

The behavioral data for the comparative part of the study were drawn from the Survey of Organizations (SOO) questionnaire (Taylor and Bowers 1972) and the Organization Survey Profile (OSP), a highly similar instrument used by Rensis Likert Associates, Ann Arbor, Michigan. These instruments grew out of the organizational research conducted at the Institute for Social Research between 1966 and 1980. The content of these instruments includes behavioral characteristics of organizations (referred to as organizational climate) as well as characteristics of the context in which a work group operates, and job design, leadership, group functioning, satisfaction, and goal integration. This range of content includes organization-level constructs and leadership, group-level, and individual attributes. The range of firms studied using either the SOO or OSP instruments allows for a comparative study at the organizational level of the impact of organizational behavior on firm performance.

The financial data used to generate the outcome measures used in this study were obtained from Standard and Poor's statistical service, COMPUSTAT, maintained on tape by the University of Michigan's School of Business Administration. This service allows access to yearly data on 130 financial measures for 2,458 firms listed on either the American or New York Stock Exchange. Data for this study were drawn from the years 1966 to 1980.

Creating an analysis file for this study involved selecting a subset of firms for which both behavioral and financial data were available. Once this match was made, behavioral data were converted from multiple versions of the survey to a common form and index structure and then aggregated to the work group level. Organization-level statistics (mean and variance) were then computed for each organization and for all indexes generated from the survey items. Thirty-four organization-level cases made up the behavioral half of the analysis file.

A subset of 17 financial measures was drawn from the COMPUSTAT tape and used to compute a set of financial ratios representing organizational effectiveness, performance, and financial health. For each firm for which there were behavioral data, all other firms in the same industry were drawn from the tape and used to compute a "standardized" performance measure, comparing each firm's performance with the performance of its competitors by year. The standardized and unstandardized financial ratios were then matched to the behavioral data to form a sample of 34 firms that would serve as a data base suitable for an examination of the relationship between behavior and performance.

The following sections of this chapter describe in detail the behavioral data, the financial data, and the process and decisions involved in creating the analysis file used to begin to address the question of organizational culture and effectiveness through comparative research. Readers who are uninterested in the methods used to construct this data base and more interested in the results may wish to scan the rest of this chapter and skip to the results presented in Chapter 4.

The Behavioral Data: The Survey of Organizations and the Organization Survey Profile

In 1966, a group at the Institute for Social Research (ISR) began a program of comparative research referred to as the Intercompany Longitudinal Study (Likert, Bowers, and Norman 1969; Bowers 1973). This comparative study of a number of firms over time demanded a common perspective, method, and research instrument. Prior research at ISR had resulted in a sizable pool of questionnaire items on many facets of organizational behavior, but had never integrated these different facets into one instrument. The initial version of the Survey of Organizations did this and served as a summary of the most valid and reliable survey items and scales, as well as a first attempt to operationalize the Likert metatheory of management and organizational functioning (Likert 1961, 1967).

The construction of this instrument was based on a number of assumptions and observations that remain as relevant and controversial now as they were then:

1. Certain behavioral characteristics, social-psychological in nature, are common to nearly all organizations and are instrumental to their performance. Thus, a valid questionnaire can be constructed with enough generality to be used in many settings without revision.
2. Questionnaire content should be descriptive and evaluative, as well as attitudinal. This is true if an instrument is to be used for either diagnosis or prediction. Reports about organizational conditions and practices, for example, should be combined with reac-

tions to such practices. Perceptions of behavior should be combined with the measurement of attitudes about those behaviors.

3. The basic structural unit of complex organizations is the work group, made up of a set of peers within a structure of authority, and linked to that structure of authority by a supervisor or hierarchical superior.

4. For meaningful diagnosis, as well as theoretical development, organizations must be studied using multiple levels of analysis: organizationwide practices and conditions, leadership, the contextual influences on a work group, the characteristics of a work group's internal functioning, and individual reactions to each of the above.

Another more general principle underlying the instrument is the general systems model of organizational functioning (Katz and Kahn 1978). The model has evolved along with the instrument and has reflected the work of many (Bowers 1975; Franklin 1973, 1975a, 1975b; Likert 1961, 1967; Likert and Bowers 1969, 1973; Taylor and Bowers 1972). All ver-

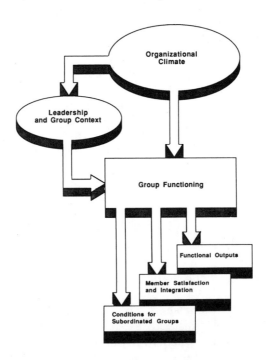

Figure 3.1 Systems model of organizational functioning

sions of the model, however, reflect a common form: organizationwide conditions and practices referred to as organizational climate, along with other more group-specific contextual factors, shape the behavior of the members of a work group. This influence process occurs predominantly through a leader who links the work group to the rest of the organization. This set of factors, along with the activities of the group members themselves, determines the functional outputs of the group, the satisfaction of the group members, and the conditions under which any subordinate groups in the hierarchy must operate. Figure 3.1 summarizes this multilevel model.

Between 1966 and 1969 the SOO was revised several times, and by 1969 a substantial archive had developed, providing the basis for most of the analyses presented by Taylor and Bowers (1972). Major revisions in 1974 and 1980 updated the instrument, but maintained some comparability with the archived data. The Organization Survey Profile, a separate version of the instrument developed by Rensis Likert Associates, shared much of the content. The research in this book has drawn from all of these sources and has focused on the set of indexes listed below. The evolution of various forms of the instrument and the current set of items and indexes are presented in Appendix B.

The set of indexes considered in the quantitative study were grouped into five areas—organizational climate, job design, supervisory leadership, peer leadership, and three outcome variables: group functioning, satisfaction, and goal integration. Each index is described briefly below.

Organizational Climate.

> **Organization of Work.** The degree to which an organization's work methods link the jobs of individuals to organizational objectives.
>
> **Communication Flow.** The flow of information, both vertically within the organizational hierarchy and laterally across the organization.
>
> **Emphasis on People.** The interest that the organization displays in the welfare and development of the people who work there.
>
> **Decision-Making Practices.** The degree to which an organization's decisions involve those who will be affected, are made at appropriate levels, and are based on widely shared information.

Influence and Control. The influence of those at the lower levels of the organization.

Absence of Bureaucracy. The absence of unnecessary administrative constraints in the organization's internal functioning.

Coordination. Coordination, cooperation, and problem resolution among organizational units.

Job Design.

Job Challenge. Variety, opportunity to learn, and the use of skills and abilities on the job.

Job Reward. Instrumentality of good job performance with regard to recognition, respect, and getting ahead.

Job Clarity. Clear and appropriate job expectations.

Supervisory Leadership.

Supervisory Support. The supervisor's attentiveness, approachability, and willingness to listen.

Supervisory Team Building. The supervisor's emphasis of team goals, idea exchange, and working as a team.

Supervisory Goal Emphasis. The supervisor's setting of high standards and encouragement of best effort.

Supervisory Work Facilitation. The supervisor's helpfulness in improving performance, planning, and problem solving.

Peer Leadership.

Peer Support. Peers' attentiveness, approachability, and willingness to listen.

Peer Team Building. Peers' emphasis of team goals, idea exchange, and working as a team.

Peer Goal Emphasis. Peers' setting of high standards and encouragement of best effort.

Peer Work Facilitation. Peers' help in improving performance, planning, and problem solving.

Behavioral Outcomes.

Group Functioning. Group members' planning, and coordination, decision making and problem solving, knowledge of jobs, trust, and sharing of information.

Satisfaction. Seven facets include satisfaction with group members, the supervisor, the job itself, the organization, pay, and current and future career progress.

Goal Integration. The compatibility of individual and organizational needs.

These measures are a complete set of the indexes that could be constructed from the survey data base. No attempt has been made, at this point, to distinguish which measures might be considered "cultural" and which should not. The first task was simply to examine the data that were available and draw conclusions about their implications for the culture and effectiveness model.

The Behavioral Data: The Organization-Level Sample

Creating organization-level behavioral measures for each firm was a complex procedure. The data came from multiple questionnaires with differing formats, index structures, and content. In addition, relatively few firms had a sample that included all of the organization's members. Many decisions had to be made about what to include, and why, as well as how. This section recounts that process in detail.

As mentioned earlier, data came from five versions of the Survey of Organizations and the Organization Survey Profile. The content varied somewhat between versions and the index structure changed several times, but the basic core items and their derivative indexes are common to all five forms. Some of the data were already a part of a large archive, but some of the individual sites were on separate tapes. Some were individual-level data, and others were already aggregated to the group level.

Computing indexes from slightly differing sets of items created several typical problems; for example, one form might include two of the three items necessary to compute an index, and another form of the instrument might include all three. The decision rule used here was the same one that covered the case where a respondent simply did not answer one of the items necessary to compute an index—more than half of the component items had to have valid scores for the summary index to be computed. Whenever possible, all indexes were computed first for individuals and then averaged to form the group mean for the index, rather than simply averaging the mean scores for the group on each of the component items of an index.

After conversion to a common format and computation of all indexes meeting the criteria, the data were aggregated to group level, with the index and item means serving as the summary statistics. At this point, all data that did not represent an intact work group with survey responses from three or more members were excluded. Although theoretically a work group is defined to be a face-to-face group with a joint product, interdependence, and regular interaction, in practice this has led to defining a work group as all those who share the same supervisor or hierarchical superior.

After the data from all work groups met these criteria, a mean and variance score for the organizations were estimated for each of the indexes in the survey. These organization-level measures were then matched with performance data from each firm in order to examine the relationship between the survey measures and performance. Several other issues also required a consistent set of decision rules.

Most of the organizations that were included in this study did not have data from all members of the firm. Nonetheless, all of the companies had samples that were large enough to be taken as a representation of the firm as a whole. Some firms also had data from the entire firm, but not all within the same year. This set of less-than-perfect samples required decision rules.

Suppose, for example, that two major divisions of a corporation were surveyed within the same year, but other divisions were not. Suppose a series of plants within one corporation were surveyed regularly, but never all within the same year. What should be included? How should they be combined? Should responses from all levels, divisions, and functions be weighted equally? How should the difference between a total sample and a survey of top management groups be treated?

In one sense, none of these questions can be answered in full. All stem, in some part, from the fact that this sample of organizations all voluntarily chose to use the SOO survey. The time of the survey, the sample obtained, and the period of time over which data were collected were, along with the financial support of this research, primarily at the discretion of the individual firms studied. This contrasts rather sharply with research that is designed to provide systematic samples with equal probability of selection for each firm in the population.

In order to carry out the analyses, some decision rules were required. First, all divisions or plants within a particular corporation were considered. In the case where data collection was spread over time, a year was selected that represented the largest possible sample of work groups available from that firm for any one year. This decision rule also implied that data from multiple divisions, collected in the same year, be combined. Different divisions within different years required that a choice be made in favor of one or the other. In fact, one example exists where different divisions of the same corporation surveyed in different years were both included. In this case, however, the survey dates were so far apart that none of the financial data overlapped, so, having met that criterion, both "organizations" were included.

A decision rule was also needed to make distinctions as to the quality of the sample from each organization and prospective quality of the match between the survey data and the financial data. Three grades of sample quality and match were distinguished: complete samples in which the entire organization had been surveyed (the highest quality, given a plus sign) were easily distinguished from those sites with small samples (<200) that did not reflect the diversity of the firm (the lowest quality, given a minus sign). Those firms falling in the middle thus had either relatively large samples or samples that clearly reflected the diversity of the firm (these were given an average quality rating, [0]). A summary of the match quality assigned to each firm, along with the survey date and the number of respondents, is presented in Table 3.1. A later section (see Appendix D) explores in detail the effects of match quality on the observed relationship between behavior and performance. In general, this analysis supports the use of the lower quality matches by showing that the observed relationship becomes weaker when cases with poorer matches are included, as would be expected. This effectively rules out the possibility that the observed relationship was, in fact, created by the poor matches and is only an artifact of the poorly matched sample of behavioral and financial data.

Even with the compromises and decisions necessary to incorporate data from as many organizations as possible, the organization-level SOO analysis file represents a unique data resource. Comparative studies of organizational behavior are rare and comparisons across a population of organizations are rarer still, even though most theories imply an organization-level outcome as a result of behavior within organizations. The existence of such a data set now allows for some of these implicit hypotheses to be tested in an exploratory manner.

Table 3.1　Description of Survey Sites

Site Number	Survey Date	Number of Groups	Number of Individuals	Match Quality
1	1979	37	259	0
2	1979	1	22	−
3	1979	90	584	−
4	1980	111	3,278	0
5	1980	11	62	−
6	1977	1,150	8,925	+
7	1978	648	2,733	0
8	1980	406	2,210	0
9	1981	5	137	−
10	1981	13	326	0
11	1981	273	799	0
12	1980	293	1,285	0
13	1980	28	132	0
14	1976	130	938	0
15	1978	126	768	0
16	1971	45	292	−
17	1970	690	2,192	0
18	1978	274	1,150	0
19	1975	147	455	0
20	1966	245	2,526	+
21	1973	75	526	0
22	1970	220	1,960	0
23	1966	34	469	0
24	1969	92	1,171	0
25	1972	108	588	+
26	1968	311	2,350	+
27	1976	109	430	0
28	1967	50	428	0
29	1977	27	144	0
30	1977	63	603	0
31	1977	159	579	0
32	1978	7	127	−
33	1979	660	4,970	+
34	1968	33	329	0
TOTALS		6,671	43,747	

The Measures of Effectiveness Used in This Study

The measures of organizational effectiveness used in the quantitative study presented here and in Chapter 4 are derived from the financial performance records of a set of firms, publicly held, that are listed on the New York or American Stock Exchange. The primary measures are two financial ratios, return on sales and return on investment. Although financial criteria such as these are plainly an important element in any operational definition of effectiveness, these criterion measures must also be set in the wider context of the literature on organizational effectiveness.

There are several distinct advantages to using financial data as indicators of effectiveness. First, the ratios are a summary measure of effectiveness and refer to the performance of the organization as a whole. Second, they are indicators of firm performance that are widely recognized by those who manage and invest in organizations. Third, they are an outcome measure quite distinct from the measure of the organization itself. "Soft" survey measure are being used to predict "hard" outcomes. Finally, these data are readily available in a form that allows comparative research to take place.

Two specific perspectives on the organizational effectiveness question directly influenced the choice of financial measures used in this study. These are the efficiency perspective (Katz and Kahn 1966, 1978) and the resource acquisition model (Yuchtman and Seashore 1967). The efficiency perspective, in its elementary form, tells us "how much of an input emerges as a product and how much is absorbed by the system" (Katz and Kahn 1978, 170). Although this construct is regarded today as simplistic when compared to the more complex construct of effectiveness, one only need look to the great variety associated with the terms "input," "produced," and "system" (particularly in light of multiple constituencies) to recognize that any such simplicity is much more apparent than real. The return on sales measure provides a direct operationalization of this construct.

Yuchtman and Seashore have also emphasized a rather simple point which has endured as a basic definition of effectiveness. They define effectiveness as the ability of an organization to "exploit its environment in the acquisition of scarce and valued resources" (1967, 897–98). To the degree that these "valued resources" can be captured in financial terms, the return on investment ratio provides a reasonable operational definition of this capacity.

Several of the theories described in Chapter 2 fit quite well with the financial indicators of performance, and others imply that financial data are only one part of the effectiveness domain. The fit of each of the specific theories of effectiveness to the operationalization of effectiveness used in the study is addressed briefly below.

Natural Systems Model. Both the efficiency and resource acquisition models grew out of the natural systems perspective and thus provide a rationale for the use of financial measures as indicators of effectiveness. The financial measures also refer to the system as a whole, and are thus a good fit in terms of unit of analysis. The causal variables in the study, organizational culture and climate, also represent some of the internal organizational processes suggested by the natural systems model. Seashore (1983), however, points out one instance where financial measures may not fit the natural systems model very well. He emphasizes that the systems model implies that effectiveness should be measured using "intact sets" of indicators. Using financial measures alone thus meets many of the demands of the natural system model, but not the need for using intact sets of indicators.

Goal Attainment Model. Many organizations explicitly or implictly define profitability as a goal or objective. If this is true, then measures of return on sales and return on investment are a good fit with the goal attainment model. At the same time, organizations hold many other goals such as growth, survival, or the domination of specific markets, which often conflict with a global measure of profitability. Organizations also constantly trade off short-term and long-term returns in a way that clouds the meaning of a measure at any particular time. Nonetheless, measures of profitability are a good approximation of effectiveness as defined by the goal attainment model.

Decision Process Model. The cultural and behavioral model of effectiveness being tested in this study is probably closest to the decision process model. Many of the behavioral variables examined might be referred to as "organizational processes and practices," and several measures address decision processes directly. Furthermore, it seems clear that a cultural theory of organizational effectiveness must be a process model, which argues that the long-term effectiveness of an organization can be determined by the characteristics of the firm's internal processes. The paradox, however, is that the financial criterion used in the study does not conform to the decision process definition of effectiveness. The criterion for examining effectiveness from a decision process point of view should be the measures of the process itself, not an independent financial measure. At the same time, it would be tautological to test a decision process model of effectiveness using a decision process definition of effectiveness. Thus, this study is best seen as a test of an organizational process model, using financial criteria, rather than a test using a decision process definition of effectiveness.

The Stakeholder Model. A conceptualization of effectiveness that emphasizes the importance of "strategic constituencies" is poorly represented by the financial definitions of effectiveness used in this study. Framing the study with respect to this perspective requires several assumptions. One must either assume a high level of consistency in the interests of the various stakeholders or ignore that good financial performance may come at the expense of some of an organization's stakeholders. Although it may be true that an organization that fails has, by definition, failed to represent an effective coalition among stakeholders, it does not follow that greater effectiveness for all stakeholders is indicated by a higher rate of return. An approach that combined financial measures with a detailed stakeholder analysis would make an important improvement in future research. Some stakeholder analysis is presented in the five case studies (Chapters 6 through 10), but this is done primarily in a historical rather than comparative way.

Resource Dependence and Population Ecology. Both of these theories present a reactive image of organizational effectiveness that is quite different from the proactive theory of culture and effectiveness presented in this book. If these theories are ''correct,'' then the measures of organizational culture and climate should do little to predict the future performance of an organization. Nonetheless, the financial measures of effectiveness used in this study fit reasonably well with the resource dependence and population ecology perspectives. These models would also make several important additions to the set of effectiveness indicators: the resource dependence model would stress the importance of controlling other nonfinancial resources, and the population ecology model would emphasize the births, deaths, and growth patterns of firms.

The process of constructing a set of outcome measures for use in the study began with the financial data available through Standard and Poor's statistical service, COMPUSTAT. As mentioned earlier, 130 financial measures were available for 2,458 firms listed on either the New York or the American Stock Exchange. For most firms, yearly data were available for the period from 1961 to 1980, and the goal was to construct a set of annual financial outcome measures for the period extending from the date the behavioral data were gathered in each firm to five years after that date.

The initial set of measures selected for this study was deliberately broad, with the expectation that an important initial step in the study would be to explore the relationships between the behavioral data and some of the financial indicators and then focus on those relationships that seemed to be the most promising. Eleven measures were initially drawn from COMPUSTAT to represent both performance and current organizational health: current assets and liabilities, long-term debt, sales, income, investment, research and development expenses, earnings per share, common equity, and working capital. From these measures, six financial ratios were computed: debt/equity ratio, current ratio, R&D/sales ratio, and returns on sales, equity, and investment.

Preliminary analysis of this large collection of financial measures showed that the survey measures were relatively good predictors of the measures of firm performance, but, as might perhaps be expected, the survey measures were not very good indicators of the current state of financial health of the sample of organizations. This led to a focus on three measures: return on sales, return on equity, and return on investment (Denison 1982). The research presented in this book concentrates on two of those measures—return on sales and return on investment—because the behavioral predictions of return on equity follow the same general pattern as the other two measures, but produce weaker relationships because of the measure's dependence on a particular firm's preferences for debt or equity financing.

The COMPUSTAT definitions and variable numbers for each of the components of the measures used in this study are presented below:

Income (018). (before extraordinary items and discontinued operations). Income of a company after all expenses, including special items, income taxes and minority interest—but before provisions for common and/or preferred dividends.

Net Sales (012). Gross sales (the amount of actual billings to customers for regular sales completed during the period) reduced by cash discounts, trade discounts, returned sales, and allowances for which credit is given to customers.

Invested Capital (037). Total investment—the sum of long-term debt, preferred stock, minority interest, and common equity.

The two summary ratios used are as follows:

Income/Sales Ratio. This ratio is a good indication of the efficiency of a company's operations, showing the return on each dollar of sales. This is a good indicator for comparing firms, particularly within industry. This ratio was computed by dividing income by net sales.

Income/Investment Ratio. This ratio shows the return on each dollar of investment and effectively adds minority interest and long-term debt to the denominator of the income/equity ratio. Thus, this is a measure of return on all sources of investment dollars, not just shareholders' equity. This ratio was computed by dividing income by total investment.

Standardization

Trying to compare the performance and effectiveness of a sample of organizations from many industries quickly runs into several problems. For example, suppose that company A in the automobile industry and company B in the petroleum industry are compared with respect to return on investment. During the early eighties, the average rate of return in petroleum was, for several years, higher than in automobiles. By the late eighties, this trend may have reversed. Attributing this difference in performance to differences in organizational culture would be an error. The industry itself may have a spurious effect on the outcome measures.

Similarly, economic cycles might be expected to have an impact on many of the financial indicators used in this study. The rate of return in 1979, for example, might well be higher than in 1974. Since the behavioral data were collected once at one point in time (from 1966 to 1981) and the financial data were then matched for a period extending for five years after the data collection, the particular years in which the financial data for year +1 were collected might also be expected to have a spurious impact on performance.

Finally, both of these effects might occur together—1981 was a bad year for savings and loans and for airlines but a good year for microcomputers. If the ratios were simply used as computed, a particular industry/year combination could also have a spurious impact on performance.

To address all three of these problems, the performance measures for each firm in the study sample were adjusted with respect to all firms within the same industry in the same year on the Standard and Poor's tape. For nearly all industries, the COMPUSTAT tape offered a reasonably large population of competing firms for comparison. This *standardization* process adjusted each firm's performance simultaneously for the effects of industry and year. Table 3.2 presents the numbers of firms from each industry in the sample and in the population against which each firm was standardized. These standardized measures of performance were then added to the two unstandardized financial indicators to make a set of four indicators of financial performance, by year, that are used in this book.

The Final Sample of Firms

Once the survey data and the financial data were both in the form described above, they were merged so that each firm had survey data for year 0, followed by financial performance data for years 0, +1, +2, +3, +4, and +5. So, for example, if a particular firm was surveyed during 1975, the six years of performance data matched to those survey data (years 0 through +5) would be taken from 1975 through 1980. This data base allowed for the analysis of the effects that a behavioral characteristic at the beginning of the period (year 0) would have on performance over the next five years (+1 through +5).

Table 3.2   Description of Industry Data Used for Standardization

COMPUSTAT Code	Industry	Number of Firms in Industy	Number of Firms in Sample
1000	Metal Mining	20	2
2200	Textile Mill Products	44	1
2600	Paper and Allied Products	27	2
1750	Commercial Printing	9	1
2800	Chemicals and Allied Products	19	2
2830	Drugs	26	1
1841	Soap and Other Detergents	10	1
2844	Perfumes, Cosmetics, and Toiletries	16	1
2850	Paints, Varnishes, and Lacquers	9	1
2911	Petroleum Refining	46	2
3140	Footwear, except Rubber	13	1
3221	Glass Containers	7	1
3350	Rolling and Drawing Nonferrous Metals	16	2
3531	Construction Machinery and Equipment	9	1
3693	X-Ray and Electromedical Apparatus	3	1
3711	Motor Vehicles and Car Bodies	9	2
3714	Motor Vehicle Parts and Accessories	27	2
3720	Aircraft and Parts	6	1
3760	Guided Missiles and Space	2	1
3940	Toys, Amusement, and Sporting Goods	15	1
4210	Trucking—Local and Long Distance	22	1
4811	Telephone Communication	14	2
4911	Electric Services	64	1
6025	National Bank/Federal Reserve System	90	2
6798	Real Estate Investment Trust	30	1

As mentioned earlier, the years for which behavioral data were collected for particular firms vary from 1966 to 1981. Since financial data were only included through 1980, it is impossible for a firm surveyed in 1980 to have financial data for years +1 through +5. Thus, there is a slight drop each year in the number of cases for which both survey and performance data are available. This drop becomes particularly noticeable for years +3 through +5.

In addition, there are two other reasons why individual firms may not appear in the final sample for a particular year. First, missing data on the financial measures make several cases unavailable for analysis. Second, as noted earlier, some of the survey indexes are unavailable for the earlier versions of the SOO or OSP. All of these examples cause a drop in the number of cases available for analysis. Table 3.3 provides a summary of the number of cases for which adequate behavioral and financial data could be paired. This gives a direct estimate of the number of cases used to estimate the behavior-performance relationship for each time period.

This table shows that the number of organizations available for analysis declines over the five-year study period. This presents several problems which must be taken into account in interpreting the results. First, the concept of statistical significance becomes somewhat irrelevant. For example, a correlation of 0.50 may be "significant" with 30 firms, but "insignificant" with 12 firms, because the criterion for significance is directly influenced by the number of firms. Rather than indulging the reader with a constant (and largely irrelevant) commentary on statistical

Table 3.3 Number of Firms in Final Data Base

SOO Survey Indexes	Years					
	0	+1	+2	+3	+4	+5
Organization of Work	25	21	19	16	12	10
Communication Flow	27	23	21	18	14	12
Emphasis on People	27	23	21	18	14	12
Decision-Making Practices	26	22	20	17	13	11
Influence and Control	27	23	22	18	14	12
Absence of Bureaucracy	12	9	9	6	3	—
Coordination	25	21	18	15	11	10
Job Challenge	12	9	9	6	3	—
Job Reward	12	9	9	6	3	—
Job Clarity	12	9	9	6	3	—
Supervisory Support	28	24	21	18	14	12
Supervisory Team Building	28	24	21	18	14	12
Supervisory Goal Emphasis	28	24	21	18	14	12
Supervisory Work Facilitation	28	24	21	18	14	12
Peer Support	28	24	21	18	14	12
Peer Team Building	28	24	21	18	14	12
Peer Goal Emphasis	28	24	21	18	14	12
Peer Work Facilitation	28	24	21	18	14	12
Group Functioning	23	19	16	12	8	6
Satisfaction	28	24	21	18	14	12
Goal Integration	12	9	9	6	3	—

significance, Chapter 4 concentrates on the *pattern* of the correlations between the survey measures and performance. Significance levels are reported in full in Appendix C.

Second, since the sample varies so much over time, a series of tests were run using only those firms that were in the sample for the entire time period. These results were then compared to the results for the overall sample, to make certain that the results reported on the entire sample in Chapter 4 were not a misrepresentation based on cases that later dropped out. This comparison generally showed that there were very few differences which were closely related to the fact that firms drop out over the period of the study.

The Analysis Plan

Since the behavioral data for this part of the study are measured at one point in time (year 0) and the financial data are measured for that year and the five years following it (years $+1$ through $+5$), the basic analysis plan follows the general form presented in Figure 3.2.

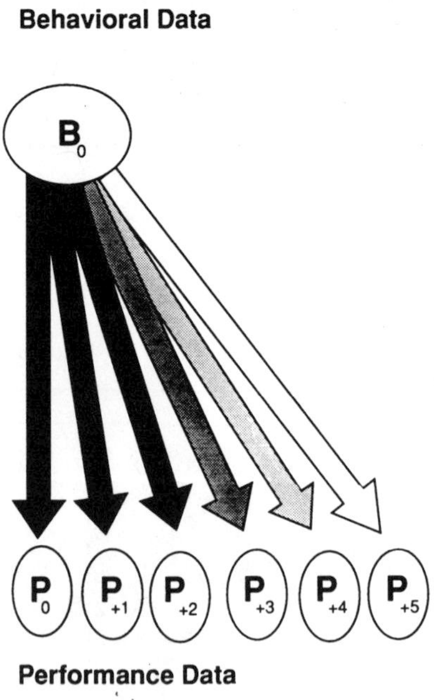

Behavioral Data

Performance Data

Figure 3.2   Analysis plan

As this figure indicates, initial differences in the survey data are used to predict the pattern of performance over the next five years. This design allows for the longitudinal tracking of performance, but not the tracking of the survey data or culture over time. The data are analyzed by looking at the actual performance of the companies over time as a function of the survey data, through both correlational analysis and direct comparison.

Although this study has some of the elements of a time-series design, it is not a true time series because of the absence of multiple measures of the behavioral characteristics. Having such measures would be very desirable and would greatly improve the study and its potential for making statements about cause and effect. As it is, any statement about "causality," however tempting, should be taken with a grain of salt. The general logic used in Chapter 4 occasionally allows some tentative statements to be made about cause and effect, but they should be regarded as exploratory and preliminary evidence about the influence that organizational culture can have on effectiveness.

CHAPTER FOUR

The Quantitative Results

This book began with a discussion of four elements of an organization's culture—involvement, consistency, adaptability, and mission—and the processes by which each of these traits might be related to performance and effectiveness. This chapter addresses that issue in quantitative terms and places particular emphasis on the empirical results that apply to the first of these elements—involvement. The results also address the elements of consistency, adaptability, and mission, but these topics in general are addressed less directly than involvement and rely more heavily on the case study analyses presented in Chapters 5 through 10.

This presentation of the quantitative results of the study compares behavioral data from the Survey of Organizations (SOO) with performance data over a five-year period for the 34 firms in the sample. This comparison and analysis takes on several different forms.

The first section of this chapter looks at the results for the "system level" organizational climate variables in the survey. Many of these variables bear directly on involvement and other elements of the theory, while others are less direct. The results are initially examined by comparing the levels of profitability of companies that score high or low on the survey indexes, and then examined in terms of the correlation, over time, between the behavioral measures and the performance measures. Some measures, as it turns out, seem to be particularly good indicators of current performance, and others seem to be better predictors of future performance. This distinction between "thermometers" and "barometers" is then addressed from a theoretical perspective. This first section ends with a discussion of the potential that organizational culture studies have for both understanding and predicting the relationship between behavioral characteristics and future performance.

The second section of this chapter presents the results from those segments of the survey that deal with the "subsystem" level variables. This includes variables such as job design, supervisory leadership, and peer leadership.[1] When the patterns of prediction using these subsystem variables are compared with the patterns shown with the system-level variables, an interesting finding emerges: the larger the unit of analysis, the longer the period for which performance can be predicted. This finding is discussed in the third section of this chapter.

Several ideas about the importance of a culture's consistency or strength are suggested by the organizational culture literature and can be tested, at least in part, by examining the SOO climate data. Foremost among these is the consistency hypothesis. The fourth section of this chapter presents a series of empirical tests comparing organization level variance scores with measures of performance over time. This crude test of the consistency hypothesis substantiates the idea that a strong culture is likely to be associated with good performance, but this relationship too shows some interesting fluctuation over time. A second test, also closely related to the organizational culture literature, examines the impact of some of the *ideals* that the members of organizations hold, and the impact that those factors seem to have on organizational performance over time. The final section of Chapter 4 summarizes these results with respect to the four elements of the culture effectiveness model.

The System-Level Results

The system-level variables in the Survey of Organizations were the first target of analysis: they are the best approximation of organizational culture that the comparative data base has to offer, and they are the best match to the unit of analysis of the performance data. Seven climate variables were analyzed, and the results are discussed here for four of these variables. The results for the remaining three climate variables are presented in Appendix C.

The original results of this study (Denison 1982) were presented as correlations between the survey measures and the performance measures over time. Some of these results are presented in that way later in this section. The simplest way to examine these data, however, is to look at the difference in performance, over time, between those companies that "have" a particular cultural attribute (or "are" a particular type of culture) and those that do not. This was the approach taken in an

---

[1]Although these variables may in several cases be less defensible as "culture" measures, the analyses are included here in an effort to contrast the system-level results with the more "micro" levels of analysis.

earlier article that presented the results for two of the climate variables, organization of work and decision-making practices (Denison 1984).

Two-group Comparisons. The climate indexes each make reference to a behavioral or cultural feature of an entire organization. For example, the organization of work index is a composite of four survey items that ask if the work methods in an organization are perceived to be sensible, if they adapt to changing conditions, and if the goals and decisions of the organization link the individual to the organization. The second index from the 1984 article, the decision-making practices index, indicates the degree of involvement that individuals have in decisions that affect them and the degree to which information is shared across levels in organizations in a way that brings the best possible information to decision makers. The impact of these two factors, both of which are clearly indicators of *involvement*, is presented in terms of two indicators of performance and their standardized equivalents: the income/investment ratio and the income/sales ratio. The first of these indicators is a measure of the effective use of resources over time, and the second is more an indicator of operating efficiency. The standardized ratios, as described in the previous chapter, compare each company to competitors in the same industry in the same year, and then express its performance in terms of a percentile score.

Figure 4.1 presents the results for the organization of work index and the performance measure, return on investment, in both standardized and unstandardized form. The highs in this figure simply represent those companies whose scores on the index are above the average for all 34 firms, while the lows represent those that are below the 34-firm average.

These figures show quite clearly that companies that are perceived to have a well-organized work system that links the efforts of individuals to the goals of the organization are likely to perform better than those that do not. The return on investment for the highs is consistently better than the lows, and is often twice as high.[2] This difference in ''culture'' also appears to have a lasting effect—the differences in performance extend three to five years into the future. The same basic pattern also emerges when the results for the standardized data are presented—the highs have a ranking within their industry that is from 15 to 50 percentile points higher than the ranking of the lows. The difference appears in all five years, and with the exception of the last year (+5), the gap between the lows and the highs appears to widen after the first year.

Figure 4.2 presents the results for the second performance indicator, return on sales. The results for this analysis are very similar, showing a

---

[2]All of the high-low differences shown in Figure 4.1 are statistically significant.

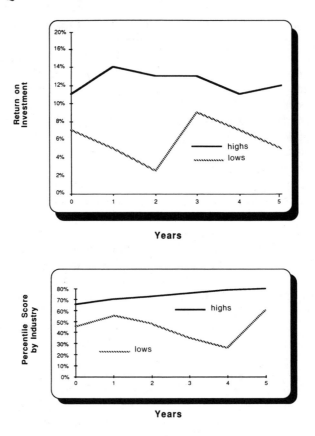

Figure 4.1 Organization of work and return on investment

consistent difference between highs and lows that appears to widen slightly over the five-year period. The difference is also quite clear in both the standardized and unstandardized analyses.

Both of these analyses show that companies with a culture that encourages the development of adaptable work methods linking the behavior of individuals to the goals of an organization are much more likely to perform well. This difference is substantial when expressed in terms of return on investment, and seems to be even more pronounced when presented in terms of the efficiency measure, return on sales.

Figures 4.3 and 4.4 present a similar set of results for the second climate index, decision-making practices. The highs and lows on this index are compared, in both standardized and unstandardized form, in terms

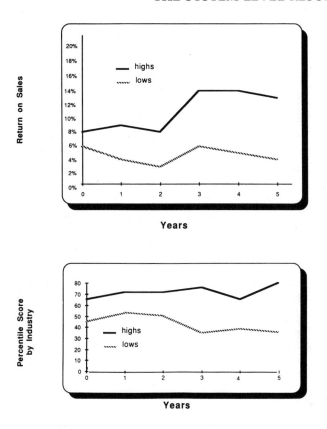

Figure 4.2 Organization of work and return on sales

of both performance measures—return on investment and return on sales.

The results for the decision-making practices index show a very different pattern from the findings for the organization of work index. Differences in the performance of the two groups of firms in the first few years are generally not pronounced, and in the case of the unstandardized analyses, the highs even appear to have slightly lower rates of return than do the lows in years +1 and +2. Nonetheless, a large and growing difference in the performance of the two sets of firms emerges in years +2 through +5. The standardized comparisons seem to show that the small initial advantage associated with a participative culture widens steadily over the five-year period. Performance relative to competitors steadily increases for the highs in this sample, generally moving

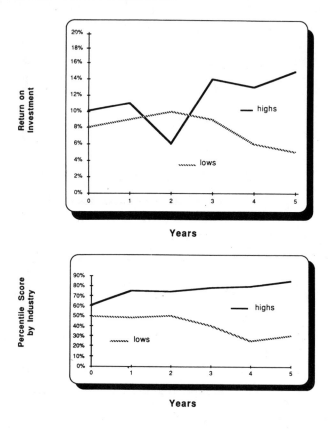

Figure 4.3   Decision-making practices and return on investment

from the 60th to the 80th percentile over the five years that these firms were studied. Standardizing the performance data by industry makes the relationship more apparent, not less apparent.

These four figures, taken together, make a persuasive case for the impact that a participative culture can have on the performance of organizations. The tests shown here address the involvement hypothesis outlined at the beginning of the book, and present some support for that idea. These results also tend to support the idea that the "main effect" of involvement is relatively strong and not totally dependent on environmental contingencies.

Correlations with Performance over Time. Another way to examine the relationship between the climate measures and the effectiveness of

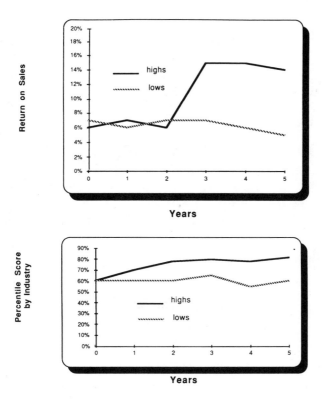

Figure 4.4 Decision-making practices and return on sales

the sample of organizations is to look at the correlations between the behavioral measures and the performance measures over time. This section presents those findings for four of the Survey of Organizations indexes, organization of work, emphasis on human resources, decision-making practices, and interunit coordination. This way of presenting the results allows for a better sense of the strength of the underlying relationship, rather than simply looking at the magnitude of the difference between the upper and lower half of the sample.

The first two indexes, organization of work and emphasis on human resources, show a similar pattern: the correlations are moderate to strong and remain quite consistent across the entire five-year period. The correlations range from 0.26 to 0.63 for the organization of work index, and from 0.15 to 0.54 for the human resources index. These results are presented in Figures 4.5 and 4.6. These survey measures are

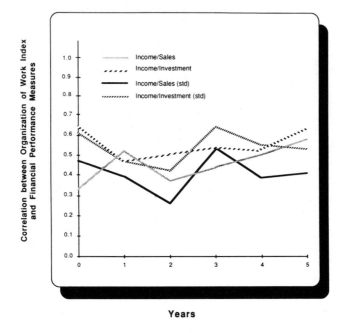

Figure 4.5   Organization of work and financial performance

good indicators of current performance but are equally good indicators of future performance. Although there are some noticeable differences in the two indicators—organization of work is generally a better predictor than is emphasis on human resources—most of the correlations remain quite stable over time. This seems to indicate that these two indexes, and the underlying organizational characteristics they represent, are good indicators of current performance and good predictors of performance in the future. The actual correlations and tests of statistical significance are presented in Appendix C.

This pattern of good concurrent prediction combined with good prediction of future performance is quite different from the pattern presented for the second pair of indexes, decision-making practices and coordination between units. These results are presented in Figures 4.7 and 4.8. Both of these measures show only a limited relationship to company performance at the time the survey data were collected. In some instances, the relationship is even the opposite of what the theory might predict—higher participation, or better coordination, seems to be associated with lower performance in year +2, for example. When perform-

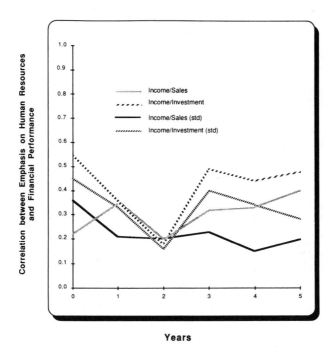

Figure 4.6 Emphasis on human resources and financial performance

ance is examined for future years, however, it appears that companies with high levels of participation, or good coordination, are better performers over the longer run, *even though they did not show higher performance initially.*

Comparing the results for this second set of indexes poses a dilemma that was unanticipated by the theory, and is largely unexpected: some of the measures act like "thermometers," while others act like "barometers." A thermometer, much like the indexes of organization of work and emphasis on human resources, tells us a great deal about conditions at a particular time but less about what might happen in the future. A falling barometer, however, is usually a good indicator of a forthcoming change in the weather, and usually precedes a storm. A thermometer is primarily a monitor, and a barometer is a useful even if not totally reliable predictor. The second pair of measures, decision-making practices and coordination between units, tend to act more like barometers in their potential for predicting performance. This may also help explain

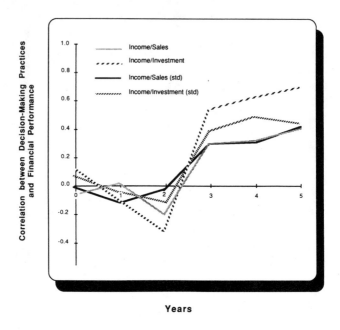

Figure 4.7 Decision-making practices and financial performance

why so many cross-sectional studies of participation have found little or no relationship to performance.

Why should one set of measures of "involvement" predict concurrent performance, and the other better predict future performance? One conclusion, which is at least partially supported by the data, would be that the two "thermometer" measures, organization of work and emphasis on human resources, are both measures of the nature of the link between individuals and organizations. They are not of themselves processes but rather are indicators of the existing state. The two "barometers," in contrast, comprise judgments about *processes* that, over time, serve to knit together an organization. The existence of these processes of coordination and participation in decision making (both elements of involvement) may contribute to the future bond between individuals and their organizations, but they do not have this impact immediately. This analysis presumes that involvement is an element of culture that is related to effectiveness and that the two sets of measures differ in that one set (the thermometers) measures the nature of the current bond between individuals and their organizations, and the second set (the barometers) measures the existence of processes that may contribute to that bond in the future.

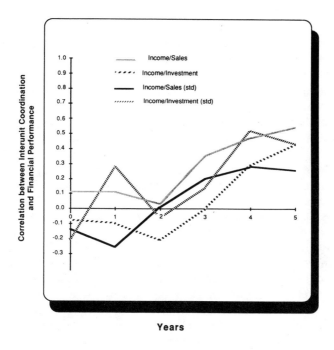

Figure 4.8 Interunit coordination and financial performance

These results seem to indicate that much progress could be made in understanding the performance of organizations if more studies were conducted that looked at *system-level* characteristics of organizations and their relation to performance over time. Many theories of organizational behavior describe microlevel processes with the assumption that these phenomena, writ large, will contribute to effective organizational functioning. In fact, such statements in the "managerial implications" section of articles directed at an applied audience seem almost obligatory. Unfortunately, they are seldom accompanied by much evidence.

If comparative research on organizational culture is going to contribute to an understanding of the effectiveness of organizations, there are a number of major obstacles to overcome. The research presented in this chapter only raises these issues and underscores their importance. The first, and perhaps most critical issue is the operationalism, in comparative terms, of the concept of organizational culture. The operational definition used here are quite far from the main thrust of the concept, and are clearly concerned with the more manifest elements of culture, rather than the underlying assumptions and values that lie at an organization's core. Better measures of culture, spanning the range from assumptions to artifacts, would enormously improve the quality of this research. The survey measures, as they stand now, have as their strength a relevance to the issue of culture and the ability to compare across organizations.

The second major issue that needs to be addressed in research of this type is that of aggregation. There are a multitude of ways that an organizational characteristic might be assessed, and this study has taken one that is simple and straightforward but can certainly be improved. Progress in theories of the meaning of internal consistency, systematic sampling of respondents within organizations, and the application of multiple measures of cultural constructs would all make important contributions to the study of organizational culture and effectiveness.

Results from the Subsystem Level

The survey data also include measures of a number of subsystem characteristics, such as job reward, job clarity, and supervisory and peer leadership. Whereas the previous section presented the results for measures that referred to an entire organization, these measures refer to units of analysis that are smaller than the entire organization: the design of jobs for groups or individuals, or the impact of leaders or peers in a work group setting. The measures are somewhat less relevant to the topic of organizational culture per se, but clearly represent some of the most popular traditional concerns of organizational behavior. Many theories imply that these subsystem factors will have an ultimate impact on organizational performance. This section of the chapter examines the impact that these variables have on performance over time, and then compares those results with the results for the system-level climate variables.

Job Design. Three measures of job design are included in the survey data: job challenge, job reward, and job clarity. Of these three, job reward and job clarity are good predictors of current and future performance and are discussed in this section. The third measure, job challenge, does not appear to be a good predictor of performance, and the results are presented in Appendix C. These results, overall, are hampered by the fact that job design measures did not appear in earlier versions of the survey; data are only available for 12 firms, and some of these firms drop out in years +3 through +5. For this reason, the results are only presented through year +3 for one of the performance measures, return on sales (standardized and unstandardized), and should be interpreted with caution.

Figures 4.9 and 4.10 present the results for job reward and job clarity. The job reward index shows a strong concurrent relationship with both

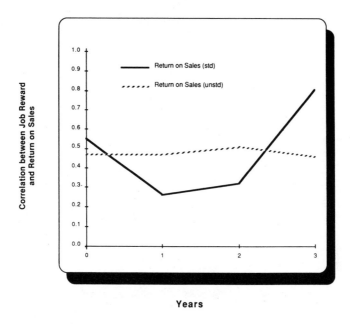

Figure 4.9 Job reward and return on sales

the standardized and unstandardized measures of performance. The correlation between job reward and the unstandardized measure of return on sales also remains quite stable over the years +1 through +3, while the correlation with the standardized measure of performance is quite high in years 0 and +3, but dips to the 0.25 to 0.35 range during years +1 and +2. Given the small number of cases available for analysis (12 in year 0, 9 in years +1 and +2, and 6 in year +3), it would be a mistake to overinterpret these results by inferring much from the fluctuation over time in the correlation with the unstandardized measure. It does appear, however, that there is a positive relationship between job reward and the performance measure of return on sales.

The second job design measure, job clarity, also appears to be a good predictor of the performance measure, return on sales. The concurrent relationship between job clarity and return on sales is moderate to strong for the standardized and unstandardized measures of performance, but, perhaps more important, the correlation between job clarity and future performance is even stronger. In the case of the correlation between job clarity and the standardized measure of return on sales, it increases steadily from 0.47 in year 0 to 0.73 in year +1, 0.83 in year

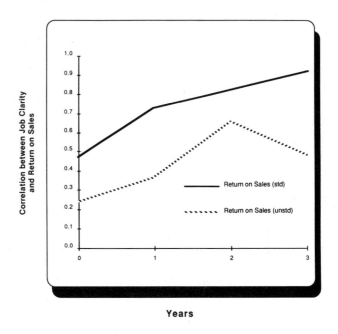

Figure 4.10   Job clarity and return on sales

+2, and 0.92 in year +3. This finding should, of course, be taken with caution given the small number of cases. Nonetheless, it is fascinating to speculate that a behavioral measure such as job clarity could possibly be such an accurate indicator of the effective functioning of an organization.

It is also important to note that the job design measures were *not* good predictors of the other performance measure, return on investment. While this difference is initially quite puzzling, there appears to be an explanation. Return on sales is a measure of efficiency; it simply compares the cost of goods and services produced with the revenues from their sale. Return on investment, in contrast, is a measure of return on all sources of investment. Poor investments, for example, could lead to declining sales, but in the case where the product is being produced at a declining cost, the return on sales margin could remain constant, or even increase. The computer industry, with its enormous development costs and rapidly decreasing costs of production, provides a classic example of this scenario. The point is that return on sales is a good measure of efficiency but not, necessarily, effectiveness. In contrast, return on investment is a good measure of effectiveness, which may or may not be a factor of the efficiency of the firm's internal functioning. Thus, job design variables, which may be taken primarily as an indicator of the efficiency of a firm's internal functioning, might be expected to be a better predictor of the efficiency measure, return on sales, than of the effectiveness measure. The results for all of the tests of the job design variables and return on investment are presented in Appendix C.

Supervisory Leadership. Another domain, or broad content area, included in the survey is supervisory leadership. This area also represents a subsystem characteristic in that the items in this section of the survey ask questions that refer directly to the respondent's supervisor rather than to the organization as a whole. Supervisory leadership practices are often strongly influenced by the overall culture of an organization, but leadership style also helps to determine culture, particularly for those at lower levels of an organization (Franklin 1975a, 1975b; Schein 1985).

The individual measures of supervisory leadership included in the survey are drawn from the four-factor theory of leadership (Bowers and Seashore 1966), and reflect the basic dichotomy between a task and a socioemotional orientation that characterized the leadership research of that era. The Bowers and Seashore formulation relied on two elements that were socioemotional in orientation—support and team building, and two elements that were task-oriented—goal emphasis and work facilitation. Although this way of looking at leadership is quite different from the current emphasis on the more symbolic role of leadership (Pondy, Frost, Morgan, & Dandridge 1984; Schein 1985), the data nonetheless present an opportunity to examine the impact of these aspects of leadership on performance over time.

This section presents and discusses the results comparing the four survey indexes and one of the performance measures, standardized return on investment. Results for the other measures of performance appear in Appendix C.

In Figure 4.11, the four supervisory leadership indexes all show a positive correlation with performance that varies in strength from modest to quite strong. The most interesting aspect of these results, however, is the fluctuation of the correlations over time: none of the four indexes is a particularly good predictor of concurrent performance at year 0. The same holds true for predicting performance in year +1. The best predictions of performance emerge in years +2 through +4, and seem to indicate that supervisory leadership practices are a potent predictor of medium-term performance; the strongest correlations occur at neither the beginning nor the end of the time period studied—they occur in the middle.

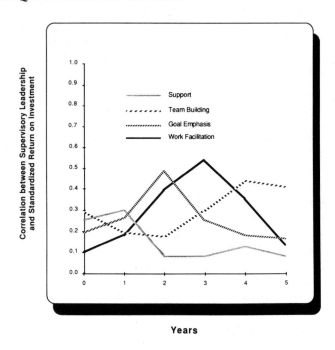

Figure 4.11 Supervisory leadership and standardized return on investment

A closer examination of these results shows that three of the indexes—team building, goal emphasis, and work facilitation—are stronger predictors than the fourth measure, supervisory support. Of these three, the two task-orientation measures, goal emphasis and work facilitation, are slightly better predictors of performance than the more socioemotional predictor, team building. The team-building measure also peaks later, showing the strongest relationship in year +4. Emphasizing goals has the earliest impact, facilitating work takes slightly longer, and building a team takes longer still. These results make intuitive sense: emphasizing clear goals for subordinates is likely to have an earlier impact than the less direct leadership processes of facilitating work or building an effective work team. Over the longer run, however, these less direct leadership processes can have an equal or even stronger impact on performance.

Peer Leadership. The peer leadership measures included in the survey also originated from the work of Bowers and Seashore (1966) and have the same four elements as the supervisory leadership measures.

Figure 4.12 presents the results for the comparison of the four peer leadership measures—support, team building, goal emphasis, and work facilitation—to the same performance measure, standardized return on investment.

These results suggest that a *very* different set of dynamics underlies the relationship between peer leadership and performance. With one exception, the four measures all show the highest correlation with performance in year 0, the year that the survey data were collected. The strength of the relationship then declines steadily, and in the case of the two socioemotional measures, team building and support, turns negative in years +3 through +5. The one measure that does not fit this pattern, peer work facilitation, shows a relationship that generally increases over time, with the strongest relationship to performance emerging in years +4 and +5.

Perhaps the most startling result in Figure 4.12 is the strong negative correlation that appears between peer support and performance in years +4 and +5. Peer support appears to have a positive impact on performance in the short term, but over the longer term, the result is not only

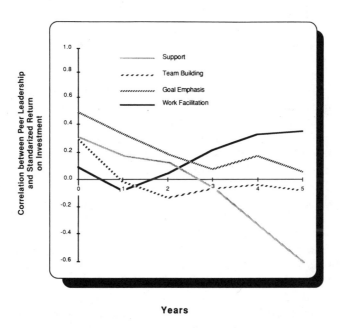

Figure 4.12 Peer leadership and standardized return on investment

negative but strongly so. This result may point to a similar finding presented by Bowers & Hausser (1977); and Bowers (1983). He found that groups with the lowest performance profiles typically had two somewhat contradictory characteristics: they operated in a very poor climate, but had very high levels of peer support. This condition, which might be referred to as the "lifeboat phenomenon," may in part explain the extremely strong negative correlation between the peer support measure and return on investment over time.

Comparing the job design and leadership variables with performance over time helps to demonstrate that subsystem characteristics of organizations can also be good predictors of current systemwide performance and performance in the future. This remains true even though the match between the unit of analysis for the survey data and the performance data is not as direct as it was for the system-level climate data. Even though these measures are quite far removed from prevalent definitions of organizational culture, these analyses do give a clear indication of the importance of these more microlevels of analysis for understanding the effectiveness of organizations.

The Effects of Inertia: Combining Units of Analysis

When the results from the system-level climate measures and the subsystem-level leadership measures are combined, an interesting picture emerges. The larger the unit of analysis, the longer into the future performance can be predicted. In contrast, with smaller units of analysis, the best prediction of performance comes in the short term. This relationship is illustrated in Figure 4.13.

This figure reflects first taking two of the measures from each of the three domains (organization of work and decision-making practices from the climate domain, supervisory goal emphasis and work facilitation from the supervisory leadership domain, and peer goal emphasis and team building from the peer leadership domain) and then averaging the correlations between those measures and the standardized measure of return on investment for each time period. The intent is to give a rough indication of the typical relationship between the variables in each of the domains and performance over time. The specific measures were chosen in an effort to help illustrate the relationship between unit of analysis and the interval for which performance could best be predicted. Thus, the "time lag" for peer leadership measures—the strongest prediction of current performance—is very short and the correlation with performance in future years quickly drops off. The time lag for the supervisory leadership measures is slightly longer—the measures are rela-

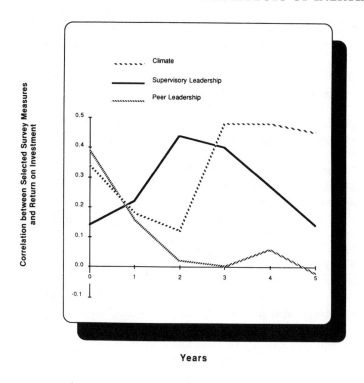

Figure 4.13 Unit of analysis and time lag

tively poor indicators of current performance, but are most useful in predicting performance in years +2 and +3. The correlations between the supervisory leadership measures and performance in years +4 and +5 drop off rapidly, suggesting a medium-term time lag for the supervisory leadership measures. Finally, the time lag associated with the climate measures is longest of all. The correlations with current performance is moderately strong, but the correlation with performance in years +1 and +2 drops off significantly. Correlation with years +3, +4, and +5, however, are much stronger, and generally support the idea that larger units of analysis imply a longer lag time.

These results seem to indicate that studying organizational processes, and using the responses and judgments of individual members of the organizations as indicators of those processes and conditions, can be a useful way to understand and predict future performance and effectiveness. Very little research of this type appears in the academic literature on climate or culture or in popular writings on the topic. One can only hope that research in the future will begin to address these problems and compile evidence that far surpasses that presented here.

Quantitative Tests of Culture Hypotheses: The Findings on Consistency

As noted in the first chapter, one of the many ideas that is unique to the recent literature on organizational culture is the concept of a "strong" culture—a culture with high levels of shared meaning, an agreed-upon normative structure, and a consensus about the basic assumptions regarding the organization and its environment. This concept of agreement, consensus, and shared meaning was not central to the earlier literature on organizational climate, but the survey data in this study do allow for this question to be addressed in an exploratory way. This section addresses the relationship between the consistency, or level of agreement in the survey responses from each firm, and the performance of the firms over time. The approach taken here is not an argument that this is necessarily the best way to study the impact of a strong culture, shared meaning, and the like, but rather is an attempt to begin to address these important issues within the limitations of the data currently available.

Figure 4.14 presents the correlations between consistency and performance for four of the climate measures discussed earlier in this chapter. Consistency was measured by taking the mean score for each group within a given organization and then computing the variance across groups within the organization. If all of the work groups within an organization had similar scores, then the variance score would be low, but if scores differed greatly between groups, that variance score would be high. Figure 4.14 presents the correlation between the variance score and a performance measure, standardized return on investment. A high negative correlation implies that the consistency, or strength of an organization's culture, is related to effectiveness.

The pattern shown in this figure suggests that a "consistent" culture is associated with better performance, particularly over the short run. The apparent advantage offered by consistency does not, however, extend very far into the future. The correlation of the variance scores with performance in later years seems to indicate that performance over the long run is not related to the consistency of the organization's cultures as defined by the survey data. Variance, in a few instances, even seems to be positively correlated with performance in the later years of the study. One explanation for this might be that a "strong" culture, through implicit coordination, helps to further immediate and short-term performance, but, over the longer run, such a culture tends to re-

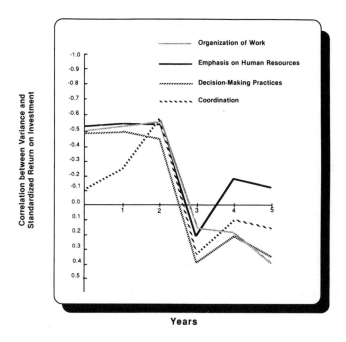

Figure 4.14 Consistency and standardized return on investment

strict the variety of options available to an organization. Since variety is needed to react to and control an organization's environment, a highly consistent, "strong" culture may sometimes inhibit this process.

The results for this section are preliminary and exploratory, but they do examine at least two novel ideas. First, cultural characteristics of an organization, whether they refer to orientation toward risk, time horizon, the meaning of particular symbols, or the level of involvement, are interesting not only because of the presence or nature of the characteristics but also because of the degree to which they are shared among the organization's members. Comparative measures of organizational culture can and should be examined for consistency and agreement along with the level of the characteristic. Such an examination should also extend to many other concepts in organizational behavior; but perhaps we should begin asking more questions about agreement, consistency, and individual differences, rather than concentrating almost exclusively on the "level" of the measured characteristics.

Second, these results present some preliminary support for a contingency theory of consistency and performance, which would predict that a strong, consistent culture is an asset to an organization in the short term, but over the longer term, particularly when an organization's environment changes rapidly, that consistency can compromise an organization's ability to adapt effectively. New bases for consistency must be continually reformulated in response to variety in the organization's environment, and these must build on the variety that already exists with the organization. When that variety does not exist, the organization has little to draw on to adapt to environmental turbulence.

Quantitative Tests of Culture Hypotheses: The Importance of Ideals

One of the most important contributions of the literature on organizational culture has been the recognition that leadership and management are often symbolic tasks (Daft 1984). Academic research in organizational behavior for many years has treated management tasks as purposeful and rational. In contrast, the culture perspective has, specifically emphasized the construction of meaning through myths, symbols, stories, and legends and the importance of these to the organizational lives of individuals and the functioning of organizations. Pondy et al. (1984) give many good examples of the implications of a symbolic role for leaders.

The survey data on which this chapter is based, in contrast, give little attention to the symbolic side of organization and management. Most of the indexes focus on management "practices"—concrete activities with purposive intent and rationale, intended to directly impact the behavior of organization members. Given this limitation, it is difficult in this stage of the study to adequately address the issue of the symbolic side of management and leadership and the relation that it may have to performance and effectiveness.

One exception is the survey data on leadership ideals. A set of questions, paralleling the four-factor leadership items in the supervisory and peer leadership areas, provide some information on the ideal type of supervisor or coworker respondents would prefer. These data have not been the target of much research, and have generally been regarded as producing little real information since they were always highly skewed in a positive direction (all respondents tend to give high scores on these questions) and typically tracked along with the items that assessed actual supervisory and peer behaviors.

Nonetheless, when these data were analyzed as a means to begin to explore some of the many issues of symbolic leadership, an interesting relationship emerges. Figures 4.15 and 4.16 present comparisons of ac-

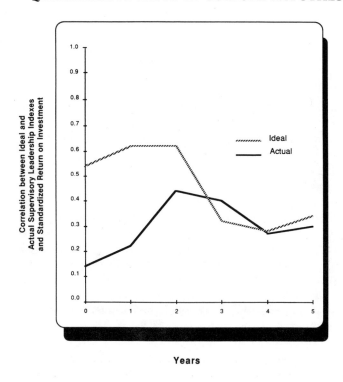

Figure 4.15 Ideal and actual supervisory leadership measures as predictors of performance

tual and ideal supervisory and peer leadership indexes as predictors of standardized return on investment.

These graphs are based on the same survey indexes that were used to represent the supervisory and peer domains in Figure 4.13. For the supervisory leadership domain the goal emphasis and work facilitation indexes are used, and for the peer leadership domain, the goal emphasis and team-building indexes are used. The correlations between each of these indexes and the performance measure, standardized return on investment, were averaged to obtain one correlation that is taken as a representation of the domain as a whole for the actual and ideal forms of the index.

The "ideal" form of the supervisory and peer leadership indexes follows the same general form as the "actual" form. Items in the questionnaire are asked in two ways—how things actually are and how the re-

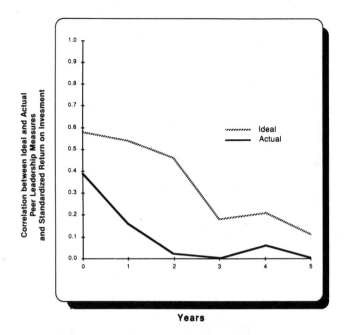

Figure 4.16   Ideal and actual peer leadership measures as predictors of performance

spondent would like them to be. Thus, the ideal indexes have the same content as the actual indexes (based on the four-factor theory of leadership), but they are projective judgments and indicate respondents' hypothetical preferences, rather than their perceptions of actual circumstances.

Both these figures reveal a rather startling finding: the ideal indexes seem to be *better* predictors of performance than the corresponding actual indexes. In the first case, the supervisory ideals are much better predictors of concurrent performance and performance in the first two years of the study, but are about equal as predictors of performance in the later years of the study. In the second case, the peer leadership ideals are better predictors of performance throughout the entire period of the study. The same set of differences also appear when all four actual and ideal leadership indexes are used.

These findings present an intriguing possibility, quite consistent with much of the culture literature: a consistent *vision*, expressed in forms both symbolic and real, can serve to tie an organization together in a way that is highly functional. Low ideals, or the absence of such a vision, can be as limiting as the actual set of conditions under which people work. Thus, the symbolic roles that managers perform may be the most important ones that they have.

The Quantitative Results: A Summary

This chapter has presented a quantitative study of 34 organizations, comparing their cultural and behavioral characteristics to their financial performance over time. The quantitative cultural data used in this analysis have been limited, but nonetheless help in the development of the culture and effectiveness model on which this book is based. The results provide compelling evidence that it is quite possible to use cultural and behavioral measures to predict the performance and effectiveness of an organization over time. This final section comments on several of the major findings in the chapter, and then closes by discussing the results with reference to the culture and effectiveness model.

The Long Lag versus the Short Lag. One of the most intriguing findings in this chapter is that some of the survey measures appear to be good predictors of short-term performance, and others are better predictors of longer-term performance. Two factors seem to influence the length of time it takes for a particular measure to show its greatest impact: the unit of analysis and the content of the measure.

The first factor, unit of analysis, is best illustrated in Figure 4.13. This figure shows that, in general, measures that refer to the organizational level of analysis tend to predict performance much further into the future than do measures with leadership or group behavior as a referent. This finding seems to point to the tremendous inertia present in cultural characteristics of organizational systems. Measures that capture system-level characteristics of organizations are more useful in understanding longer term trends, but more microlevel measures may often be better for understanding short-term impacts.

The second factor, the content of the measures, is somewhat more complex. As noted earlier in the chapter, some of the measures appear to be analogous to thermometers—they predict current performance but do not indicate much about future performance. Other measures are more like barometers—they provide a better indication of future performance than of current performance.

This difference appears to parallel the difference between an *indicator* of integration and an underlying *process* that contributes to future integration. Although the best example of this comes from comparing two "thermometers," organization of work and emphasis on human resources, with two "barometers," decision-making practices and coordination between units, the same pattern also recurs several other times within the chapter. In supervisory leadership, for example, work facilitation and team building, both measures of integrating *processes*, appear to predict performance further into the future than supervisory support, which is primarily a measure of integration itself. Similar results also appear with respect to the peer leadership measures.

The results help to underscore the importance of introducing *time* into organizational studies. Not only does the impact of culture extend over time, but, as these results have shown, different aspects of culture have very different lengths of time over which they exert their influence.

The Culture and Effectiveness Model

Involvement. The quantitative findings probably bear more directly on involvement that on the other four elements of the model. The content of the survey instrument is heavily weighted toward involvement and participation, and explores these dimensions with respect to leadership and group behavior, as well as to the overall climate of the organization. The findings that most directly support the involvement perspective come from the analysis of four indexes: organization of work, emphasis on human resources, decision-making practices, and coordination between organizational units. These results all provide support for the idea that both formal and informal sources of involvement contribute to organizational effectiveness.

Consistency. The quantitative results speak much less directly to the issue of consistency, since this concept is not directly included in the survey instrument. The results do, however, address this issue in an exploratory way by looking at the variation in survey responses across work groups within each organization as a measure of consistency. Obviously, this is only a partial approach to the complex issue of the consistency of an organization's culture, but it does yield some intriguing results. These results show that high consistency is associated with high performance in the short term, but is not a predictor of high performance over a longer period of time. In some cases, the evidence may even suggest that high consistency results in lower performance in the future. Although these results are only exploratory, they suggest that future research on consistency and effectiveness may produce more evidence regarding the impact a "strong" culture has on performance.

Adaptability. The evidence for the impact of adaptability on effectiveness is also limited, but encouraging. Most of the measures that support the adaptability concept are the same measures that support the involvement concept. Responsiveness to input and the organization's ability to adapt work systems to changing conditions are both captured to some degree by the organization of work and decision-making practices indexes. These two indexes help to begin to quantify the positive impact that adaptability can have on performance.

These results, unfortunately, only address those aspects of adaptability that have to do with internal flexibility. Other aspects of adaptability, particularly the linkage of an organization to its external environment, are not addressed. Ideally, adaptability must be studied in a way that encompasses both the capacity to adapt organizational systems to changing conditions and the capacity to perceive those changing conditions and translate them into changes in internal organizational systems.

Mission. The positive impact that an organizational mission can provide is addressed indirectly by several measures in the quantitative analysis. Most significant, the impact that the leadership ideals have on performance suggests that a vision or desired state can have an impact on an organization's effectiveness beyond what might be attributed to actual leadership practices. In addition, measures of job clarity and goal emphasis are also good predictors of organizational performance, and seem to point to the impact that a strong sense of direction can have.

In order to extend the culture and effectiveness model beyond these encouraging preliminary findings, Chapter 5 now lays the groundwork for a radically different approach to studying culture and effectiveness— a series of case studies that compose Chapter 6 through 10.

CHAPTER FIVE

The Qualitative Results: Introduction and Overview

The quantitative results in Chapter 4 presented an important story. The results support the idea that corporate culture has a measurable impact on bottom-line performance, and that involvement, consistency, adaptability, and mission are significant elements of culture that help determine future effectiveness.

Nonetheless, the statistics in the last chapter only tell part of the story. They make a broad generalization about culture that tells us little about what actually occurred, and they imply that the process by which culture influences effectiveness will be the same in all cases. Even if the theory were "correct," there are many exceptions to any rule and much could be learned about culture and effectiveness by taking a closer look at the individual firms. Or, as Freud put it, "La théorie c'est bon, mais ça n'empêche pas d'exister" (The theory may be good, but that doesn't keep things from happening).

The inherent limitations of comparative research also suggest that, at some point, greater gains can be made by looking more closely at individual firms. If the logic of comparison used in the last chapter were continued, it would soon require examination of a host of other factors that might influence culture and performance. Considering size, structure, market share, maturity of the organization, turnover in top executives, and fluctuations in regional economies would only be a beginning. A complete list would go on and on, and it quickly becomes apparent (at least in this study) that many more *factors* need to be taken into account to understand the relationship between an organization's culture and its effectiveness than there are organizations to compare. At this point, the logic of comparative research breaks down. The theory cannot progress beyond the methods used for study.

Because of these problems, and the need to address culture in far broader terms than in Chapter 4, the remaining chapters take a different approach to studying the relationship between culture and effectiveness. Using the findings from the last chapter as a springboard, this chapter selects five companies for the detailed case studies that appear in Chapters 6 through 10. The cases examine the history and development, the business, and the culture of each of the five companies. These cases are used to expand on the conclusions in Chapter 4 and to look further at the four elements of the culture and effectiveness model.

The perspective taken in this chapter emphasizes a qualitative understanding of the unique nature of each firm and the context within which it developed over time. This approach draws from several different yet complementary methods as models: business ethnographies such as Thomas Rohlen's *For Harmony and Strength*; phenomenological treatments of culture such as Clifford Geertz's *The Interpretation of Cultures*; the case study method so often used in business schools; the anecdotal approach often taken by management best-sellers; and the clinical approach to diagnosing organizational cultures (e.g., Schein 1985). All of these methods share an emphasis on understanding the structure of a specific situation in qualitative terms, and typically grow out of direct contact with the organization under study. An explicit discussion of the methodologies used in these cases studies is presented in Appendix E.

Chapter 5 is divided into two sections. The first section presents a critique of the comparative survey method and the "hypothesis-testing" approach to understanding organizations. This critique also serves as a rationale for the case study approach taken in this book. The second section describes the way in which the five companies chosen for case studies were selected. These five case studies include companies that fit the pattern described in Chapter 4, as well as companies that did not.

The Limits of Comparative Research

The carefully constructed generalizations and comparative frameworks that academics are so fond of often collapse when confronted with reality. The complexities, the rate of change, and wide differences in individual perceptions and interpretations make it difficult to generalize about an organization's culture and even more difficult to generalize about the relationship between that culture and the organization's success or failure. Furthermore, although perceptual data, such as those presented in the last chapter, help to predict future performance, they do not describe the *process* by which those characteristics determine future performance. In addition, prediction alone does not always mean that the same process will occur in the future. History seldom repeats itself. This section highlights several of these major limitations of comparative organizational research and their implications for this study.

Dealing with Complexity. Comparative methods often serve as a "filter" to simplify the complexity of an organization. They help ensure that the researcher will encounter little or no information that contradicts his or her preconceptions. In order to remain convinced that one's "filters" are appropriate, it is usually best for a researcher to get in, grab the data, and rush away—staying too long may force him or her to acknowledge the incredible complexity of any large firm and begin to doubt whether or not he or she was asking the right question to begin with. The researcher may also be forced to listen to the explanations of those who do not know "the theory," and who often have a way of proposing situational explanations for important events that defy generalization.

Most often the goal of comparative research is the reduction of the incredible complexities of human behavior to a set of simple linear relationships. That is, behavior is captured as "variables," and the goal is to show how one unit increase in "Variable A" results in one unit increase (or fraction thereof) in "Variable B." Despite some remarkable efforts to go beyond such obvious oversimplification, most research inevitably falls back on the simple linear model. As Larry Mohr (1982) has shown, this orientation tends to focus attention on explaining the variance in behavior rather than understanding the process by which it occurs.

Theory Testing versus Theory Building. Another important limitation of comparative research is its bias toward theory testing rather than theory building. Testing a theory usually consists of laying a logical template on the organizational world and then deciding if it fits. Over time, the theory tester comes to see the organizational world more and more in terms of conformity and departure from the template. As Chris Argyris (1980) and others have pointed out, many times this approach is not a "learning system"—research often consists of deciding "what's what" beforehand and then going out to find support for those ideas. If research only tries to gather information on previously defined concepts, then there is little room for creative discovery. This is one of the reasons why theories often persist despite the lack of supporting evidence, or even in the face of evidence to the contrary.

In contrast, building a theory often requires an inductive rather than a deductive approach to a problem (Sutton & Rafaeli 1988). Induction requires that information be gathered before the logical structure necessary to "pull it all together" is constructed. This approach to research requires a creative integration in order to make sense out of one's data. Despite the risk of "rediscovering the wheel," new ideas are found to emerge when an inductive approach is taken.

Inference and Probability. Another significant limitation of comparative research is its reliance on inference and probability. The typical study tries to demonstrate "statistical significance" at the $p < 0.05$ level, and, with a large enough number of cases, often does. A correlational study with 15 cases will conclude that a correlation of 0.30 is almost meaningless, whereas a study with 150 cases will conclude that the same correlation is highly meaningful. These criteria, as much as any other, probably account for the extraordinary number of organizational behavior studies that deal with individuals and the small number that deal with groups or organizations. Within social psychology, the same criteria probably account for a tendency to study the "social cognitions" of individuals rather than their actual behavior in groups. In each of these cases, the "tail wags the dog"—the criteria of inference and probability are determining the way in which social and organizational processes will be studied.

A second major problem with the criteria of inference and probability normally used in comparative research is that they often turn attention away from the unexplained part of the problem. Suppose, for example, that a study showed a significant correlation of 0.30 between the strength of an organization's culture and its short-term effectiveness. The typical reaction is to (1) presume that this hypothesis is "correct" and (2) react to competing explanations by either denying them or incorporating them into the existing framework. Both of these reactions tend to draw attention to that part of the problem that has already been explained rather than to those aspects of the problem that are unknown.

An alternative approach to this situation would be to focus on the examples that do not fit the pattern so that the goal is learning more, rather than finding support for one's original ideas. This implies that unexpected findings should often be of as much or more interest than the findings that were expected. The results of this study, as presented in Chapter 4, stand as a case in point. The correlations are often strong and frequently reach statistical significance. The case could be made, based on the criteria of inference and probability, that the involvement and consistency fostered by an organization's culture determine its effectiveness. Following the rules of "normal science" one could conclude that these two hypotheses were "correct" and ignore (or incorporate) other explanations of culture and effectiveness. The far more interesting alternative, however, is to step into the buzzing, blooming confusion of the organizations themselves and try to find out what really happened.

The case studies presented in the coming chapters address many questions that would be difficult, if not impossible, to study using survey research. These questions are central to understanding the relationship between culture and effectiveness and require the use of a wide range of methods to resolve. Although there are many questions that might be asked, those below seem to be among the most important.

- How did the organization's culture develop? Was it purposefully created or did it develop spontaneously? How was the development of the culture related to the development of the business itself?

- What is the current culture of the company? How rapidly is it changing? Does the observed culture resemble the picture of the organization presented by the survey data?

- What is the relationship between the meaning system, the deeply rooted values of the organization and the overt management practices and behaviors that structure the organization?

- What is the process by which the organization's culture contributes to effectiveness? How do the members of the organization perceive this link? How does this compare to the culture and effectiveness model?

These questions help to guide the five case studies presented in the book. The first step in this process was to select companies for case study.

Selecting Firms for the Case Studies

Selecting a case for detailed study is always a crucial step. Ideally, a case should be selected to provide a compelling example of a principle or situation the author wants to illustrate. In reality, cases often develop because of a researcher's prior involvement or experience rather than because of the principles or issues they could illustrate. This serendipitous approach usually helps solve problems of access to the organization but not problems of illustration. The "planned" approach, in contrast, must solve different problems—finding a case that illustrates the principle and then gaining access.

Both approaches often face common criticisms: How representative is the case being studied? Can generalizations be made? What are the limitations?

The problem of representation is addressed by using the quantitative analyses in Chapter 4 as a springboard. The findings are used as a framework for selecting firms. For example, a central finding from Chap-

ter 4 shows that there is a close relationship between the level of involvement in the 34 firms studied and their performance two to three years
in the future. Does this mean that all firms followed the same pattern?
Are there some firms that showed a different combination of participation and performance?

Figure 5.1 compares the scores of 18 firms on the decision-making
practices survey index with a return on investment (ROI) measure expressing future return on investment in relation to competitors in the
same industry. The ROI measure is scaled as a percentile score, that is,
50 percent equals the industry average. The decision-making practices
index was chosen because it seemed to provide the best contrast of firms
that fit the pattern with those that did not. Using the organization of
work index gives very similar results, and the term *involvement* is used
to refer to a common dimension that underlies both decision-making
practices and organization of work. Other central findings from Chapter
4, such as the relationship between consistency and effectiveness, were
also considered as a framework for selecting cases, but seemed less reliable.

The return on investment figures are from the period three years after
the survey data were gathered. Thus, this chart shows the relationship
between decision-making practices and *future* performance. The one ex-

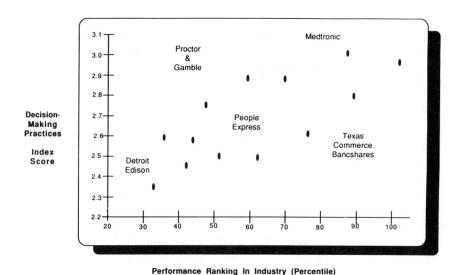

Figure 5.1   Organizations selected for case study

ception to this three-year time period is People Express Airlines, for which a two-year time interval was the only measure available. Picking the actual cases for study involved comparing both actual ROI and the adjusted ROI scale shown in the figure.

The five companies shown in this figure are the cases chosen for more detailed study. All had good survey samples. They were chosen because they represent several of the possible combinations of involvement and performance. In the upper-right corner, Medtronic, the major producer of implantable cardiac pacemakers, represents a high-performance, high-involvement organization, which was surveyed in 1969. In the middle of this chart is People Express Airlines, the well-known, low-cost airline born of deregulation in the early 1980s. Survey data for People Express are from 1982. Surprisingly, when only the survey and performance data are examined, People Express represents a moderate-involvement, moderate-performance organization. In the lower left corner, Detroit Edison, southeastern Michigan's public utility, appears to be a low-involvement organization with financial performance that is below average for a utility. Survey data for Edison were gathered in 1977. These three organizations, at least on the surface, appear to support some of the general findings presented in Chapter 4.

The case studies include two organizations that appear to contradict the findings of the last chapter. Procter & Gamble, the well-known consumer goods company, when surveyed in 1966, appeared to be a high-involvement organization with somewhat lower than average ROI during the period studied. In contrast, Texas Commerce Bancshares in Houston achieved very high performance relative to competitors, even though the 1977 survey data show that levels of involvement are slightly below average. These two organizations, it is worth noting, are the most significant departures from the general pattern of findings. Procter & Gamble is the only firm in this sample that has exceptionally high-involvement scores combined with below average performance, and Texas Commerce is the only firm with exceptionally high performance that falls below average on the involvement scale.

Working from this framework gives a general orientation as to what one might expect to find. But most of the important questions are still unanswered. Culture and effectiveness are far broader concepts than survey measures can convey, and their evolution over time as a result of internal and external forces must be carefully unraveled. This can only be understood through an analysis of each company and its history, the nature of the business and the industry in which it competes, and the ideologies, norms, and strategies that have evolved from the past and help to determine the future.

All the case studies follow a similar outline. First, the history and background of the company and the influence of leaders and founders are described. Then the culture of the company—its ideology and belief system, as well as its normative system and management practices—is portrayed. Particular attention is paid to the way in which culture has emerged from the organization's adaptation to its environment and the way in which it has contributed to performance and effectiveness. Last, each case is analyzed in terms of the culture and effectiveness model, and ends with a consideration of the lessons that each firm provides for the understanding of organizational culture.

CHAPTER SIX

Medtronic

From the quantitative analyses in Chapter 5, Medtronic appears to be a perfect example of a high-involvement, high-performance company. When surveyed in 1969, the corporation had high scores on most of the survey variables, and clearly outperformed its competitors during the five-year period from 1969 to 1973. A closer look at the company reveals a unique culture, a powerful mission, a charismatic founder, and a fantastic growth record. A closer analysis also shows the importance of technology, the problems posed by the life cycle of the company, the increasing competitiveness of the industry, and the problems of leadership succession. On balance, this case helps in understanding the cultural dynamics of a successful high-involvement, high-technology organization as it grows and faces increasing competition.

Medtronic is best known as a producer of implantable medical devices, designed primarily to support the human cardiovascular system. Its primary products are pacemakers, although the corporation has diversified into heart valves, neurological stimulation, and other implantable devices. The Hall-Medtronic mechanical heart valve is an integral part of the Jarvik-7 artificial heart, and its pacemakers have sustained life for well over 1 million patients worldwide, including former Soviet Premier Leonid Breshnev. The company today employs more than five thousand people and does business in 85 countries worldwide. Its corporate headquarters are located in suburban Minneapolis.

History and Background

The company's history is dominated by its founder, Earl Bakken. The firm was started, quite literally, in a garage by Bakken and his brother-in-law, Palmer Hermundslie, in 1949. After nine years of making and selling custom-made electro-medical equipment, Bakken, in response to a University of Minnesota heart surgeon's request, developed the first wearable external pacemaker. Two years later, Medtronic signed an agreement to produce and market the world's first implantable pacemaker. In 1962, after nearly going bankrupt when the first year's production costs outstripped the company's cash flow, the company began what would be 24 consecutive years of growth in sales and earnings.

By 1969, Medtronic had grown from 50 to 500 employees, and up to $15 million in net sales. In 1969 and 1970, it expanded manufacturing facilities, increased operating capital, and added several staff departments and direct domestic and international distribution. Production capacity was expanded to $50 million, and in 1972 the corporation shifted to a 36-hour, four-day workweek. Sales growth ranged from 20 percent to 50 percent per year. Roughly 10 percent of sales was spent on research and development in an R&D program with the joint goals of improving the reliability and effectiveness of pacemakers and diversifying into related areas.

Medtronic established the pacemaker industry and dominated it during these early years, always capturing at least 50 percent of the worldwide market for pacemakers. The domestic competition, primarily made up of former Medtronic employees, was limited, and, prior to the late 1970s, it never challenged Medtronic's technological or market lead.

By 1974 the company had grown to 1,600 employees and $5.3 million in earnings on $54 million in sales. Medtronic was highly profitable, had very bright prospects for growth, and was a "sweetheart" of Wall Street, with stock trading at up to 100 times earnings. With a strong market position in a growing industry, the company's future looked very promising.

Beginning in the early 1970s, Medtronic's leadership began to change. Thomas Holloran, an executive vice-president for many years, served as president from 1973 to 1975 and Dale Olseth, a member of the Medtronic board since 1973, took the position of president and chief executive officer from 1976 until 1985. Both of these changes marked the decreasing role of the founder, Earl Bakken, in the day-to-day management of the firm. He still remained very active as chairman of the board in the planning and direction of the firm. Since 1985, Winston Wallin, a former Pillsbury executive, has served as chairman, president, and CEO, while Earl Bakken remained actively involved as founder and senior chairman of the board.

A second major change to jolt Medtronic came shortly after Olseth became president and CEO. A product problem with the Xytron pacemaker developed, which could potentially cause the device to shut down quickly. Because the device was implanted inside the body, this was a serious problem. In the few cases where the pacemaker actually sustained rather than regulated the heartbeat, a failure could be life-threatening. Xytron began an era of periodic product problems and increasing government regulation and oversight that were unknown in the early days of Medtronic. Acknowledging and overcoming these product problems has been an important part of the evolution of the Medtronic culture and identity.

A third major change is one that occurred in the health care industry. By the early 1980s, it became clear that the future would be far more competitive in all areas of health care. Prior to this time, costs could easily be passed along to maintain a profit margin because very few customers ever "bought" a pacemaker. Physicians simply made the "best" decision, and insurance companies and national governments paid the bill. The new cost consciousness in health care meant that the industry would become price competitive and that many of the purchase decisions would for the first time be made by administrators.

The company received an enormous amount of negative publicity focusing on both quality and cost issues in the early 1980s when it came under investigation by the U.S. Food and Drug Administration. The investigation concluded that pacemakers were prescribed too often for elderly people, with little cost control, and recurring product problems. Although Medtronic's quality record is better than most of its competitors, as the industry leader it often received most of the publicity.

As a result of this combination of difficulties, in 1985 Medtronic broke its string of 24 consecutive years of growth in sales and earnings. Confidence and morale fell and the organization seemed to struggle to define its identity and direction. By 1986, however, the organization had rebounded with a successful new product, a change in leadership, and a confidence that it had reestablished a new sense of direction that was consistent with its history and mission.

These major changes in the corporation, and the accompanying changes in its culture, expand tremendously on the findings about the company's culture and its presumed relationship to effectiveness presented in the last chapter. A simple relationship between involvement and effectiveness, even though it might be a fair characterization of the years 1969 through 1973, does not entirely explain or predict the changes that occurred after 1975. The simple involvement-effectiveness hypothesis also does not allow for a full understanding of the rich ideology and culture that developed within Medtronic.

The Medtronic Culture

Once I began studying the Medtronic culture in detail, it quickly became apparent that it was a powerful and complex system that was intimately related to the organization's adaptation over time. The organization has a clear and explicit ideology, a unique set of behavioral norms and approaches to management, and a rich collection of stories. Most of the organization's members strongly believe that these factors were an integral part of the company's early success, and most also believe that these factors have at time been an obstacle to the firm's attempts to adapt to the changing health care industry.

The early years of the company's history are often characterized in mythical terms. Everyone knows the story. The Garage was the company's origin and symbolized an unfettered state where technical genius and creativity could be applied for the betterment of mankind. The early death of Earl Bakken's partner and brother-in-law, Palmer Hermundslie, seemed to add a spiritual tone to the origins of the organization.

In 1961, during a meeting of the board of directors, Earl Bakken went to the blackboard and, with the help of the board, wrote down the first formal statement of Medtronic's six corporate objectives. Twenty-five years later when I interviewed him, he produced a small card with those same six corporate objectives. In between, each new Medtronic employee had had lunch with Earl and reviewed those same corporate objectives. They provide an explicit mission, which is very well known throughout the corporation.

1. To contribute to human welfare by application of biomedical engineering in the research, design, manufacture and sale of instruments that alleviate pain, restore health and life of man.
2. To direct growth in the areas of biomedical engineering where we display maximum strength and ability; to gather people and facilities that tend to augment these areas; to continuously build on these areas through education and knowledge assimilation; to avoid participation in areas where we cannot make unique and worthy contributions.
3. To strive without reserve for the greatest possible reliability and quality in our products; to be the unsurpassed standard of comparison and to be recognized as a company of dedication, honesty, integrity, and service.
4. To make a fair profit on current operations to meet our obligations, sustain our growth, and reach our goals.
5. To recognize the personal worth of employees by providing an employment framework that allows personal satisfaction in work accomplished, security, advancement opportunity and means to share in the company success.
6. To maintain good citizenship as a company.

These corporate objectives spelled out a powerful mission of caring and commitment that served as a magnet to build the organization's early work force. The objectives, plus a close working relationship with the surgeons who implanted Medtronic's pacemakers, seemed to serve as strategic plan, operating procedures, and norms for behavior within the organization. Several people described the organization at that time as a "scientific engineering club," with little internal control or accountability. It is a powerful example of the direction that can be derived from a few simple principles that are widely understood within an organization.

The early days also involved an enormous amount of risk sharing with its primary customers—cardiologists and surgeons. Earl Bakken took great pride in holding a locker at the University of Minnesota Hospital, which put him in direct contact with the surgeons. Medtronic people were, literally, in the operating room during many of the early implants. Bakken believed very strongly that "if you spend your time out in the field, your customers will make your [strategic] plan for you." The company relied heavily on the contributions of the most innovative, progressive cardiovascular surgeons of the day, who willingly assumed the liabilities associated with these new and invasive procedures.

Bakken's career plans originally called for a life as a research engineer. Profit and growth never stood as ends in themselves, but only as means necessary to pursue his humanistic and technical goals. His attention naturally gravitated to the technology and the needs of customers and patients, rather than to the management and structure of his rapidly growing organization.

Bakken's approach to management was very personal. He made a practice of having lunch with all new employees to talk with them about the company and its mission and simply to get to know them. He was always called by his first name, whether he was being addressed by his executives or by the custodian. He was often described as paternalistic, but not as a directive authority figure. Employees had great autonomy and trust, and, at least when the organization was young, had little bureaucratic interference.

Several stories of Bakken's resistance to the bureaucratization of his company are widely known. The first concerns his opposition to the development of policies for dealing with customers. Bakken's own approach was to stay extremely close to customers and to find a way to accommodate their needs while establishing and building a bond of trust. When he found that corporate policies were starting to get in the way, he chose to make his point at an annual winter retreat of the company's top executives at a rustic resort in northern Minnesota. He walked into the living room where the group was sitting in front of a large fireplace. Chained to his leg were the corporation's policy manuals and regulations, a symbol of what he felt was the company's increasing bureaucratization. Dragging these behind him, he crossed to the fireplace, unchained the books, and threw them in the fire. The management team watched as their policies and regulations burned in the roaring fire.

Bakken also advocated an approach to research and new product development that stemmed from his early experience. As mentioned earlier, the Garage was seen as the source of creativity and inspiration, and, if left to their own, creative researchers would uncover new methods of applying technology to medical problems. This led to a philosophy of diversification that some characterized as "let a thousand flowers bloom." The principle seemed to be that if the *process* of the company's original discoveries was replicated, then the invention of the "next pacemaker" was only a matter of time.

As the company continued to grow, nearing two thousand people and $100 million in sales in the mid-1970s, the culture began to change. The company slowly began to reject some of its history, such as the four-day workweek, the informal organization, and lack of bureaucracy, in response to the competitive demands of the business environment. Responding to the perception that the company was "undermanaged," a new group of professional managers entered, emphasizing the economic goals of the company and beginning to build the infrastructure required to operate the larger corporation that Medtronic had become.

The "New Culture"

The "old culture" of Medtronic arose primarily from the founder's mission in the early days and gave the company's employees a strong sense of meaning and direction. The corporation enjoyed tremendous success, which reinforced these emergent principles, and they were seen by many as the foundation of the company's success. Nonetheless, with changes in leadership, an increasingly competitive environment, and a large and growing corporate structure, many perceived the need for change.

This debate within the company resulted in a strong push for a "new culture" that was a results-oriented professional meritocracy—a sharp contrast to the old paternalistic, egalitarian ways. The "old" culture was increasingly perceived to be a barrier of insularity and entitlement that prevented adaptation and change. The company had been largely a mission and needed to become a business; it needed to become competitive rather than continue to deny that worthy competition existed; it needed to introduce an element of confrontation into the management of the corporation rather than always to find ways to avoid conflict.

Many of the company's members also felt a strong need to alter the organization's decision-making processes. Most felt that many decisions were made on noneconomic grounds and that the organization attached more importance to input and process than to the actual decisions and their results. Many perceived the corporation to be "undermanaged" and felt that resources were wasted as a result. Indulgence and a taste for first-class style without economic justification also needed to be changed.

Another element of the "old" culture was also under attack at this point. That was the sense that the corporation was infallible. After years of "sweetheart" status on Wall Street, media attention for its tremendous contributions to human health, innumerable examples of saving lives, and a strong bond of trust with the world's most innovative cardiovascular surgeons, the company began to have product problems. The people in the company were "devastated," "grieving," and (figuratively) "jumping out the window." Another described these days in the company as "going into Vietnam." "Some never came out," he agonized, "some ran away—others went underground. The trust of the customer was devastated."

This crisis quickly undermined the belief of the company's employees and executives that they were "infallible"—an organization of high integrity that could do no wrong. This part of the mythology of Medtronic had been built up slowly over the years from its remarkable record of accomplishments, and it was difficult to let it go. Nonetheless, from 1977 on the company was subject to continuing controversy over the quality of its products, its "overuse," and its cost. The media always found Medtronic newsworthy, whether it was for its life-saving accomplishments, product problems, or as scapegoat for the pacemaker industry and example of the skyrocketing costs in health care.

The organization's reaction to this publicity and attention was in keeping with its established identity. It was difficult for the employees and executives to question their own integrity, honesty, and good intentions, and they did not always react well to adverse publicity. This, coupled with Medtronic's position as industry leader in pacing, often left it as a target. Management often seemed to feel its duty was to bear the general criticism directed at the industry, even though this occurred at a time when Medtronic's competitors were steadily gaining market share.

Thus, by the mid-1980s, when I began studying Medtronic directly, the company had two clearly contrasting "cultures" The old culture, with Earl Bakken as symbolic leader, was benevolent, tolerant, and patient, and had tremendous expectations coupled with self-criticism. Accountability was low, and penalties were seldom imposed. Seniority and entitlement were the primary bases for reward, and the corporation seemed unwilling to accept its failures but unable to celebrate victory. In contrast, the new culture, with CEO Dale Olseth as leader, promoted a much more active style of management, with much higher account-ability and a tougher approach to running the company. In a company with a clear memory of four-day workweeks, layoffs were required for the first time in order to remain competitive. The new culture held that the size of the company limited the degree to which trust and a shared sense of mission could be the basis for management. The new competi-tiveness in the health care industry was seen as an impetus for the change and the painful, yet necessary, set of conditions to help promote that badly needed change.

One illustration of the changed approach to actively managing the company comes from the company's attempts at diversification. As mentioned earlier, the traditional philosophy toward diversification was described by some as "let a thousand flowers bloom" in the hope that one of the flowers might be the next pacemaker. Recognizing that this approach had not led to many profitable new businesses, the company began to develop a concept of diversification that built from the existing customer base, rather than simply trying to continue to leverage the technology base. In addition, diversification efforts were grouped within a new ventures structure, rather than in operating groups or in research units. Although this process was guided by the attempt to re-create the Garage as a research setting, it also ensured that diversifica-tion efforts were carried out with at least one eye on the marketplace.

Reconciling the "Old" and "New" Cultures

By late 1985, with Win Wallin as CEO and new leadership in place, the immediate objective was to improve quality and focus the wide range of technologies into five diversified but related businesses. Each of these businesses was planned to be viable on its own and was intended to stay on the cutting edge of commercial technology in the industry. In each of the businesses, this required introducing new products through both internal development and external acquisition. Perhaps more im-portant, a renewed commitment to the corporate mission as a worthy goal and a historic strength of the company reaffirmed the importance of Medtronic's core values.

Interestingly enough, in developing a renewed commitment to the mission, the conflict between the old and new culture became less im-portant—both humanistic commitment to noneconomic goals and shrewd business decisions by talented managers were required to fulfill the challenging mission that the company had defined for itself. Recon-ciling the two cultures meant reaffirming the central mission and then viewing both the old and new cultures as valuable sources of compe-tency, which could be brought to bear on the objectives. "Culture" as such was discussed less frequently because the word connoted the conflict over *means* represented by the old and new cultures. In the end, this conflict was less important than the mission itself.

At the same time, during the mid- to late 1980s, changes within the industry made Medtronic "one of a kind" once again. By 1988, all of its competitors had been acquired by major corporations such as Siemens or Eli Lilly, making Medtronic the only independent pacing company remaining. This change allowed Medtronic to be more flexible, entrepreneurial, and autonomous than its competitors and in some ways meant that the company was once again primarily competing with itself. The mission, rather than bureaucratic control systems, was once again used to create a sense of urgency.

Results since 1985 are phenomenal. The company's market share in pacing, which had dropped steadily from 60 percent to below 40 percent over the past decade, regained 10 to 15 percent. A new pacemaker, which adjusts the heartbeat to a patient's level of activity, has provided a surge in both market share and confidence. One of the "thousand flowers" bloomed, despite the earlier dissatisfaction with the new product development process. Innovation and diversification outside the pacemaker business have also occurred through both acquisition and internal development, and three of the five core businesses are highly profitable.

Although economic and noneconomic goals now seem much more compatible at Medtronic, this is not to say that the humanistic culture and management culture have been fully reconciled. For example, at least one step remains in reconciling the mission and the management: executive succession. In April 1989 it was announced that William George, a Honeywell executive, will be appointed president. George, succeeding Win Wallin and Dale Olseth, will be the third successive outside executive appointed to lead the company. All three, interestingly enough, have come with broad management experience from major Minneapolis corporations, with the goal of improving the management system while building on the core mission and values. One of the clear criteria for selecting each of them was their commitment to the mission. Nonetheless, a truer sign of the integration of management and mission at Medtronic will be when the system itself has produced a hybrid—a homegrown manager who can lead the mission and the business.

The Culture and Effectiveness Model

Using Medtronic as a case study helps to begin to uncover some of the complexity underlying each of the four elements in the culture and effectiveness model, as well as to illustrate the utility of this model in analyzing an organization's culture.

Involvement. Involvement is clearly one of the means by which the organization's early success was achieved. Nonetheless, involvement and participation have two very different meanings during the "old" and "new" periods in this organization. During the "old" period, involvement is held as the very fabric of the organization's tremendous success, but during the "new" period involvement and participation are more often treated as evidence that the organization has "gone soft" and has become indecisive. Can both be true at once?

The answer seems to lie in the difference between an *external* and an *internal* focus for the processes that are characterized by involvement and participation. The sources of involvement in Medtronic in the early days were a combination of empowerment and autonomy bolstered by a shared mission. The reason for getting involved was simple: it was to bring the technology to bear on the needs of the patient. The goals of involvement were external to the organization itself.

Over the years, however, the importance of this connection became less obvious. As a result, involvement increasingly took the form of a concern with internal process, and, therefore, a growing insularity. The traumas of product problems also created self-doubt and introspection that contributed to the internal focus of the organization. Involvement became directed at the maintenance of the social system itself rather than its adaptation to the external business environment. During the "reconciliation" period, involvement again became focused on the mission and the external business environment.

Consistency. Under the old culture, consistency was based on a shared perception of the needs of patients and surgeons, which was forged through direct, frequent, and continual contact. These beliefs, coupled with an ultimate faith in the potential for technology to address human needs, provided a system that integrated and regulated the behavior of organizational members. The struggle between the old and new culture can be interpreted as an evolution from the implicit system of integration and consistency described above to a consistency based on the shared perception of Medtronic as a *business* organization. Bureaucracy and internal control systems were unnecessary in the old culture because of the small size of the organization, the potency of the normative system and shared values, and the organization's monopoly position in a cost-plus environment. The emergence of a competitive market, the discovery of its "fallibility," and the requirement that it respond to the demands of a broader range of stakeholders for quality, cost, and the like all brought on a greater need to construct an explicit system for monitoring and ensuring consistency, rather than relying on integration to emerge from shared values and mission.

But the introduction of management systems designed to control the "old culture" inevitably created another inconsistency, symbolized by the clash between the "old" and "new" cultures. Thus, the history of the organization, viewed from the perspective of consistency and normative integration, appears in three stages: first, the organization as an implicit humanistic, scientific, and technical mission; second, the layering of explicit management systems in an attempt to bring "business discipline" to the organization; and third, the integration of the business and humanistic perspective in pursuit of the mission. Consistency was high during the first stage, lower during the second stage when necessity forced a competing system of logic and integration on the system, and high again during the third stage when these two systems began to converge.

Adaptability. The Medtronic case also helps to elaborate the concept of adaptability because it gives examples that are both positive and negative from the same culture at two different points in time. One of the best examples of adaptability is the concept, mentioned above, of "sharing risk." Early pacemaker implants were based on an extraordinarily high level of trust between innovative cardiovascular surgeons and Medtronic experts. Both were at risk in every operation. Both understood that the consequences of their interdependence went far beyond the simple economic transaction of buying or selling a pacemaker. The company's salespeople knew the liabilities and the intangibles associated with the sale of their product, and the rest of the organization supported this broad-based (and often noneconomic) understanding of the value associated with their product.

Product problems compromised many of these relationships, and the nature of the customer relationships themselves began to change. Since pacemakers were at that time changing from a "leading edge" technology to a known technology, Medtronic's products were more likely to be chosen by less innovative cardiologists or by administrators concerned primarily with cost as a criterion. The organization had far less collective knowledge about dealing with these relationships in a constructive way, and thus had a much lower level of adaptation. The internal focus noted above also resulted in an overemphasis on the internal bureaucracy rather than on the increasingly important needs of this new type of customer.

Mission. As mentioned earlier, Medtronic in the beginning did not *have* a mission but rather it *was* a mission. In a manner reminiscent of Selznick's (1957) discussion of an organization's mission as the "institutionalization of a societal need," Medtronic developed an organization devoted to the needs of patients and their surgeons. Money was not the object. The direction of the organization was extremely clear and the roles of particular individuals within the organization were highly meaningful. Economic and noneconomic goals seemed highly compatible. Because of this strong sense of meaning and direction, few administrative controls were necessary to ensure coordinated activity.

Difficulties arose when the single-minded pursuit of the mission no longer ensured the viability of Medtronic as a business organization. Competition and fallibility underscored the necessity of responding to the needs of Medtronic as a business organization as interpreted by the board of directors and shareholders. It is important to note that this redefinition of the Medtronic mission was required because of changes in the external business and regulatory environment. The mission stayed the same, the environment changed, and the "institutionalization of societal needs" thus required a change in orientation by the organization. Emphasizing the requirements of the company as a business organization at first appeared to be highly inconsistent with the historic values, but over time both came to be seen as compatible means to pursue the corporate mission.

Lessons Learned from the Medtronic Culture

A host of lessons can be learned from studying culture and effectiveness at Medtronic. At first glance, the organization appears to strongly confirm the general ideas about involvement and effectiveness uncovered by the quantitative analyses. On the basis of those data, I expected to find a high-involvement, high-effectiveness organization. What I found was a complex culture that was perceived by nearly all of those interviewed to have an intimate relationship to the performance of the firm. This culture combined a strong mission, an explicit and shared ideology, and an enormous sense of commitment. The foundations of this culture were symbolic, spiritual, and central to the identity of the organization and its members. A compelling mission had, in the minds of most, fueled the growth of an enormously successful organization.

Nonetheless, when the company's entire history is examined, a far more complicated explanation is required to understand the relationship between the company's culture and its effectiveness. The same culture that was credited with the company's early success was, for a time, seen as an obstacle, but is now once again seen as the foundation of success. What can this paradox tell us about corporate culture and effectiveness?

Culture and Causality. It is quite clear from this analysis that the periods of time when the organization performed best coincided with periods when the culture was most positive. Poor performance occurred during times when involvement was low, inconsistencies were difficult to resolve, adaptability was a problem, and the basic mission was in question. What is not so clear is "which came first, the chicken or the egg?"

One interpretation suggests that the nature of the culture helped determine the effectiveness of the organization. Most members of the organization would agree with that statement and would cite the commitment of the organization's members as a key competitive advantage. Most would also cite the mission and culture of the company as a prime reason why they liked to work there.

Nonetheless, five years ago, many would have argued that the culture was an *impediment* to effectiveness because it primarily represented feelings of entitlement on the part of the organization's employees. This line of argument suggests that "culture" is a result of effectiveness and that slack resources will be consumed to create a more "positive" culture.

In the final analysis, there is truth in both perspectives, and they must be considered jointly to truly understand the ebb and flow of an organization's culture and its link to effective performance. Considering either perspective alone only tells half the story.

Cultural Inertia. The culture and effectiveness model suggests that the consistency of a culture and the ability of a culture to change and adapt should both contribute to an organization's effectiveness. The Medtronic case suggests a close relationship between these two characteristics of consistency and adaptability. That is, the greater the consistency of an organization's culture, the more difficult the culture is to change. Consistency and adaptability contribute to effectiveness, but it is difficult to attain both at the same time. In Medtronic, the capacity to adapt could only be attained by challenging and refuting the original culture. Adaptability, in practice, meant the creation of a subculture with antithetical values.

The original culture grew in response to the organization's early adaptation and success under the influence of the founder. It was not the deliberate product of an active management effort, but reflected some of the implicit values necessary to link the technology to the customers. The "new" culture, in contrast, was an explicit, proactive management attempt at cultural change. Thus, it is instructive to look at the way in which this change was attempted.

The first steps in this change were quiet. The professional management component of the company was steadily increased and moved into positions of authority. Then the issue of cultural change was made an explicit one and the "new" culture was portrayed as a means of adapting to an increasingly competitive and hostile environment. The positive aspects of the "old" culture were then "reinterpreted" with respect to the new environment, and the inconsistencies were downplayed.

This pattern of change implies that culture is managed not by some elaborate process of reengineering the values of those in the organization, but rather by changing the control of the organization to those who have different values. One meaning system declined as the other ascended. Their coexistence was tense. Organizational members needed to see this as a clear-cut difference between competing ideologies in order to change their own behavior and conform to the new system. Over time, and with a considerable amount of struggle and adaptation, these competing ideologies came to be seen as consistent.

Technology. It is also improtant to consider the central role that technology played in the growth and development of Medtronic. The periods of time in which the organization enjoyed its greatest growth were those when it was making incremental improvements in its basic technology and held a dominant position in the marketplace. Earl Bakken not only built a "better mousetrap," but also improved it faster than the competition for nearly 20 years. Even since 1985, the major success in the company has been an incremental improvement in pacing technology. Perhaps this success and maturation process is simply a normal cycle for organizations based on new technology. Maybe the concept of culture should be considered a lagging indicator rather than a leading indicator.

In the final analysis, the history of Medtronic and the development of its culture can only be understood as a complex set of interactions among the life cycle of the technology and the products, the succession of leaders within the company, and the changes within the business environment as the organization's size increased. All these factors had clear impacts on the form of the Medtronic culture and effectiveness.

CHAPTER SEVEN

People Express Airlines

Much has been written about the second case study, People Express Airlines. This innovative discount carrier was spawned by the Airline Deregulation Act of 1978 and introduced "flying that was cheaper than driving." The airline brought bargain-rate fares to many cities and helped create unprecedented competition within the industry during the early 1980s. A key element in the strategy of this organization was the commitment and motivation of its members and the innovative and humane approach taken to managing people. Partially because of these innovations, the culture of this organization is a strong and distinctive one.

More recently, however, the People Express story has changed. Since the company's acquisition of Frontier Airlines in late 1985, the growth and dynamism that led People Express to become one of the fastest growing corporations of the 1980s could not overcome the growing disenchantment of the stock market and the members of the organization or the steady flow of red ink. By March 1986 it became clear that the airline needed to divest itself of Frontier in order to survive, and, when a near-deal with United Airlines fell through, People Express itself emerged as a takeover prospect. Soon thereafter, Texas Air Corporation acquired People Express, helping to make Texas Air the nation's largest carrier. Ironically, the small group who started People Express in 1981 came primarily from Texas International Airlines and was led by Donald Burr, its former president.[1]

---

[1]Texas International Airlines became a holding company, Texas Air Corporation, which acquired Continental, New York Air, People Express Airlines, Frontier Airlines and Eastern.

109

The quantitative data that represent People Express in Figure 5.1 are a puzzle. The data seem to describe an organization that is solidly mediocre. The level of involvement is average, as is performance in comparison to airline industry averages. Both of these measures clash badly with the image of a highly participative organization that grew from nothing in 1981 to a billion dollar per year corporation in 1985. Resolving this discrepancy demands a closer look at this organization's history and culture.

History and Background

People Express began operations on April 30, 1981, with three Boeing 737s and 120 employees, flying out of Newark International Airport's dilapidated North Terminal. The airline had been incorporated about one year earlier by a small group led by Donald Burr.

The members of this founding team set out to find a different way to run an airline. Their aim was to design an organization that would allow the maximum possible growth and development of the individuals within the organization. This led to the development and application of management practices that were highly innovative and creative: minimal hierarchy and specialization, work that could be done by teams, a reliance on "self-management" rather than formal administrative oversight and authority, and a compensation system which included stock ownership and profit sharing for all employees. All employees of the organization were considered "managers," entrusted with the management of the firm's resources and responsible for maintaining a high level of service.

The basic philosophy of the company was prescribed by a brief set of precepts, developed within the first year of the organization's operation by the top management team:

1. Service, commitment to the growth of people.
2. Best provider of air transportation.
3. Highest quality of leadership.
4. Provide a role model.
5. Simplicity.
6. Maximization of profits.

These precepts reflected the assumption that it was People Express's mission to revolutionize air travel by building a simple organization, designed to meet the needs of its employees and its customers by creating a service for which there would be tremendous demand.

After an incredible burst of enthusiasm and creativity at start-up, the airline entered a period of continual rapid growth. The initial group of 17 planes were arriving at the rate of about one a month, and this committed the airline to hiring and training people, staffing and maintaining the aircraft, and selling tickets fast enough to match the rate at which aircraft were arriving. Four months after start-up, the air traffic control strike occurred and greatly restricted landing slots at many key airports to which the airline needed to expand. The firm narrowly avoided an early bankruptcy by focusing on the Florida market during its first winter of operations.

The airline's simple structure in these early days grouped all managers into one of four categories: the managing officers and general managers—the top management team of the organization; the customer service managers (CSMs)—those who worked in ground operations, reservations, staff work, or as flight attendants; flight managers (FMs)—the pilots; and maintenance managers (MMs)—those who supervised the maintenance and servicing of the aircraft. Within each of these groups, jobs were rotated frequently. Flight attendants did staff work, pilots did scheduling, and even the managing officers regularly did customer contact work. Little formal hierarchy or conventional lines of authority existed between the top management group and those who flew and provided cabin service during flights.

Morale and motivation during this phase of the airline's development were at unprecedented levels (Denison 1989a). The flexible and informal structure allowed for a tremendous sense of ownership and commitment on the part of all managers. This psychological ownership was reinforced by literal ownership; many of the company's members took advantage of regular stock offerings (in addition to the required purchase of stock by each employee), and were profiting financially as the price of the stock rose.

By early 1982, however, as the size of the airline neared one thousand employees and about $100 million in annualized revenues, it had clearly outgrown this simple structure. The issue of how the existing structure should evolve was controversial. After nearly six months of discussion, a new structure with about 40 CSMs, FMs, and MMs designated as "Team Managers"—a formal position linking the general managers and the rest of the organization—was created. This restructuring process is described in greater detail later in this chapter.

This structure, plus an aggressive plan for new cities, new aircraft, flights to London, and a new reservations system, led the airline into two years of continual growth. This period was the most successful and the most profitable in the airline's history, and resulted in tremendous publicity for the airline and its innovative ideas. People Express became the largest air carrier in the New York area, one of the 10 largest airlines in the country, and had a substantial impact on the air travel market. Fare wars became widespread in the industry, and the airline competed head-to-head with major carriers in major markets. Despite the competition, the airline's low costs per seat mile (about six cents per mile versus the industry average of eight cents) and high load factor (60–70 percent versus an industry average of 50–60 percent) allowed it to remain profitable. *Time, Newsweek, Business Week, Fortune*, and *Inc. Magazine* all did cover stories or major feature stories on the airline, and these attracted the interest of managers, executives, scholars, and consultants across the country.

By the summer of 1984, however, the airline was once again bursting at the seams of its structure. With 4000 aircraft employees and 70 aircraft, the airline moved to an operating group structure that created 11 separate organizations with approximately 350 employees each. This restructuring, described later in this chapter, was an attempt to return to a system that gave individual managers a sense of belonging and an opportunity to self-manage with a structure that was small enough to respond and show the impacts of their efforts.

During this period, the airline was struggling. It lost money in the last quarter of 1984 and the first quarter of 1985, and several of the original core group that made up the top management team left the company through firings and resignations. By the spring of 1985, the airline began to reduce its rate of growth and concentrate on the operation, with Chairman Don Burr saying several times that the airline needed to consolidate rather than grow for the rest of 1985. Nonetheless, by October 1985, People Express had acquired the Denver-based Frontier Airlines for approximately $90 million.

The cultures of these two companies were very different. Frontier was a classic unionized firm, which had grown up as a regional carrier, and was now having great difficulty competing for the Denver hub in a national market. People Express quickly coordinated the schedules of the two airlines and cut Frontier's fare structures and service to People Express levels. This alienated many of Frontier's traditional travelers as well as the travel industry. Denver travel agents, reluctant to make reservations on People Express because it did not pay the same commissions and overrides as other airlines, instituted a service charge on all flights under $100.

For the next few quarters, Frontier contributed roughly $20 million a month loss to People Express's already dismal financial picture. In addition, the terms of the agreement anticipated that the Frontier management team would stay in place, thus imposing considerable limits on the active management of Frontier by People Express. The spirit of the arrangement was that, over time, Frontier would adopt many of

People's principles, realizing their value through experiencing it first-hand. Unfortunately, there was not much time. The departure of most of the Frontier management team by January 1986 only made matters worse.

By the spring of 1986, People Express was actively looking for a buyer for Frontier as a necessary step to avoid bankruptcy itself. After a near-deal with United Airlines fell through, Frontier declared bankruptcy in August, and by September 15 Texas Air Corporation acquired both People Express and Frontier for about $170 million. On February 1, 1987, People Express was folded into the Texas Air system, thus ending one of the more remarkable chapters in the history of the American airline industry.

The People Express Culture and Management Practices

The culture of People Express is a compelling subject. The organization's culture was an integral part of the firm's management strategy and structure, and closely linked to the airline's rise and fall. It is, without question, an example of "strong" culture and a pervasive meaning system, and presents a direct link between ideological principles and management practices. The culture also is one that has integrated many of the innovative ideas that have come out of the field of organizational behavior in the past decade, and has combined them in a way that made it clear that this was a new way of doing business.

Founder and Chairman Don Burr was the central figure in the creation of this culture. He was teacher, preacher, strategist, and role model; a "Streetwise" pied piper leading an organization that was, in his own words, designed "to unleash the power of the individual." Burr and his cofounders conceived of People Express as an instrumental path to self-actualization—individuals, the corporation, and consumers could all benefit from this fundamentally different way of doing business. And in doing so they could bring air travel to the masses in a way that had never happened before.

The mission was infectious. The belief that a humanistic organization could revolutionize the industry, that commitment and involvement as equal team players could fulfill individual career ambitions, and the vision that an organization of owner-workers could prosper together, all combined to produce phenomenal levels of activity and commitment. Everyone ate, breathed, and slept People Express in the early days.

This quasi-spiritual mission also translated into a distinct set of management practices and principles. These links between the precepts and the practices made the culture of People Express far more than just an ideology—they made it a different way of doing business. Five of these practices in particular stand out:

Self-Management. Each manager in the company was expected to make autonomous decisions on a daily basis in the best interest of People Express. Decisions were often made without "supervision" because everyone in the airline was a "manager" entrusted with the management of the resources of the company. Managers who asked someone in a position of authority for help or advice about a problem were often told to "self-manage" the problem—solve it using your own approach without relying on someone else for direction.

In the early days of the airline, before its unique approach was well known, this principle occasionally caused confusion among customers. A customer who had a complaint might say, "Let me talk to your supervisor." The People Express manager would respond, "I don't have a supervisor, I'm a manager." Such conversations usually ended (after some exasperation) with the manager describing the philosophy of self-management that was so central to People Express: Everyone is a manager; no one depends on the hierarchy for supervision and direction; peers help train, inform, and regulate; thus top managers are free to concentrate on setting the general direction for the company as a whole.

As the airline grew and then began its decline, however, self-management sometimes took on a very different meaning. Several managers described it as a way to sometimes stifle criticism that came from the lower levels of the organization. As one manager put it, "Every time I disagreed about something, my general manager would tell me that I should 'self-manage' that problem. After a while I stopped speaking out about things I disagreed with." Self-management was empowering in the early days, but sometimes became a sign of an unresponsive hierarchy as the airline grew larger.

The Team Concept. Work in the airline was performed by teams wherever possible. In the cabin of the aircraft, on the flight deck, in the terminal, and in staff and management jobs, an effort was made to design work in a way that self-regulating teams could operate with autonomy and responsibility. Among customer service managers teamwork was particularly important. When new CSMs were hired, they went through a six-week training session, part of which involved joining a team of three that would then work together after they began flying. Considerable effort was devoted to building a team during training. When the new team began working, they were scheduled together, and each month bid on the type of work they wanted to do the following month. The work in other areas of the airline sometimes was impossible to design around teams (e.g., pilots are prevented by the FAA from flying with the same people regularly), but the principle was clear: Committed individuals often made their contributions through a team structure. Good teamwork was essential to the success of the airline, and, to be successful, individuals needed to work well within teams.

Cross-Utilization. Within the broad employment categories outlined earlier, each manager in the airline typically performed a wide variety of tasks. Customer service managers, working as a team of three, might spend one month working as flight attendants, a second month working in ground operations, and a third month working as individuals in various staff jobs. Maintenance managers often split their time between day-to-day coordination of aircraft maintenance and longer term engineering projects. Pilots, who in most airlines have highly specialized jobs, worked as flight managers, many of whom alternated between flying and doing administrative work. Even general managers and managing officers occasionally did in-flight work, and it was not unusual for Gil Roberts, the chief operating officer and a pilot, to leave a meeting in his office sometime during the day to fly to Boston, Pittsburgh, or Washington and back.

Highly specialized work was deemphasized in the airline's culture. The principle was that by doing varied work and moving from one part of the organization to another, individual managers could choose the work they wanted and come to understand how the entire system fit together. In addition, this design provided a high-variety work environment for individual managers, coupled with many opportunities for growth and development.

Like the team concept, cross-utilization was, quite obviously, not possible in all situations. Skills in planning the airline's monthly schedule, for example, were not widespread; the task typically fell to those who had the most experience or liked the job most. Individuals and teams also tended to select those jobs that were the most attractive. Some CSMs liked to fly, some liked to work ground operations, and some were anxious to secure staff jobs. Teams often formed and reformed to allow managers to pick the type of work they wanted.

Despite the airline's attempt to make all jobs appear as equal and as necessary as possible, some jobs were much more attractive than others. As the airline grew and tried to keep costs as low as possible, staff work was at a premium, and many CSMs had to spend nearly all of their time "flying the line." Thus, although cross-utilization was a central part of the organization's culture, it increasingly became part of the organization's ideology rather than the actual practice.

Ownership and Profit Sharing. Each new manager at People Express was required to purchase at least 100 shares of discounted stock as a condition of employment. They also were offered regular options to buy more stock at discounted rates each time new shares were issued, and could pay for their stock through payroll deductions. Approximately one-third of the airline was owned by the employees, and many of them became serious investors during the early days when the stock was trading at up to 40 times earnings. The managing officers of the company were all heavy investors in the corporation.

Profit sharing was also an important part of the compensation system. Quarterly profit sharing was, on average, 20 percent of earnings and could amount to 25 percent of a monthly paycheck. The airline paid $15.8 million in profit sharing between 1982 and 1985. Had People Express remained profitable, the plan was that increases in compensation would continue to be directly tied to the profitability of the airline. Increases in base salary would level off after five years of employment, and future increases would be based on profitability.

These two principles of compensation, when the airline was vital and growing, gave managers a strong sense that their own efforts were contributing to the success of the company and were having an impact on the price of the stock and the profitability of the company. As the airline grew but its stock price and performance declined, this perception disappeared; managers in the company no longer thought that their efforts had much connection to the airline's performance.

Flat Organization and Democratic Values. As mentioned earlier, formal hierarchy, much like specialization, was de-emphasized in People Express. As a consequence, the organization did not have as many status differences as a conventional organization with more formal hierarchies. Employees at all levels tended to be involved, committed, and rewarded. Levels of leadership evolved slowly and involved broad spans of control.

The principle of self-management also meant that authority was widespread in People Express. Control and influence were more equally distributed than in a conventional organization in which people at the top have all of the authority and people at the bottom have none. Although in reality there were substantial differences in formal and informal authority between the top and bottom of the organization, democratic values were a central part of the People Express organization.

The flat structure and democratic values did result in a few unique problems for the organization. As noted later in this chapter, because of the bias toward a flat organization, decisions about adding levels of leadership were always difficult. Furthermore, once a multilevel hierarchy had emerged, managers who had grown up in the organization when it had very few levels sometimes had difficulty learning to operate in the new multilevel system.

Subcultures: Flight Managers and Customer Service Managers

Another example of the importance attached to minimizing status differences comes from the relationship between two of People Express's strongest occupational subcultures: flight managers and customer service managers. In most airlines, the status differences between these two types of employees is very clear: Pilots fly planes and have high status; flight attendants serve customers and have low status. People Express radically redefined this relationship, in part because of the belief that effective customer service work was of equal importance to effective work by pilots in the satisfaction of customers and successful operation of an airline.

The history of People Express shows that the status differences between these two groups were quite minimal at the beginning. In 1981 and 1982 the airline industry was in a downturn, and labor was a buyer's market. At that time, FMs received somewhat less salary than their counterparts at the major airlines, but CSMs received as much or more salary than flight attendants at other airlines. Nonetheless, many FMs perceived their overall compensation to be acceptable because of the rapidly escalating price of the stock and the discounted options that were available.

The influence of these two groups in the airline was also nearly equal. Many times an ambitious, talented yet relatively inexperienced CSM could have as great an impact on the operation of the company as older FMs with years of airline experience. The general management of the company seemed, at least to the FMs, to support and encourage this.

Over time, however, as the airline grew and the labor market changed, the FMs were given salary increases and a stronger say in the operation of the airline. A flight manager became chief operating officer, and many other FMs assumed major roles in the operation of the company. The Air Line Pilots Association made several attempts to organize the FMs during this period but was unsuccessful.

Many other characteristics also support the idea that People Express was not a homogeneous culture and that FMs and CSMs represented two occupational subcultures with interests that occasionally conflicted. For example, flight managers had a number of characteristics that made them, as a group, somewhat less receptive than customer service managers to the People Express approach. Older, predominantly male, with far more airline experience, most FMs had a military background. They often saw the People Express culture and management innovations as a way of depriving them of their rightful status, and as a group were far more interested in the operating efficiency of the airline and their own advancement. They were also far more likely to be commuters—living far from the Newark hub and being present only when it was necessary. When the job market for pilots improved, many FMs were quick to move back into a more traditionally structured airline. Pilots were also more likely to speak up when they disagreed, and some of them perceived that this could lead to trouble.

Customer service managers, as a group, contrasted quite sharply with FMs. The CSMs were younger, often just out of college, with equal numbers of men and women. People Express exhaustively recruited talented, ambitious people, but they were often individuals who had little airline experience or even work experience. As such, they frequently fit the value system of the airline better than the pilots. In addition, CSMs, being less experienced, were far more malleable, and they had fewer outside demands and obligations, such as family and other responsibilities.

The third major occupational group, the maintenance managers, also had a distinct subculture. Maintenance managers usually had many years of experience in the airline industry, usually in traditional organizations with extensive hierarchies and an established division of labor. In many cases, MMs had come to People Express after being laid off by another major airline. At People Express, most discovered they did not have the enormous depth of resources that they had relied on with their previous employers. Managing maintenance required them to be resourceful and to master a variety of tasks.

Maintenance managers also had the unusual assignment of managing the maintenance workers themselves. People Express did not employ maintenance workers and instead contracted for ground service with other organizations. A similar arrangement was used for reservations workers and baggage handlers because these were perceived to be boring blue-collar jobs with low-skill requirements, repetitiveness and few opportunities to grow and develop. If workers in these occupations were an integral part of the organization, it was feared they would become sources of infectious discontent. Maintenance managers were assigned the difficult task of managing across these boundaries; the innovative practices that applied within People Express (which were foreign to the MMs to begin with) did not apply in dealing with the maintenance workers. In order to deal with this subculture, the MMs needed to fall back on practices more in keeping with their previous, more traditional employers. Nonetheless, the traditional practices used with the maintenance workers could not be applied within the airline itself. This posed a difficult dilemma for several MMs, who often had had only limited managerial experience.

A fourth subculture also warrants mention. The group of founders, known as "the start-up team," was, as the name suggests, around at the beginning. Experiencing the tremendous growth, sharing the importance of the ideology and meaning, and seeing the reward of an idea put into practice set this group apart from the rest of the organization. They were, with a few exceptions, "believers." They accepted the People Express mission, ideology, and strategy, and remained strongly committed to the organization in a way that those who joined later could not always duplicate. In addition, they enjoyed some celebrity status— they were part of the family and were well known by the top management group.

The existence of such disparate cultures within one organization reinforces the idea that a "strong" culture is a complex phenomenon, not to be directly equated with simple homogeneity or conformity. The differences between subcultures, and the ways in which the shared value system helped reconcile them were as much a part of the culture of the organization as the precepts, the management principles, or the charisma of Don Burr.

The "Cult" in Culture

Many organizations have unique terms to describe those members of the company who are very strongly committed. For example, in Caterpillar, they describe loyal old-timers as having "yellow blood" (Caterpillar paints all of its equipment yellow). In AT&T the "Bell-shaped man" has a similar connotation. People Express had its own term; those who were unquestioningly loyal were referred to as "Kool-Aid drinkers." This refers, of course, to the tremendous charisma and persuasive powers of Don Burr, and likens those powers in rather sardonic fashion to those of the Reverend Jim Jones, whose followers committed mass suicide in Guyana in 1979 by drinking poisoned Kool-Aid. Those who used the term tended to interpret the People Express mission and its meanings as an exploitive myth that was not in the best interests of the members of the organization.

But for those who did believe in the People Express mission, it is clear that the organization had some of the characteristics of a cult. The organization had a powerful meaning system, an extraordinarily charismatic leader, and unprecedented success and attention. These factors combined to make their work role central to their lives and identity. Outsiders could not know the "People Express way" in the same sense that an insider could, and this was reinforced by making the only path of entry into the organization from the bottom up. During times of trouble, the airline resisted bringing in new management talent from outside the organization, and returned to a predictable formula: create autonomy and opportunity through organizational growth.

It seems inevitable that an organization with a strong culture will begin to take on many of the characteristics of a clan or a cult. People Express remains of high interest, despite its decline and fall, because it set out to create a distinctive organization, and it did so quickly and successfully. The airline also remains of high interest because of the ways in which the culture may have contributed to both its success and decline.

The Growth and Restructuring of the Organization

As mentioned earlier in this chapter, the initial structure of the airline was very simple. The three major employment groups had direct access to the managing officers and general managers (MO/GMs) group, with no intermediate level of authority. This structure, represented in Figure 7.1, lasted from start-up in April 1981 until summer 1982. During this time the organization grew from 100 to nearly 1,000 employees with very little formal hierarchy between the top management and the rest of the organization. The system relied on an informal network of coordinators, most of whom had been a part of the start-up of the airline. The coordinators had little more "formal" authority than other CSMs, FMs, or MMs, but managed through their influence and experience. This group of 20 to 30 managers linked the MO/GMs and the rest of the organization and helped knit together the rapidly growing organization.

By early 1982 when the airline was approaching a size of 800–900 employees and $100 million in annual revenues, this structure was stretched to the breaking point. The company was highly dependent on the coordinators who linked the MO/GMs and the rest of the organization, but this group was extremely overworked and received no formal recognition of their contributions and no increase in conventional rewards like pay or benefits. The "coordinator problem" was growing along with the airline itself.

The decision to add a formal layer of hierarchy was not easy. The discussion began in late 1981 and continued until a solution was reached in the summer of 1982. Part of the difficulty in the decision was that it

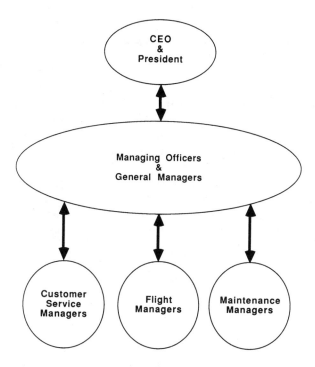

Figure 7.1   People Express Airlines initial structure

went directly against the assumptions of equality and strong collective values on which the organization was based. Even if the decision to add a layer to the organization was clear, it was unclear *how* decisions should be made or how the changes should be implemented. Managers from all parts of the airline had input into the decision, to the satisfaction of both the managers and the senior officers of the corporation. As Hackman (1984) notes, when consensus was reached on a general direction for the structural change, it served to unite the organization.

The decision was further complicated because there was very little task-based feedback on individual performance in the airline. "Performance" was difficult to define objectively and was difficult to use as the criterion of selection for those who would become team managers. Therefore, advancement was often influenced by five factors: (1) perceived merit, (2) membership on the start-up team, (3) support for People Express's values and mission, (4) reputation for performance among peers and MO/GMs, and (5) the degree to which an individual was known to the MO/GMs who made such decisions.

In the end, about 40 team managers were chosen, some from each employment group. They had more formal responsibility within these employment groups, but the team managers still functioned as a team rather than having explicit authority over a special subset of CSMs, FMs, or MMs. This second structure took the form presented in Figure 7.2.

This structure lasted from summer 1982 until summer 1984 and served as the basic framework with which the organization grew from just under 1,000 employees to nearly 4,000, and from $100 million in annual sales to $500 million. During this time the airline introduced international service with 747 aircraft, introduced 727 service on many routes in the United States, and nearly tripled the number of aircraft in service—from 18 to more than 50. By the time the organization had grown to 3,500 employees in the spring and summer of 1984, it was becoming clear that the work environment was no longer a personal one

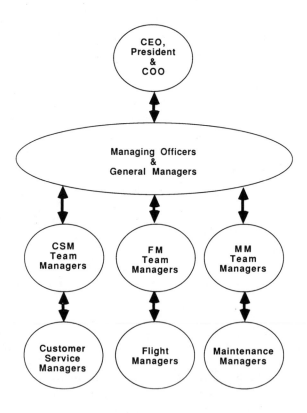

Figure 7.2 People Express Airlines second structure

that fostered strong commitment and a sense of belonging on the part of organizational members. Instead, People Express was rapidly becoming a large, anonymous bureaucracy. The structure was once again bursting at the seams, and some divisional structure seemed necessary if the airline was to regain the internal work environment that had helped it grow so successfully.

The concept that emerged was that of the operating group. Creating operating groups would restructure the airline into units of approximately 350 managers and provide a "home base" for each manager. An operating group would be led by one managing officer and three general managers, and would be formed around a particular aircraft type. The schedule would be divided among the operating groups each month so that the most desirable routes were evenly distributed. By September 1984, the first operating group was created on a trial basis, and began functioning with some autonomy from the rest of the airline. Once this test case proved that the principle was viable and helped to recreate a favorable work environment, the plan was laid to reorganize the entire airline along this model. Figure 7.3 presents the structure for an individual operating group, and Figure 7.4 the structure for the entire airline.

These 11 units of 200–300 people generally resembled the structure of the entire airline in the early days, but with several important differences. First, two new categories of positions were created: team leaders in the CSM, FM, and MM ranks and flight manager recruits and customer service representatives. Leadership positions were *elected* within each operating group, and team managers and team leaders assumed responsibility for communicating and coordinating a subset of the managers in that operating group. Team leaders were elected for a six-month period, and during that time received $6,000 per year in additional pay. About 10 to 12 team managers were elected in each operating group.

The second set of new positions, customer service representatives and flight manager recruits, were also created. Customer service representatives were temporary, part-time employees, often college students, who did customer service work on the ground in Newark and in other city terminals. A source of less expensive labor, they also were a well-trained pool of applicants for future CSM openings. As FMs in training, flight manager recruits often filled the flight engineer seat. They were hired at a substantially lower salary than regular flight managers.

In addition to these new positions, there were several other important differences between the operating group structure and the original People Express structure. First, the operating group structure had far more hierarchy than the original organization, even though they were approximately the same size. At least five distinct layers were present in the new group structure, although the original organization had only

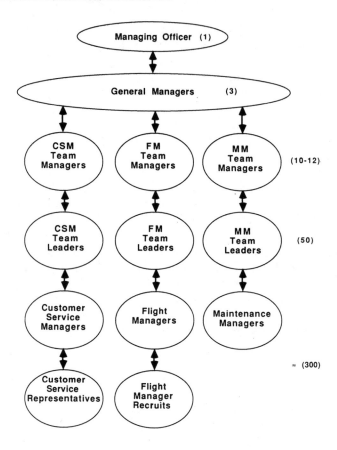

Figure 7.3 People Express Airlines' operating group's internal structure.

two. In addition, the original organization had 12–15 general managers and managing officers at the top, but each operating group now had only one managing officer and three general managers. Perhaps the most important difference was that each of the operating groups did not have a Don Burr at the top.

Managing through the levels of leadership posed a new challenge for People Express. It now had a hierarchical structure, but little experience at managing such a structure. The values and assumptions, which had guided the organization and its development, favored doing things without a hierarchy wherever possible, so when these expectations were coupled with the current hierarchical structure, some very inconsistent messages were given.

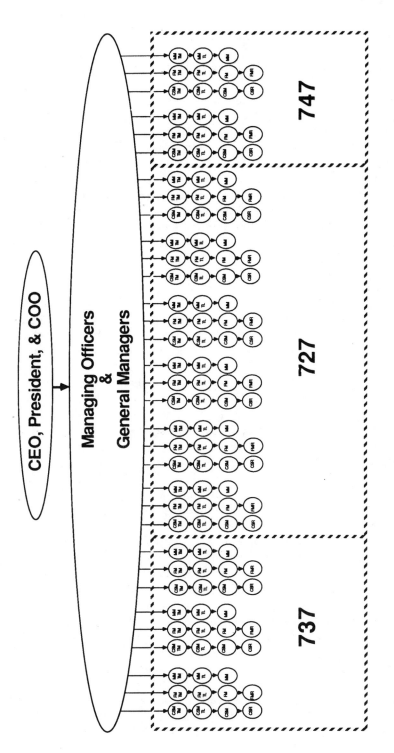

Figure 7.4 People Express Airlines operating group structure

Analyzing the interaction between the cultural values and the structural growth of People Express helps to point out some of the dilemmas that were created as a highly ideological organization grew into a large, complex bureaucracy. The structural demands of growth eventually required more levels of leadership, and, at the same time, the culture and values resisted hierarchy. One can even argue that part of the reason the organization was able to grow so quickly was because of the lack of hierarchy. Using "empowerment" as a substitute for hierarchy and structure also seemed to require continued organizational growth to create individual opportunities. This continued organizational growth, however, seemed to require that hierarchy eventually had to be substituted for empowerment. This paradox reappeared regularly as the People Express system evolved.

Effectiveness

A number of aspects of the company's strategy were central to the airline's early success and were clearly not related to its human resource strategy. These factors must also be taken into account in any assessment of the organization's effectiveness. People Express bought aircraft in a buyer's market at reduced rates and recruited most of the early flight managers under similar circumstances. Increasing both the number of seats and the load factor in each plane by pricing well below the going rates allowed it to have the lowest costs in the industry and still have hopes of turning a profit. Founded during a recession, the airline survived 21 percent interest rates, skyrocketing fuel costs, and the air traffic control strike in its first year.

The continual growth was in part fueled by acquiring aircraft. Once a contract was signed committing People Express to a delivery schedule on new aircraft, the airline had little choice but to expand as quickly as possible to avoid going out of business. Numerous episodes in the airline's history point out the risks associated with this approach as well as its use as a business strategy. Profitability and consolidation took a back seat to continual growth. Nothing held as much appeal to the chairman or the rest of the organization as expansion.

The organization's innovative management practices were clearly an effective strategy for managing the growth stages of the airline. They were not, however, a substitute for some of the technical aspects of competition in the industry after 1985. Foremost among these fundamentals was the development of *yield management software* in major airlines such as American and United. This software allowed airlines to match People Express fares by selling a few seats at a low price and filling the rest of the plane with much higher fares. With this tool the proportion of seats sold at each fare could be adjusted by route, by day, and by time so demand could be managed both to yield high revenues and to offer the lowest possible fares. People Express did not have this capacity, and without it its price advantage was ruined.

Part of the allure of Frontier Airlines was that it appeared to offer the computer capacity necessary to implement such a system. Unfortunately, building a competitive system based on Frontier's computers would have required more time and resources than People Express could muster.

This case has pointed out both the effectiveness and the ineffectiveness of People Express. Shrewd business decisions and innovative personnel practices helped the organization become one of the successful new start-ups of the 1980s but they were not enough to make the transition from an entrepreneurial start-up to a major carrier in the industry. The decision to rely solely on an internal labor market and promote only from within was perhaps an excellent long-term strategy, but was nevertheless a strategy that left the organization with limited managerial depth at a time when the Frontier acquisition placed a heightened, if not impossible, set of management demands on a technologically disadvantaged organization in an increasingly competitive environment.

The Culture and Effectiveness Model

Analyzing the People Express organization in light of the culture and effectiveness model provides a summary and extension of the insights provided by this case.

Involvement. The conditions created within People Express during the first two to three years of operation clearly led to high levels of involvement on the part of employees. Furthermore, this involvement was, without question, key to the airline's tremendous growth and early success. Sustaining this involvement as the organization grew, however, was another matter. The involvement was precedented on values that were difficult to sustain and redefine as the organization grew larger and encountered increasingly difficult competition. The People Express environment was characterized by incredibly high involvement, but involvement did decrease as the organization grew, despite improvements such as the restructuring into operating groups.

Consistency. The strength of the People Express culture led to a consistency of values and behavior that was unusually high. Much like involvement, this was a tremendous strength to the organization in the early days. The direction and control necessary to manage a rapidly growing organization came from a shared vision and shared values, rather than a system of administrative oversight. Over time, however, the consistency, which was an early strength, was seen by some as an emphasis on conformity rather than a means to function effectively and create a humanistic work environment.

Adaptability. The airline's first two years of operations displayed an adaptability and ingenuity without which it could not have survived. Strategies could be devised one day and implemented the next, and in several cases actually were. Nonetheless, adaptability also suffered as the airline grew. In particular, the airline's commitment to a market niche that was becoming increasingly competitive and its inability to expand beyond that niche had severe consequences. The moves in May 1986 to raise fares and add first-class service to compete for business rather than seasonal travelers tend to underscore this difficulty in adapting. Adapting to the business travel market depended more on the perception of improved on-time performance than on a simple increase in fares and level of service.

Mission. People Express was a powerful example of a mission-based organization. The mission combined a business strategy, a career strategy, and individually meaningful work into one driving force and identity. This combination of meaning and direction left many outsiders astonished as the airline planned and then executed the seemingly impossible. The root of this mission—nothing was impossible for an organization that could unleash the power of the individual—may also have helped create the assumption that the organization could not fail. The Frontier acquisition was in part a consequence of the assumption that People Express could not fail, feeling of invulnerability which had come from previous conquests. The mission was also weakened because of the growing discrepancy between the original vision and ideology and the day-to-day work of each member of the airline as the stress on the organization increased.

Lessons Learned from the People Express Culture

Several specific lessons about the relation between culture and effectiveness can be learned from studying People Express. This chapter concludes by discussing the way that the culture contributed to the organization's decline and failure; the inherent conflicts between individual and collective interests; and the problems that may be associated with quantitative measurement of culture.

How Did the Culture Fit into the Decline and Failure? It is tempting to point to the innovative People Express system as an explanation for both the success and failure of the airline. This argument suggests that the entrepreneurial culture, which provided for the early growth, did not provide the stability and control necessary for a mature organization. The discussion earlier in this chapter of the difficult transition from a small, highly personal and ideological organization to a large bureaucracy is one example of this type of problem. Nonetheless, it must also be recognized that a large part of the chaos, pressure, and strain, which characterized the organization after 1985, was brought about by increased competition and the desperation moves required for survival, rather than by any inherent limitations of the organization itself.

The more compelling explanation of the link between the culture and the decline of the organization is that the culture created blind spots as well as strengths. The most significant of these, in hindsight, was the emphasis on the human side of the organization and neglect of the technical side. The working assumption, until early 1985, was that the airlines dealt with relatively known technology and that innovation on the product and organization side was the most effective strategy. This assumption would eventually prove very costly. Concentration on the organizational innovations, valuable as they were, tended to create a focus that was slow to recognize innovation in other areas and the threats they posed to the airline.

Tensions between Individual and Collective Values. The principles used to organize and manage People Express made some fundamental assumptions about the nature of individual and collective values, their malleability, and their relation to the effective functioning of an organization. These central values, and the way they were expressed in the series of structures and conflicts that accompanied the growth of the airline, provide a deeper look at the culture of this firm.

The organization seemed to make at least three assumptions about the nature of collective values, all of which grew from the basic assumption that individual achievement could be accomplished through a strong commitment to the collective.

First, collective organizational values could be enculturated through a selection and socialization process within a society (and an industry) that emphasized individual values. The collective values reinforced through the structure and management practices could be central to the success of the business. Teamwork was wholly compatible with individual autonomy and did not need to subordinate the individual to the team. The tensions between the organizational values and the industry or societal values could be constructively managed.

Second, the functional demands of a growing organization could be met without alteration of these basic collective values. Big organizations were just small organizations writ large. Implicit coordination could meet most of the needs for integrating the divergent functions of the airline. Thus, there was little emphasis on training in the conventional management skills associated with coordinating a large multilayered bureaucratic organization.

Third, when hierarchy and structure were needed as a response to the organization's growth, it was assumed that the core values could be retained, but their application, as defined in practice, altered. Thus the meaning of a central concept, such as "self-management" (which implies individuals will manage themselves effectively in the interests of the collective and without direct supervision), could be redefined regularly without altering individuals' commitment to the basic principle. In practice, the first time one of the team members was promoted and another was not, it became difficult to retain the belief that all members of the organization were "equal." The second time it was much harder.

These assumptions were central to the controversies that continued as the organization grew from 100 employees to 4,000. The inevitable restructuring, which occurred along the way, consistently aroused this same set of issues and created a series of crises for the airline. These issues are fundamental concerns in the design of any organization, and several valuable insights can be gained from the People Express example.

Problems with Quantitative Measurement. At the beginning of this case, the quantitative results were presented as a puzzle: How could an organization that had revolutionized the air travel industry appear as "average" with respect to the measures of both involvement and effectiveness? What does this tell us about "measuring" organizational culture? What does it tell us about the performance and effectiveness of the airline?

Two ideas have come out of this analysis of the organization's culture that help explain why the decision-making and involvement scores were only average. First, the responses to a survey item are a product of individuals' perceptions of an attribute and their expectations regarding how much of that attribute is "some," "a lot," or "not very much." People Express managers had extremely high expectations about the level of involvement they would have in the organization and, by comparison, saw their level of involvement as moderate.

Second, the rapid growth of the airline is quite different from the stable, established set of companies that are represented in the norm bank to which these data were compared. Comparisons of the behavioral characteristics of new, rapidly growing organizations and organizations with stable populations should be interpreted with caution.

Finally, the performance data to some degree tend to misrepresent the effectiveness of the airline. When the performance data used in Figure 5.1 were collected, People Express was one of few profitable firms in a break-even industry. It was, however, one of the most profitable periods in its history. Furthermore, return on investment was not necessarily the target the airline was shooting for: growth, expansion, and attaining a critical mass were, instead, the measures of effectiveness that the airline defined for itself.

CHAPTER EIGHT

Detroit Edison

Detroit Edison, the third case, is an electric utility in southeastern Michigan. The company today has more than 10,000 employees and generates approximately $3 billion per year in revenues. With jurisdiction over 13 percent of the state, the company serves more than half of Michigan's population. The survey data, collected in 1977, portray Edison as a relatively low-involvement organization with below-average performance in relation to other utilities. As such, Edison fits the general pattern between involvement and performance shown in Figure 5.1. Unlike the other case studies in this book, however, Detroit Edison operates in a highly regulated environment: rates, profits, and capital investment must all be approved by the Michigan Public Service Commission; and operation of the company's 1,100-megawatt nuclear power plant, Fermi 2, is closely monitored by the Nuclear Regulatory Commission. This regulation and oversight, as well as the historical development of the organization, have helped create a distinctive management style and organizational culture.

History and Background

Detroit Edison, like many U.S. utilities, was formed in the early 1900s through a consolidation of several independent utilities in the region. Driven by the rapid industrial growth of the Detroit area, the company has traditionally been a very progressive utility and a leader in the industry. The company has been led by several legendary executives who were closely involved with the evolution of public utilities nationally and internationally.

The first of these, Alex Dow, led one of the company's predecessors, Edison Illuminating, as early as 1896. Dow was a self-educated Scottish immigrant, who saw himself as a steward of the new world order being created by the application of the sciences. In the words of Detroit Edison biographer Raymond Miller (1951, 1971), Dow saw the company as a "machine entrusted to him" (p. 57). With a "Presbyterian's sense of duty and responsibility," (p. 56) Dow established a simple formula for operating an electrical utility: "(1) maintain the plant and equipment, (2) pay the going wage or a little better, (3) pay enough on capital to guarantee more when you need it, and (4) any other income should benefit the customer in lower prices" (p. 57). His pragmatic obsession with function, along with his mission as a reformist and scientific revolutionary, set him apart from most of the executives of his time.

Dow, a major figure in the consolidation of regional utilities that created Detroit Edison, led the company from 1917 to 1940. His pragmatism, simplicity, and commitment made a permanent impact on the Detroit Edison culture. A major company award, given for service, commitment, and scientific achievement, still bears his name.

Walker Cisler, the second of Edison's legendary early executives, was known worldwide throughout the utility industry. Cisler's Edison career began during World War II, at about the same time he was commissioned an officer and assigned to Allied headquarters in Europe, with the function of restoring civilian and military electrical service in the wake of the advancing Allied troops. His continued international activity as a key figure in the Marshall Plan and later service as the first American president of the World Energy Conference helped give Edison prominent national and international stature. Many Edison managers benefited from the international exposure offered by a tour of duty in western Europe, Asia, or a developing third world nation.

Edison grew rapidly, along with Detroit and the automobile industry, from the 1920s through the early 1970s. Growth in the demand for electricity during this period was so consistent that utility experts developed the rule of thumb that the demand for electricity would double every decade. With a predictable 7 percent annual growth, the most important management function was to plan the continual construction of generating stations and distribution systems. This set of conditions fostered a combination of predictability and dynamism that helped create a unique organizational identity.

By the early 1970s, however, all of this changed. Three factors combined to alter both Edison and the industry. All represented changes driven by forces *outside* the organization, and they altered forever the assumptions by which the organization had been managed for the past 50 years.

The Energy Crisis. Beginning with the oil embargo in 1973, fuel prices skyrocketed, bond ratings dropped, and the growth in demand declined to 1 to 3 percent per year. Several years saw actual declines in total kilowatt hour sales. All construction was halted. When combined with the slow process of obtaining rate relief from the Michigan Public Service Commission, these factors resulted in severe liquidity problems in 1974. The energy crisis also threw Detroit's automotive industry into chaos and led to further decline in the region, with slower growth in residential and commercial demand and several years of decline in industrial demand.

By 1978, the utility had begun to recover from the initial shock of the oil embargo, only to plunge into the recession of 1979. Total sales fell more than 7 percent, and sales to the auto and steel industries fell nearly 20 percent. Significant growth did not resume until the early 1980s as the recession ended. Thus, the energy crisis ushered in an era of unprecedented economic uncertainty, coupled with steadily increasing vulnerability to factors beyond the organization's control.

Nuclear Power. Detroit Edison's involvement with nuclear power dates back to its central role in the planning and construction of the first breeder reactor in the 1950s and early 1960s. When this early promise of a technology that produced more fuel than it consumed proved unsuccessful, the company began planning and construction of a thermal reactor, Fermi 2, announced to the public in 1968.

Fermi 2 construction began in 1972, and was halted in 1974 by the recession, the oil embargo, and soaring interest rates. Construction resumed in 1977, but was delayed pending investigation of the Three Mile Island accident in 1979. As a result of the investigation, the Nuclear Regulatory Commission imposed design changes and new regulations causing another delay of 21 months for Fermi 2. Two years after resuming construction in 1981, the work was 95 percent complete. Nonetheless, it was not until early 1985 that Edison obtained a full-power license. Incidents during testing in 1985 resulted in another year-long delay, and it was not until January 1988 that the plant completed the testing required for final approval and went into commercial operation.

The story is a classic case of the problems associated with the nuclear power industry. Fermi 2 was conceived in 1968 as a six-year, $228-million project. Now, about 20 years later, estimated costs have risen to more than $4 billion. The company's future now depends on keeping the plant on-line at full power, at a time when many of the company's executives admit that few, if any, nuclear power plants will be built in this country in the near future.

Fermi 2 also had a direct but far more subtle influence on the company. Edison was once an organization that prided itself on engineering expertise. Construction of conventional plants had been carried out by the company itself, and represented an important source of vitality, dynamism, and pride. With Fermi 2, however, it relied more heavily on outside experience. Thus, the 1970s not only began a period of little or no growth but also a period that tended to increase the company's dependence on outsiders rather than demonstrate its independent engineering expertise and leadership.

Affirmative Action. The third major change in the 1970s was in affirmative action. In a highly publicized lawsuit in 1973, attorneys from the U.S. Justice Department's Civil Rights Division, representing black Edison employees, charged the company with racial bias in hiring practices. The court decision ordered that the 8 percent proportion of blacks in the company be raised to 30 percent, and that the company pay $4.25 million in damages to the victims of discrimination. Two of the company's unions were also found guilty of ignoring pleas from black members who tried to initiate grievances. The company was also ordered to undertake a court-ordered affirmative action program, which stipulated that one black must be hired for every two whites who were hired, and that one black employee must be promoted for every white employee who was promoted.

Implementing this change under court supervision posed another difficult challenge for Detroit Edison. After considerable resistance, the company's leadership of the time began to adopt a pragmatic approach toward integration, and later became more progressive. Change at the top, however, was easy compared with change throughout the rest of the organization.

As one executive put it, the company changed relatively quickly at both the top and the bottom, but very slowly (and with great resistance) in the middle. Foremen, supervisors, and mid-level line managers saw affirmative action as a major threat to their carefully planned (and sometimes promised) promotions, and protested accordingly. The mandated policies were implemented, but with reluctance, resignation, and a lack of commitment in the middle and lower levels of the company. It is not unusual today, 15 years later, to sense bitterness on the part of older employees over the way they were treated when the company was being integrated. For more than a few, this still appears to be one of the major events in their careers at Detroit Edison.

The company's forced integration also altered the strongly paternalistic culture and sense of family that had characterized the company for years. It created racial barriers within an organization that had traditionally held a set of remarkably egalitarian customs for informal socializing both on the job and outside of work. These changes all took place, of course, against the backdrop of a city torn by racial conflict in 1967 and eroded by the "white flight" to the suburbs in the years that followed. These changes, along with the other forces hitting the industry, made the 1970s a time of turmoil and transition for Detroit Edison.

The three changes were the result of forces that were beyond the control of the organization. After nearly a half century of planning how to accommodate the steady increase in demand for electricity, the organization, over a relatively brief period, had to cope with a complex, multifaceted environment that was changing rapidly. The forces that would determine the future of the Detroit Edison organization now lay outside the company, rather than within.

The Detroit Edison Culture

Several distinctive characteristics help define the Detroit Edison culture. First is the traditional stability of the work force and the long tenure of many employees. Even today, someone with 15 years of service is considered relatively junior, and it is not unusual to find employees who have been on the job 40 or more years. The company has traditionally been a "good employer" and old-timers will be certain to recall that the company did not lay anyone off during the Great Depression. Particularly until the turbulence of the 1970s, employees saw themselves as a family, and many of the management practices were highly paternalistic. Many employees, for example, told stories about being given a suit and an overcoat by their first boss, or about being loaned money to pay tuition for night school. Traditionally, Edison employees socialized outside work, often centered around luncheon clubs or their Edison Boat Club. In these settings, it was commonplace for employees of all levels to interact freely, which helped contribute to the sense of family. Although the company today is not nearly the "family" it once was, the pleasant and respectful manner of interaction developed over the years is still present. One reason for this is that open conflict has traditionally not been tolerated, and thus issues that might raise conflict often have been avoided.

The lore of the line organization stresses technical expertise, around-the-clock flexibility, and the ability to respond in time of crisis. As one of the managers interviewed told it, this ethic stemmed from "the myth of the boomer lineman." The "boomer lineman" refers to the early days of the industry when independent traveling linemen moved continually from one location to another stringing up power lines. Although the current lineman is far more likely to hold his or her job because of the nine-to-five security it offers, the resourcefulness and independence of these early days are still highly valued. When an occasional thunderstorm disrupts service, it is not unusual for linemen and operators to work around-the-clock until service is restored, and in the process reaffirm some of the same values held by the original boomer linemen.

Traditionally, Edison has also been a male culture. Top executives have nearly always been men, and the operating organization is almost entirely male. Until the early 1960s, Edison had a rule that women must quit work when they got married, and, with the exception of a few career executive secretaries in the past, until recently there have been few influential women in the company. Women now work primarily in support positions, although there are a few women executives.[1]

Edison has also been, for the most part, an organization dominated by engineers. Thus, the occupational culture associated with engineers—a view that the world is primarily a rational, objective, quantitative, and technical place—pervades the organization. Engineers are an elite group in the company, and over the years they have provided much of the strategic thinking that has directed the organization. They have also influenced the internal structure of the organization. Lines of authority and areas of responsibility are clearly drawn, and the organization, for the most part, operates like a machine.

During the 1970s however, the organization began making a number of changes designed to broaden its executives' view of the world. Before then, nearly all positions within the company were filled by engineers. When a position opened in Government Affairs or Public Relations, for example, management would just ''move someone over,'' as one executive put it. This meant that the organization often suffered from chronic groupthink—the tendency of a highly homogeneous group to reach consensus (and sometimes poor decisions) without considering all the alternatives. Many engineers denied the impact of the political, social, and governmental influences on the company, and longed for the simpler days when they needed only to worry about building bigger and better power plants.

The top management, however, must operate differently. It links the organization to the community, the Michigan legislature, Public Service Commission, and the Nuclear Regulatory Commission, as well as other regulators and constituents. Top managers must function as politicians and consider problems within a broad set of social and political parameters, rather than the narrow and precisely defined set of parameters with which most engineers are comfortable. Interestingly enough, both the engineers and the ''politicians'' within the organization use the word *reality* to describe what they are responding to. Engineers do not always

---

[1]It is also important to note that Detroit Edison was one of the first companies in the industry to appoint a woman, Sarah Sheridan, as vice-president.

respond to politics, regulation, or the company's culture because, as one engineer put it, "We can't accept it in the political sense because we are trained to deal with the realities of the world." In contrast, another executive, more accustomed to dealing with state government, kept referring to the "real-world aspects of an issue," and commented that "some engineers seemed to be interested in the real world, but don't always know how to deal with it."

The "engineers vs. politicians" dynamics within Edison provide a classic example of conflicting subcultures and a clear example of top management acting as a "buffer" to try to preserve the efficiencies of a stable technical core. The logic of the technical core often contradicts political and social considerations, and there are inevitable trade-offs between providing consumers with options and choices and providing them with the most efficient low-cost electricity.

A final characteristic of the Edison culture stems from working in a regulated industry. Many executives commented that they often worked with the feeling of someone "looking over my shoulder." The company can be (and *is* often) required to provide any type of information its regulator requests, and this information can be used to the company's disadvantage in rate cases or in the interpretation of regulations. Thus, many of the organization's members have a style that is simultaneously forthcoming and secretive. They know they must provide a gracious and timely response to any question posed by the regulator, but do not, of course, have to respond to the "unasked question." In this environment, formulating a competitive strategy often means trying to keep a step ahead of the regulator by posing the next set of questions, rather than waiting to be asked.

Management Practices

In addition to the cultural factors, the organization has several distinctive management systems and practices. Most of these systems tend to reinforce the stability and formality of the operating organization.

For example, career tracks in Detroit Edison are quite clearly defined, and managers often know well beforehand what their next position will be. In regard to future advancement and promotion, one manager went so far as to say that "promises are made, and they are kept." This helps create a high level of stability and predictability, both in the organization and in individual careers.

At the lower levels of the organization, this means that promotions are often based on "time-in-grade" as well as on performance. This practice is less apparent toward the top of the organization. At the higher levels, the practice of designating the successor for a position is still very common, but here the system places less importance on senior-ity and allows bright and capable people to rise quickly. In an attempt to bring well-rounded managers to the top the organization is com-monly offering broadening experiences as part of management training. This type of experience, however, is rare in the operating organization.

Until the early 1970s, all upper management positions within the company were filled by insiders. Thus, critical appointments in Public Affairs or Government and Community Relations were often filled by engineers, with little explicit training or expertise in the area, rather than being covered by experienced professionals. Then, however, the com-pany began bringing in "outsiders" at very high levels in an effort to make itself more responsive to external factors. Slowly, the newcomers began to change the style of top management and achieve integration of the organization with the community and the state. These changes occurred through recognition that many of the most important decisions of the future were going to be made by those outside the company.

Management practices within the operating organization are very conventional and focus on the control of existing activities and opera-tions. As one manager put it, "Day-to-day operations are not a strategic issue. We can run the pants off a power plant, put up lines, and main-tain 'em very, very well. We have very talented people." The objective to obtain a high level of efficiency, in a stable, capital-intensive environ-ment contrasts drastically with the objective at the top of the organiza-tion: fitting a public utility into the world around it.

Several managers also commented on the influence of the regulatory process on the management practices and culture of the organization. In addition to engendering the feeling of "someone looking over your shoulder," regulation seems to make managers look backwards, thus restricting the organization's ability to change. A classic example is the continual concern with rate cases. Rate requests or other legal actions typically take up to 5 years to resolve, and cases that continue for 10–15 years are not uncommon. Thus at the same time Edison is arguing one point of view in court, it is often making decisions in its current planning and operations that contradict that point of view. Even though this is an adaptive response (because the situation may have changed drasti-cally since the original case was introduced), it often gives the impres-sion that the company is being inconsistent. These pressures lead the company to always try to behave in a way that is as consistent with the past as the current circumstances allow. Clearly, this constrains its ability to change and adapt to (or help create) its future environment.

Edison has great skepticism about innovative human resource prac-tices. Several of those interviewed made the point that culture and inter-nal organization are irrelevant to the company and that such things were best left alone. Although some managers acknowledged that their operating employees were not always as productive, focused, or challenged as they could be, most did not see this as an area that needed fixing. Thus, the organization, for the most part, favored a conventional human resource function, concerned primarily with selection, training, and performance appraisal. Innovations were perceived to risk raising expectations unnecessarily, and were usually approached with caution. Or as one manager put it, "Why rattle the cage if you aren't going to feed the animals?"

Effectiveness

Determining the effectiveness of a regulated public utility is often problematic. Many constituencies must be served, and key decisions are often made by outsiders. Profitability is only one criterion of performance. Rates are set, and the regulator needs to ensure that the utility makes neither too high nor too low a profit. A utility cannot be allowed to fail because the public would lose its investment. At the same time, if a utility is too profitable, the public may be paying too high a rate for its electricity.

Several geographical factors also have an impact on Edison's financial performance. Most fuel must be imported into the state, and the state has fairly strict environmental standards and a high level of industrial emissions. The region's wage rates are relatively high, and are driven by those of the auto industry.

Nonetheless, it seems clear that Detroit Edison is a relatively high-cost producer, and generally falls in the next-to-lowest quartile when compared to a national sample of utilities. Industry analysts who have examined Edison's earnings, cash flow, interest coverage, profit and expense ratio, and dividends generally paint an unfavorable picture, and the company's costs and financial performance are often taken as an indication of its effectiveness. Managers and executives can readily explain why these performance issues are beyond their control, yet the general trend persists.

A clearer sign of the limitations that the organization's culture may place on its effectiveness comes when one examines the company's attempts to adapt to factors such as a low-growth environment and the possible deregulation of the utility industry. One response to the low-growth environment has been to try to diversify. The company's major attempt at related diversification is its wholly owned, for-profit subsidiary named SYNDECO. For the past five years, SYNDECO has attempted to diversify by building on the organization's expertise and resources and by forming new service-based companies to provide an alternative to a totally regulated environment. SYNDECO is an interesting study in the clash between an entrepreneurial culture and the traditional Detroit Edison culture. But with less than 0.05 percent of the corporation's revenues, SYNDECO has yet to have a real impact on Detroit Edison.

The potential of deregulation also requires Edison to begin to consider adapting to a changing future. Deregulation could change the regional monopolies that utilities have enjoyed by forcing them to transmit to customers power they themselves have not generated. Deregulating the transmission lines could allow non-Edison producers of power to sell to customers on the Edison system. This innovation poses several difficult technical problems, but would provide customers with *choices* that they do not now have. This change would also bring into play a complex set of competitive forces in an area that has traditionally been a monopoly.

A second innovation, which has already begun, is cogeneration—or the production of power by independent companies. Cogeneration requires a utility to purchase electricity generated by its customers at peak rates, but still be prepared to sell electricity back to those customers when they need it. This allows private industry to generate electricity for its own use and sell it to the utility when it is not needed.

Both of these innovations require a new type of flexibility. Nonetheless, the organization still seems to view these changes as a departure from the normal (and proper) way of doing business, rather than as an early sign of the nature of its future business. These problems of adaptation probably provide the best example of the limitations that Edison's culture places on the organization's future effectiveness.

The Culture and Effectiveness Model

Historically, Detroit Edison has enjoyed conditions that most organizations would envy: rapid and steady growth in the demand for its product and no competitors. Within this context it was a relatively high-involvement organization with a consistent and distinct approach to managing. Only one form of adaptation was required—building bigger and better power plants. Its engineering-based culture met these demands extremely well. Today, however, and during the period when the survey and performance data were collected, the picture looks quite different.

Involvement. During the study period (1977–1981) and still today, Edison appears to be a low-involvement organization. This is particularly true in the highly stable operating organization, which is no longer challenged by the growth and construction of the early years. In addition, the operating organization now makes up a larger proportion of the company.

Involvement in other parts of the organization may well be much higher than in the operating organization. The top of the organization has changed considerably in response to outside forces, and it appears to have developed a style that incorporates diverse viewpoints, values innovation, and contemplates the impact that regulatory decisions may have on future business. Other areas of the company such as SYN-DECO and Fermi 2 also appear to create work environments characterized by higher involvement than the operating organization.

Although much of the efficiency of a utility is driven by capital investment and the characteristics of the region served, both the quantitative analysis and the case study make it difficult to rule out the possibility that low levels of involvement are one of the features contributing to lower-than-average performance over time.

Consistency. Despite the many changes that have hit the organization in the past 10 to 15 years, much of the Detroit Edison organization remains a very stable, consistent, and inbred culture. Again, this statement rings particularly true in the operating organization, and is less applicable in other parts of the organization, such as the top, where a conscious effort has been made over many years to broaden the parameters by which decisions are made. These changes have helped to reduce consistency and conformity and to create a culture that has more variety than in past decades, when the company's operating and construction objectives were unchallenged and highly successful.

Forces that have helped reduce the high level of consistency that Edison traditionally has had include more active intervention by government and regulators, a higher profile public image, and a racially integrated work force and management staff, which more closely represent the composition of the community the company serves. Forces that have helped maintain this cultural consistency include the tremendously capital-intensive nature of the utility, the way in which the operating organization is buffered from the environment by top management, the power of the occupational culture of engineers in the company, and the tremendous inertia of the culture itself.

The consistency of the organization's culture has changed appropriately to reflect changes in the organization's environment, but the balance must necessarily continue to shift toward diversity and variety as Detroit Edison continues to adapt to future demands.

Adaptability. It is clear that the adaptability of the organization has generally increased over the past 10 to 15 years, but it is also apparent that the nature of its adaptability has also changed. For years, adaptability simply meant responding in a timely manner to predictable linear growth in the demand for electricity. During that period, the organization was highly adaptable to a very limited set of factors. Adaptability in more recent years has come to mean responsiveness to outside influences and accommodation of the needs of a larger set of stakeholders. In contrast to the earlier years, the organization has adapted more slowly (and with more difficulty) to a much broader set of influences.

Despite the quantum leap in adaptability, it is still apparent that many of these changes have taken place primarily at the top of the company and, to some degree, at the bottom. The middle management seems to feel the greatest pressure to stay the same and also the greatest risk in changing. In the future, as demands for adaptability and responsiveness to outside influences continue to grow, adaptability at all levels of the organization will become more important. For now, the organization's ability to adapt and change appears to be the most critical factor limiting its future performance.

Mission. The mission of Detroit Edison has changed substantially in the period discussed in this case study. These changes in mission can be directly traced to a changing definition of what it means to be a *public* utility. As noted throughout this case, for a half-century being a public utility meant adding capacity in a predictable and efficient manner. But for the past 20 years, being a public utility has increasingly meant responding to the public's demands, represented through the political system, for cost-effective options and safeguards. Thus, the mission of Detroit Edison is to steward the state's existing capital investment while assessing the options available for electrical power in the future. Complex issues such as cogeneration and deregulation of transmission lines imply a trade-off between traditional economies of scale and options for the consumer. The utility's expertise in *balancing* this equation will be the criterion of success—a stark contrast to the old mission of maximizing capacity.

The difficulty is that the first mission is still alive and well in the hearts and minds of many of the organization's members. The second mission is seen as a challenge or a threat to the long-established traditions. The existing organization includes many systems and values designed to the original mission, and these change very slowly. Some of the systems are compatible with both the old and the new mission, but many are not.

Lessons Learned from the Detroit Edison Culture

The clearest lesson that comes from studying culture and effectiveness at Detroit Edison is the tremendous inertia that a culture can develop over a long period of time, and the restrictions that inertia can place on an organization's ability to adapt. The culture in this case has many roots: an engineering occupational culture; a long period of stable growth, which defines for many the meaning of a public utility; a belief in personal control over destiny; some strong assumptions about race and gender; and a paternalistic organizational family. This particular set of assumptions, nurtured by five decades of success, probably reached its peak sometime in the late 1950s, or early 1960s. Then the changes began.

As this case analysis has pointed out, the 1970s were a decade of incredible turbulence, and challenged nearly all these basic assumptions. The energy crisis, nuclear power, affirmative action, and the end of construction required that the organization adapt to influences by those *outside* the company. "Fixed costs," stemming from its tremendous capital intensity, clearly limited its ability to adapt, but not nearly so much as the "fixed costs" associated with its time-honored mind-set and behavior. With such inertia, change could occur only through great pain and turmoil.

Cultural change, in this organization, did not occur without *massive* change in the organization's business environment. Even then, this turbulence was countered by the tremendous inertia that the Edison culture had built up over time. Personal careers, management and personnel systems, strategic plans—all were called into question by the new environment. The tendency was to adopt a defensive posture and attempt to "buffer" the core of the organization from these changes. One may, in fact, learn most about this organization by asking how it has been able to stay the same in the face of such large-scale environmental change.

The conclusion, then, must be that culture is like any object with *inertia:* the more momentum the object gains, the larger the disruption necessary to change its course, and the smaller the deflection from its original path. Only over a period of time comparable to the development of the original culture, with constant pressure from both inside and outside the organization, can a substantial redirection of a culture occur. Thus, even the incredible turbulence of the 1970s and the concerted efforts of a generation of executives have left an organization in which Alex Dow himself might still feel at home.

CHAPTER NINE

Procter & Gamble

The fourth case study is Procter & Gamble (P&G), a company widely known as one of the nation's premier consumer marketing organizations. The company is more than 150 years old, and many of its products have long been household words. Well-known products such as Ivory Soap, Tide, and Crisco have been market leaders for decades. The company has the incredible growth record of doubling its sales volume each decade of its existence, and is the first career choice for hundreds of highly talented graduates of top American universities each year.

The survey data portray P&G as a high-involvement company with financial performance slightly below average for the industry. The survey data, as noted in Chapter 5, were gathered in 1966 and compared to performance data that came from 1966 through 1971. It is important to remember, however, that performance in these analyses was equated with return on investment and return on sales, and not with growth over time. Clearly, if the criterion for performance was long-term growth, P&G would be an outstanding performer.

The corporate culture of P&G is intriguing. Its legendary emphasis on thoroughness, market testing, and ethical behavior is transmitted to new employees through unique recruitment and socialization practices that combine internal competition and internal promotion. Only the "victors" in this "tournament" eventually assume leadership roles at P&G. These practices have led to a strong and distinctive culture that past and present members of the organization perceive to be closely linked to P&G's effectiveness.

History and Background

P&G was founded in Cincinnati in 1837 by William Procter, a candle-maker, and his brother-in-law, James Gamble, a soapmaker. During the week, Procter managed sales and finance and Gamble ran production, and they met regularly on Saturday night to discuss the business. The founders' basic values and beliefs established principles that strongly influence the corporation to this day. Their mission was to produce relatively inexpensive household products, technically superior to the competition, that were quickly consumed and were an integral part of their customers' life-style. By serving their customers' everyday needs through quality products, they sought to "foster growth in an orderly manner, to reflect the standards set by the founders, and to plan and prepare for the future" (Schisgall 1981).

Building on its early success, the company grew rapidly during the Civil War, when it supplied the Union Army with soap and candles, its two main products. The emptied packing crates, with P&G's famous "moon and stars" trademark, served as furniture in Union tents and as reminders of the company's products.

The company's early innovations came both in the product arena and, perhaps more important, in marketing and advertising. In 1887, when a New York chemical analyst discovered that P&G's new bar soap had only 0.0056 impurity, young Harley Procter wrote the ad copy classic, "Ivory Soap is ninety-nine and forty-four one-hundredths percent pure." This campaign has been used to sell Ivory ever since, and helped begin a long tradition of excellence in advertising and marketing. Other soap products were soon added to the P&G line, and were followed by food products such as Crisco, beginning in 1912. Sales of all these products benefited from an increasingly well-tuned marketing system.

The company has always relied heavily on research and has valued objectivity. The reliance on research led it in two complementary directions: the development of "technically superior products" and the development of innovative ways to advertise and market. Producing a "technically superior product" meant beginning with an objective customer need and then developing a product noticeably better at meeting that need than any existing product. Until it had produced such a product, P&G typically would not enter a market, even though it might have been profitable to do so.

To gain more objective information about the marketplace, P&G formed an economic research unit in 1923 to ask customers what they thought of the company's products. As the research became more systematic, this unit became the forerunner of the market research function in major corporations, which in turn prompted the P&G penchant for research to extend to understanding the marketplace, as well as developing new products.

To bring its message to the public through "wholesome family entertainment" (a medium in keeping with the corporate values), P&G invented a new form of entertainment, the "soap opera." The company served as sole sponsor of these radio programs in the twenties through the forties, and then on television in the 1950s. Classics such as "Search for Tomorrow," "As the World Turns," and "Edge of Night" were developed and sponsored exclusively by P&G, and the firm has traditionally maintained television's largest advertising budget.

Several organizational innovations, developed during the 1920s, endure as a mark of the P&G style. The first of these was direct retail sales. Once it discovered that selling directly to retailers would work in the New York area, P&G moved to eliminate brokers altogether and to sell directly to retailers across the entire country. This allowed them to respond to a stable demand for its products, rather than the volatile demands of wholesale brokers. Although P&G eventually retrenched somewhat and relied on brokers to sell to very small outlets, the company succeeded in drastically changing its pattern of consumer marketing and reducing the turbulence associated with selling through wholesale brokers. In addition, the persistent image of the P&G sales representative carefully examining the shelf space allocated to P&G products provided the company with a new way to ensure that its products captured the consumers' attention.

A second organizational innovation, which took place in the 1920s and 1930s, was the evolution of the brand management system for which P&G is so well known. The system developed, in part, in response to Camay, the company's new soap product and a potential competitor for Ivory. Without separate marketing and advertising, argued Neil McElroy (who was later to become CEO and chairman of the board), how could a new brand be expected to compete freely with an established brand? The brand management system created a separate organization for each brand and ensured that the development of new brands would not be hindered by the attention paid to older, more established products. This form of internal competition ensured that brands would vie for resources and that no brand would be forced to subsidize a less profitable product.

The company has had a long history of influential leaders, all of whom have made their own contribution to the organization's culture. The early leaders came primarily from the Procter family, most notably Harley T. Procter and William Cooper Procter. Harley Procter was the first to convince the P&G board that making consumers *aware* of the company's products was a worthy investment. The first advertising budget of $11,000 allowed Harley to develop the ads for Ivory Soap, a name he had devised. The genius of P&G advertising and the constantly increasing advertising budget can be traced to Harley's innovations.

With a long history of being a progressive employer, P&G management has continually searched for ways to merge the interests of the company with those of the employee. Cooper Procter was largely responsible for these traditions within the company. Practices such as profit sharing for employees, employee conference committees, in which employees had the opportunity to question the top leadership on a regular basis, the shortened workweek, and the assurance that each regular employee would be guaranteed 48 weeks of steady employment during each calendar year were all in place by 1923. Profit sharing, one of Cooper's earlier innovations, began in 1887! Because he was personally responsible for many of these innovations, employees raised funds, when he died, to build a monument in recognition of Cooper Procter's contributions to their well-being.

The first company president from outside the founders' families was Richard Deupree, who rose from the very bottom of the company to become one of its most distinguished chief executives. Deupree's contributions were many, but his implementation of direct retail sales, brand management, and P&G-sponsored soap operas on the radio certainly number among his major contributions.

More recent leaders of the corporation have also made their unique mark on the company and its culture. Soon after his graduation from Harvard, Neil McElroy established his reputation at P&G by proposing and implementing the brand management system. He also continued a tradition of involvement in national politics, begun by Cooper Procter, by serving as secretary of defense under Eisenhower. McElroy was followed in the company presidency by Howard Morgens, who presided during a period of explosive growth and directed the introduction of many diversified products. During this time, Morgens also attained an unprecedented level of stable and predictable performance. John Smale, the most recent chairman, reemphasized the importance of scientific objectivity to the corporation's marketing strategy through his dogged pursuit of the American Dental Association's endorsement of Crest as "an effective decay-preventive dentifrice. . . ." This was the first time the ADA had endorsed such a product. John Pepper, Smale's successor as chairman, faces the challenge of leading P&G into a future where it must rediscover the company's historical strengths and expand in new areas such as food products and specialty markets to continue the company's remarkable growth record.

The Procter & Gamble Culture

Procter & Gamble is an excellent example of a strong culture. The system is based on a simple set of values, well understood throughout the organization, and a socialization process designed to pass those values on to successive generations of managers. The result of this system is that individual identity is always minimized and sometimes lost. There are few individual accomplishments; most are team accomplishments. A new recruit soon learns to say "we" instead of "I."

Several personal statements help underscore the importance of the whole and the unimportance of individual identity. As one manager put it, "Everyone at P&G is like a hand in a bucket of water—when the hand is removed, the water closes in and there is no trace" (Pascale and Kaible 1982). Several managers noted that this deemphasis of individualism was made particularly clear when someone left the company.

> When an individual left P&G (usually Friday afternoon), his office would be totally gone Monday morning. There would be a wall where the door was, since [both walls and doors] were movable panels. It was as though they attempted to totally erase the memory of the departed manager.

Another manager also commented on what happened when someone left the company:

> When people leave the company abruptly, everything that they had worked on could be reconstructed from the files in a matter of hours. The system just picked up where they had left off.

To work successfully, this system requires tremendous conformity. "Conform and you succeed; question and you are gone" was the way one manager described it. Many talented managers learn the P&G system, but leave because of the emphasis on doing everything "the right way." Suggestions about finding a better way are often met with a blank stare or a quick lecture on why it is unnecessary. Being procedurally correct is often more important than being right.

One advantage of this conformity is a thorough and methodical approach to doing business. To quote past Chairman Richard Deupree, "Even though our greatest asset is our people, it is the consistency of principles and policy that gives us direction, thoroughness, and self-discipline." The result is a carefully engineered and highly redundant system of making decisions. No single link can cause a failure.

An integral part of this thoroughness is the strong emphasis on research. The expressed intent of P&G research is to "remove personal judgment from the equation" by "testing, retesting, and testing again." The P&G approach has been to create a product, based on research, that is technically superior to the competition and will win consistently in a blind test. Presumably, this allows the product to eventually dominate the market.

Stories about the importance of research and testing within the company abound. A classic is about the systematic testing performed when P&G was trying to make a choice about replacing the carpeting in its elevators. Before making a choice, P&G did an extensive "market test" on a sample of elevators. This story underscores the importance given to research data, and the importance of the market research logic to the decision-making process. Misrepresentation of data is one of the greatest "sins" in P&G, and it seems that almost no issue is too insignificant to escape scientific investigation.

Another example of P&G's extreme thoroughness is in the use of memos. The P&G culture emphasizes written rather than oral communication in order to communicate facts and remove individual judgment. All significant events and decisions are preserved in writing, and the record can be recreated at any point. Managers are often required to "boil it down" to fit a one-page format. Specific protocols for each type of memo are designed for efficient communication. Thoughtfully designed forms and protocols are everywhere. This system is used to convey facts and recommendations upwards in the organization so that decisions can be made. The individual who initiates an action usually become anonymous because ownership of the substance often moves up the hierarchy with the memo.

New P&G recruits tell horror stories about their first memos being ripped to shreds by the boss. After 8 to 10 rewrites, most eventually boil it down to a one-page memo to suit the high standards of written communication and the established format for conveying such information. The classic story describes an endless series of revisions culminating in the final memo, forwarded to the boss, with an attached handwritten note, by the brand assistant. The memo came back with a note from the boss: "Congratulations! Your memo looks fine. Now, about your handwritten note. . . ." The "niggling" (the process of repeated suggestions, comments, and revision to a P&G memo) never ends.

Thoroughness has created a system that is, in many ways, foolproof. Checks, counterchecks, and an emphasis on the product characteristics and customer preferences ensure that rational decisions can be made and are a central part of the P&G system. As one manager put it, "P&G has created a system where it is possible that a good idea is lost, but a bad one seldom survives."

This system is kept in place by an extensive socialization process that begins with the first job interview and seems to continue as long as an employee remains with the company. The system is designed to preserve the P&G way and to develop a highly motivated and talented set of new recruits into a new cohort of P&G managers. All new employees in the marketing organization enter as a part of a class or cohort against which their progress will be measured. About one-third of these new recruits are "peeled off" each year (the language of one P&G veteran), and only about one in four or five eventually reaches the level of brand manager. There is a rigid time line for promotions and it is made clear when someone is falling behind his or her cohort.

Despite this competition, the bond among the members of a cohort is very strong and often continues for the rest of their career. New employees are friends and coworkers and "go to strange towns, work together all day, and see the same people on weekends." It is not unusual to find members of a P&G cohort who are still in close contact, even though they may have left the company 10 years ago. The cohort, to a large degree, socializes itself, with its members competing with each other to perform well and adapt to the company culture.

Careful socialization to the do's and don'ts of P&G culture also takes its toll. Because of the company's emphasis on conformity, many highly talented managers leave and pursue successful careers in the consumer products industry, often using the methods and systems learned at P&G. Many managers also pointed out that once you learned the rules, "you can absolutely bank on them" because you know for certain that others will behave in the same predictable way. It may be difficult to innovate, but you are guaranteed due process.

A final element of the P&G culture is a high level of secrecy. This posture also has a long history within the company. For example, in 1895, several years after becoming a public corporation, the company stopped giving detailed financial reports to its shareholders because it felt that shareholders might misuse the information. The New York Stock Exchange protested and refused to trade P&G stock until this policy was rescinded. Consequently, the stock was not traded on the New York exchange again until 1929. More recent accounts of the corporation's disclosure practices (e.g., Solomon 1987) confirm that financial information is still very closely held and that the company maintains a mistrust of outsiders who are overly curious about P&G. New employees are instructed not to talk about the company to outsiders, and those who leave are counseled not to give out proprietary information. When this factor is combined with the internal promotion system, the result is an organization that has very distinct and impermeable boundaries.

Management Practices

The P&G culture is supported by and expressed through a set of concrete management practices. Nearly all the managers interviewed saw a very close link between these practices and the actual culture and value system. This section outlines several of the distinctive approaches to management taken at P&G, and often expands on a general theme introduced earlier in this case.

Possibly the most distinctive management practice within P&G is its policy of only promoting from within. The company aggressively recruits top M.B.A. and B.A. graduates of major universities and places them in a highly competitive situation. Those who cannot learn the system and begin performing immediately are weeded out and encouraged to seek employment elsewhere. Young managers compete on relatively objective grounds, and are subject to regular reviews by their bosses. Developing and mentoring younger managers is a highly valued management skill.

Because of this system, no one can reach the middle ranks, much less the upper levels of P&G, without 5 to 10 years of very close scrutiny and training. This creates a homogeneous leadership group with an enormous amount of common experience and a strong set of shared assumptions. As one manager described it, the internal promotion system also makes the slightly risky assumption that the "solution to tomorrow's problems lies with the current 'corporate gene pool'." Some of the effects of inbreeding and conformity are addressed further in the section on effectiveness.

A second distinctive aspect of the P&G management system is the delegation of tremendous responsibility to those at the lower levels of the organization. New recruits may assume major responsibility for a project almost immediately and typically are given as much responsibility as they can handle. Responsibility is also given a very personal touch at P&G. For example, rather than speaking of typos on a P&G memo, they are often called "thinkos."

New employees alternate between challenging project assignments and extensive periods of formal training. The company makes a large investment in each employee through training, mentorship and supervision, and extensive contact between new and seasoned managers. It expects that young managers will return this to the company in terms of motivation, dedication, and long hours spent working on challenging projects. The company invests a lot in a new employee and expects a lot back in return.

Despite the high levels of responsibility given new employees and employees at all levels, many jobs carry very little individual authority.

The authority to make real decisions is usually held far up the hierarchy, and decisions are usually made by hierarchical groups. Nearly everything must be approved through the memo process by several layers of management.

To illustrate that there is little authority at the lower level of the organization, there are many stories about relatively trivial decisions going all the way to the top of the company. Supposedly, the decision regarding the color of the lid on Folger's coffee was made by the CEO, and market testing to decide the shape of the Folger's jar continued for four years. Another story illustrating the tendency of decisions to float to the top describes a group of vice-presidents making changes in the recipes on Duncan Hines cake mix boxes. Truth value aside, these stories help illustrate the perceived lack of authority at lower levels in the organization.

A third classic P&G management innovation is the brand management system. In many ways, this system has become the archetype for running a consumer marketing business. Brands compete for internal resources, do their own advertising and marketing, and are independent cost centers. Brands have a clear pecking order within the company, and assignment to an obscure brand is the P&G version of Siberia. Application of this concept at P&G preceded the idea of the strategic business unit in other organizations by *decades*.

The brand management system creates a separate organizational structure for each brand. The brand manager is in charge and directs a staff of several assistant brand managers and a number of brand assistants. Career advancement usually means taking a better assignment at a different brand, and moving up the ladder to brand manager. Responsibility is highly decentralized in the brand management system, but authority is very centralized. Each brand maintains a separate marketing and advertising budget and separate product identity in the marketplace.

The innovative approach to management also extends to the manufacturing side of the organization. It was among the earliest American corporations to adopt new ideas about plant design that emerged in western Europe and the United States in the 1960s and 1970s (Walton 1972). In an attempt to move beyond the traditional assembly line mentality, plants were designed or redesigned to create a system of responsible, autonomous workers, decentralized decision making, broad job classifications, and a lean management structure and work force. This system also included a "pay for knowledge" approach to advancement and promotion, in which employees were rewarded for the acquisition of skills and knowledge, not for their progression in a hierarchy.

These innovations are consistent with P&G's traditional emphasis on creating a system that encouraged the employees to personally identify with the organization, the enterprise, and the product they are producing. Cooper Procter's philosophy that the corporation and the employee can jointly prosper was as alive in the late twentieth century as it was a half century before when he implemented profit sharing, and more than 70 years since he instituted 48 weeks of guaranteed work per year.

Effectiveness

An interesting example of an effective organization, P&G has pursued a specific form of effectiveness, and within that definition has been very successful. Effectiveness at P&G has meant growth over a long period and dominance of selected mass markets. Typically only active in those markets where it has the best or second-best product, P&G will not enter a market unless it has a superior product. As several managers stated, P&G has created a system that will not make big mistakes, but will sometimes be beaten by faster, more risk-oriented companies.

Profitability is an important criterion, but being exceptionally profitable is not important. The most impressive profitability statistic for the company is that between 1957 and 1974, the years that Howard Morgens led the company, profitability averaged 6.8 percent per year *and never varied more than 1 percent*. The rate itself is not particularly impressive, but the stability is astonishing. It is also worth noting that the rule of thumb for long-term growth in P&G was the same as in the utility industry in its heyday—the organization would double in size every decade.

The organization has traditionally targeted a mass market that warranted the tremendous costs associated with product research, market research, blind tests, and so on. Effectiveness has been defined as dominance of those markets. In more recent years, P&G has also attempted to enter more specialized markets and markets that tend to emphasize "taste" rather than objective product characteristics. They have not fared as well in these markets, in large part because competing favorably implies a departure from the traditional system and a challenge to procedures and values that are well-adapted to a mass market.

Another intriguing issue in the effectiveness of P&G is its system of recruitment and socialization. The "up and out" system means that P&G serves as a training ground for the consumer products industry, providing its competitors with well-trained and experienced managers. Opinions differed about the function of this system and its contribution to P&G's success.

One set of responses was that the system is highly functional. P&G gets its pick, and "never lost anyone it wanted to keep." The selection and socialization process is necessary to ensure consistency in the future. P&G gets enough work out of those who are being trained so that there is little loss in investment when most of them are gone after five years. The positive results of internal competition are greater than the loss of highly trained and skilled personnel.

A second set of opinions was that the system is somewhat disfunctional. The criteria for advancement are primarily conformity and fit, and the resources devoted to training are lost on those who leave the company. Worse yet, those who are well trained but resist conforming to the P&G system are the most dangerous competitors: they have more to gain by leaving P&G than by staying. Those who held this opinion pointed to many examples of highly successful managers who left the company and went to outstanding careers elsewhere.

On balance, the internal promotion and socialization system at Procter & Gamble is a powerful strategic tool. It funnels talented recruits into the organization and gives lots of feedback about their performance and adaptation. The system is highly powerful as long as the organization's mission remains fixed and fits the demands of the business environment. When the environment or the mission changes, the socialization process must reflect (or, better yet, anticipate) that change. To the degree that it does not—and a strong argument can be made that the system does not fit some of P&G's recent attempts to diversify into specialty markets, then the system need fundamental redirection.

The Culture and Effectiveness Model

Using the culture and effectiveness model as an analytic framework provides a useful way of summarizing the Procter & Gamble culture. This section discusses the company with reference to the four dimensions of culture: involvement, consistency, adaptability, and mission.

Involvement. A high-involvement organization, P&G has succeeded in developing a system in which the goals of the individual and the goals of the organization are largely compatible. The company's long tradition of trying to reconcile the interests of employee and employer has undoubtedly contributed to a high level of involvement. Involvement also seems to be aided by its system of internal promotion and its geographic location in Cincinnati, which offers few comparable career options.

At the same time, however, much of the high level of involvement that characterizes the organization stems not from merging individual and organizational goals, or from formal and informal systems of participation. Instead, much of the involvement comes from the intense internal competition to which most employees are exposed. Without becoming totally involved in the work and the organization, one is quickly passed over for advancement, and soon asked to leave the organization. Thus, the high level of involvement has a coercive side.

Consistency. A much more distinctive cultural characteristic of P&G is its consistency. The high level of consistency stems from strong underlying values that stress thoroughness, objectivity, and the efficiencies associated with a mass market. The weight of tradition, the emphasis on forms, memos, and protocols, and the socialization process all contribute to an incredibly consistent approach to managing and organizing. Even managers who were trained in the P&G system, but left to pursue their careers elsewhere, use some of those same systems 20 years later.

The consistency of the culture is an important element in P&G's legendary ability to move in a deliberate fashion. Decisions may be slow, but the company's ability to implement once it has chosen a course of action is impressive. This strategy has served the company extremely well in its efforts to grow and expand in mass market consumer goods.

Consistency appears to create at least two significant problems for the company. First, many talented managers and future executives rebel and leave the corporation after a few years' training. They are in high demand because of their skills, and they often leave for more entrepreneurial pursuits. Second, the values and procedures, which are at the root of this consistency, place limits on the organization's ability to change. These two problems seem to fit together—those who are most likely to change and innovate are also the most likely to leave.

Adaptability. The P&G culture allows for a high level of adaptability in the consumer goods mass market. It responds very well to market research and product research and combines those two forms of objective knowledge to introduce technically competitive, well-positioned products. It adapts well to consumer needs in the mass market.

The irony of P&G's adaptability, however, is that when it moves outside its traditional markets to specialty markets, or markets driven by "taste," the company has more limited ability to adapt. Several managers described the company as being "good at science, not at art." Responding to markets that are structured differently seems to present problems: the company tends to make the assumption of a mass market in a way that is no longer true of many consumer products markets. Its efficiency at exploiting a known set of mass markets clashes with its effectiveness at entering new markets. A recent account of P&G's attempts to enter the Japanese market ("They didn't listen to anybody" 1986) shows how the assumption that a new market will be like an old market can be very costly.

Mission. The P&G mission has traditionally been very strong and widely shared. Much of that strength continues today. As the discussion has pointed out, however, its mission was very well suited to a mass market and led to a culture that is overadapted to mass markets. The complementary mission and method enhance its ability to compete in traditional areas, but limit its ability to diversify beyond those areas. Thus, P&G is an excellent example of a strong mission that may be better suited to the company's past than to the future. Alternatively, future growth and performance might be better served by "sticking to the knitting" and pursuing growth in those areas that are best suited to the organization's traditional mission.

Lessons Learned from the Procter & Gamble Culture

The P&G culture is very distinctive and closely intertwined with the performance and capabilities of the organization. As such, it provides several lessons about culture and its relationship to effectiveness. This final section of the case analysis focuses on a few selected lessons about culture that come from this study of P&G.

Dynamics of an Internal Labor Market. The company has the unusual combination of the exclusive use of internal promotion practices, intense socialization procedures, and a policy of secrecy toward outsiders. The potency of this system suggests that *the strength and uniqueness of an organization's culture is a direct function of the impermeable nature of the organization's boundaries.* When there is only one way to enter an organization and clearly defined steps on the ladder, then it is much more likely that there will be one set of socialization norms and many opportunities to shape the behavior of those who will eventually lead the company. When an internal labor market exists, a high level of consistency and a strong sense of direction are far easier to achieve. The power of culture is greatly enhanced once "the border" is closed.

In contrast, when an internal labor market does not exist, an organization has a far more difficult time creating a distinctive culture and a sense of mission. Where there is no internal labor market and socialization process, occupational, regional, or ethnic cultures are more likely to dominate the organization and result in a less distinctive culture, or one that is less attributable to the organization itself.

Committing to an internal labor market, however, means a major commitment to a long-term course for the future of the organization. Recruitment and socialization must be directed at a clear future vision and strategy, but add to the inertia that must be overcome if a change in direction is required.

Time and Inertia. One of the most fascinating aspects of the P&G story is the development of the culture over so long a period. At each point in its history, the company's leaders made the best decision they could, informed by their own insights and the organization's past experience. As time passed, the volume of history informing the corporation's decisions grew, and the culture became richer and more complex. Beliefs about "the right way" to do business were reinforced by the company's success, and no major crises intervened to cause wholesale rethinking of the beliefs and values that structured the system.

The longer this process continued, the greater the strength of the culture. This means that if the mission and strategy are still appropriate, then the culture will continue to contribute to effective performance. This also means that, over time, cultures become much more difficult to change.

Selecting Performance Targets. Organizations define their own targets, and these are difficult to capture with a small number of performance measures. Rather than "maximizing profits" in the conventional sense, the target for P&G has been steady growth and moderate profitability. The organization's consistency in achieving these objectives (like the consistency of its culture) is very impressive.

Only with a measure such as average growth over five decades or lack of variation from 7 percent profit per year over 25 years could a "performance" measure really begin to capture the target toward which P&G has aimed. The performance pattern complements the company's culture very well, even though P&G's concept of performance and effectiveness is far different from many American corporations.

CHAPTER TEN

Texas Commerce Bancshares

The final case study in this book focuses on Texas Commerce Bancshares (TCB), a holding company headquartered in Houston with 82 banking locations throughout Texas. The bank itself was formed through a 1964 merger, but its predecessors had roots deep in the history and origins of the Houston region. With a loan portfolio balanced between energy, real estate, and national and international loans, the bank has pursued a combination of aggressive growth and cautious lending that has allowed it to outperform consistently other Texas banks through boom and bust. The organization grew very rapidly through the oil boom of the seventies and early eighties, but it has avoided some of the worst impacts of the drop in oil prices, which have recently driven many Texas banks to the brink of failure and to the doors of the Federal Deposit Insurance Corporation.

The quantitative data presented at the beginning of Chapter 5 portray TCB as an anomaly. The survey data show a low-to-moderate level of involvement and participation in 1978, but financial data show an unusually high level of performance relative to firms in the same industry during the years that followed. On closer inspection, the bank's financial performance is even more impressive—65 quarters of continuous growth in profits from 1969 to 1985, and a level of profitability that has been consistently higher than the large money-center banks. This combination of low involvement and high performance was quite rare in the quantitative study of 34 firms presented in Chapter 4.

A qualitative analysis of the culture of TCB tends to confirm the survey data: the organization is tightly controlled, has well-defined methods and objectives, and is highly centralized, even though geographically decentralized. The bank has been led for nearly 20 years by Ben Love, CEO and chairman, whose demanding, compelling, and systematic style permeates the organization. The bank's culture and its success pose an important question: What implications does a low-involvement, high-performance organization have for the development of the culture and effectiveness model presented in this book?

History and Background

The history of TCB and its predecessors, like all Texas banks, is one of consolidation of small regional banks, which were caught between the ever-increasing credit needs of a growing economy and the state's populist mistrust of big banking and concentrated wealth. Historically, large loans had always come from outside banks because the credit required for big projects was far beyond the loan limits of Texas banks.[1] The growth of the oil industry, beginning in the 1930s, provides a classic case. The credit demands of the major oil companies, such as Gulf and Texaco, far exceeded the lending limits of Houston banks, but at the same time the risks of lending to the small independent oil companies were deemed too great for the conservative bankers, who were primarily accustomed to financing the cotton trade. Until some innovative financier learned how to lend money based on proven underground oil reserves, Texas banks were only able to lend to local oil executives whose personal business reputations could serve as collateral.

Even though Texas Commerce Bank itself was formed in a merger in 1964, business historians Buenger and Pratt (1986) trace the bank's origins through the century-long evolution of the Houston economy and banking industry. The merger that formed TCB involved two Houston banks—the National Bank of Commerce and Texas National Bank, each of which brought a distinct cultural heritage to TCB. Both of these banks originated in the early twentieth century and reflected the dependence of the Houston economy on cotton, lumber, and real estate.

Texas National Bank was itself formed from a merger of two Houston banks—Union National Bank and South Texas Commerce National Bank. Both had a history of conservatism, with roots in the predictable lending to the cotton trade, and a disdain for the laxity of the "jazz banking," which accompanied periods of rapid growth in the Houston economy. Union National and South Texas Commerce National shared a reluctance to change until their founders, who led the banks from the

---

[1]For example, a 1978 survey by the Federal Reserve Board of the 42 largest companies in Texas found that 80 percent of their loans and loan commitments were from banks outside the state.

mid-twenties until World War II, finally relinquished control. Partly because of this leadership crisis, Union National and South Texas Commerce merged to form Texas National Bank (TNB) in 1953.

In order to survive in the postwar boom era, TNB steadily became less conservative and began to develop an impressive cadre of professional young bankers and managers through training and recruitment. Over the next decade, this created a first-rate professional management team that helped make TNB an attractive partner for the merger that created Texas Commerce Bank.

The National Bank of Commerce (NBC), the other partner in the merger that formed Texas Commerce Bank, also has a rich history, closely linked to the wide-ranging career of Jesse Jones. Jones, in rough chronology, was a lumberman, banker, newspaper publisher, public figure, government official, and spokesman for the Houston business community. After making his original fortune in lumber, Jones was the major stockholder in NBC, and its chairman of the board from 1929 until his death in 1956.

As a national and public figure and representative of the Houston business community, Jones served in the Roosevelt administration as head of the Reconstruction Finance Corporation and as secretary of commerce. He brokered the Houston banking community's response to the banking crisis of 1931, avoiding the bank failure that plagued much of the rest of the country and providing the basis for a stable recovery for the Houston region.

Like many great leaders, Jesse Jones was a hard act to follow. He tried repeatedly to find his own successor, but died before one could be found. After several unsuccessful attempts at replacing the bank's aging leadership, merger with Texas National Bank became an attractive option. It was a way to reestablish NBC's position as the largest bank in Houston and capture a large and talented pool of professional managers.

In 1964 the two banks merged, with the agreement that Texas National's young president, J. W. McLean, and his able cadre of young professional managers would soon take over the top position from the aging Robert Doherty, chairman of NBC. But in an eleventh-hour coalition of NBC interests on the board of directors determined that the top position would stay within NBC's control, and McLean and some of his most talented managers left the bank. John Whitmore, an NBC senior vice-president not previously targeted for the top spot, was chosen to lead the newly created Texas Commerce Bank.

After a transition period of three years, Whitmore recruited Benton F. Love, CEO of River Oaks Bank and Trust, a small, rapidly growing bank in a fashionable Houston suburb, to serve as a senior vice-president. Love quickly rose to become president (1969) and then chairman (1972), and has remained in that position ever since. Love's leadership began a transition from a loyal clan, based on the charisma of Jesse Jones, to "a hard-driving organization strongly committed to quantitative measures of performance" (Buenger and Pratt 1986, 301). This period was also marked by expansion through acquisition, the continued development of professional management within the bank, and the final separation of the bank's ownership and management.

The rapid growth of the 1970s and early 1980s was driven by the booming oil and real estate business and by changes in the Texas laws governing bank holding companies. Prior to the 1970 amendments to the Federal Bank Holding Company Act of 1956, Texas law allowed only a single location for each bank. After that amendment, there was a rapid consolidation of Texas banks into multibank holding companies. In 1971, Texas Commerce Bancshares became a bank holding company and, over the next 15 years, TCB acquired and absorbed more than 60 Texas banks. This gave the bank a strong presence in every major market in Texas, even though its major concentration (about 70 percent) remained in the Houston area. This rapid growth was necessary to ensure that TCB maintain a leadership position in Houston, and by 1983 the bank was the second largest in Texas and among the twenty largest banks in the United States. Its return on assets was consistently at the top of the list for all U.S. banks and its earnings increased steadily for 65 consecutive quarters, averaging 15–20 percent growth per year over this period.

This spectacular growth and performance continued until 1983 when the price of oil began to plunge. The reversal quickly ended the era of acquisitions, and resulted in a decline in earnings growth and growth in deposits. In 1985, for the first time in Ben Love's reign as chairman, the bank reported losses. Despite this downturn, TCB still absorbed the shock better than most other banks in Texas and the Southwest because the bank's conservative lending approach had limited its participation in troubled energy and real estate loans.

In September 1986, Texas banking laws changed again, this time allowing for interstate banking and the acquisition of Texas banks by banks from other states. Ben Love and TCB had worked for many years to see these laws change and were quick to take advantage of them. By December 1986, amid mounting losses, TCB announced it was merging with Chemical Bank of New York for $1.19 billion, a record for interstate bank acquisitions. At the age of 62, Ben Love resolved the future of his bank in the way of several of his predecessors—merger and consolidation.

The Texas Commerce Bancshares Culture

The legacy that TCB inherited from its predecessors was one of a quasi-public institution and major stakeholder in the economy of the Houston region. The allure of a public figure, in the model of Jesse Jones, as the spokesperson for a major Houston bank was an enduring one. This prodevelopment regional orientation and Jones's underlying philosophy of pragmatic liberalism were tempered by the conservatism of TCB's predecessors, which had developed from the predictability of the cotton trade. The synthesis of these two threads in the 1970s and 1980s was brought about through the combination of enthusiastic sales ability and tight internal controls brought on by Ben Love. This era coupled a regionally focused, progrowth strategy with a highly conservative, risk-limiting approach organized around the principles of industrial management. Beginning in the 1970s, "return on assets, return on equity, and the P/E ratio replaced a pat on the back by Jesse Jones as the measure of performance at Texas Commerce Bancshares" (Buenger and Pratt 1986, 256).

In this system, performance was defined almost exclusively by statistical goals. Every employee—from the officers to the tellers—understood the primary organizational goal of "at least 15 percent growth in earnings per share each year". Subgoals for different parts of the organization were also spelled out in great detail, and performance relative to these goals was monitored monthly by the "blue books," a series of notebooks that carefully tracked the performance of each bank, each loan, and each manager. To quote Ben Love directly, "Organizing human resources in the pursuit of statistical objectives is uppermost in my philosophy of management" (Buenger and Pratt 1986, 256). All of those interviewed emphasized the critical importance of "knowing the numbers" and meeting the goals.

These ambitious performance goals were enforced by a strong system of control. Those who did not meet goals were dismissed, and the system treated everyone the same. This fostered the sense of an elite meritocracy, closely linked to the market. "There is no emotion in it. The numbers are there for all to see, and everyone is treated on the same basis" (Stuart 1979, 128).

Strong pressure was applied from the top on down to enforce this system, and it seems to have created high levels of personal responsibility and tireless workers who expected the same from everyone else. The link that held this system together was Ben Love who, in a smooth but forceful style, kept up the pressure. There were many who did not stand up to these goals, pressures, and expectations, and a number of them left the organization over the years. Love is quick to recognize his influence, and acknowledges that "there was a time when the pressure that I individually exerted on people might have seemed a little untenable, and that people exited for that reason" (Welles 1983, 116).

One of the main arenas in which Ben Love set the standards and expectations for the bank was the loan committee meetings where proposed loans were presented and critiqued. Many current and former high-level officers of the bank tell stories about Love's smooth and methodical questioning, which often led to the downfall of a presenter who did not know the details of the loan inside out. Once on the defensive, few recovered. Loan meetings were public events, and many of those who were embarrassed in that setting did not regain momentum in their careers at TCB. Several of those who left the organization described a career sequence of rising through the organization based on merit, having an embarrassing confrontation at the loan committee meeting or other public setting, and then leaving the organization. Another example of this style comes from a story about Love's response when a junior officer fumbled during a presentation to a client. Love said nothing during the meeting with the client, but later, in the presence of colleagues, told the junior officer, "You have embarrassed me personally, and the bank" (Stuart 1979, 125).

The bank's culture also strongly reflects its ties to the Houston regional economy. Billboards leading into Houston proclaim "Let's Succeed Together" and "Texas Commerce Means Business." The TCB logo is a red, white, and blue design patterned after the Texas flag. A consummate marketing and sales organization, TCB is as enthusiastic as it is systematic. An interesting example of the interplay between these market-oriented values and the values that stress internal control was related by a former vice-president. The story described a loan meeting where a loan was presented with the recommendation that it be approved at an interest rate of 9 percent. As Ben Love began his smooth and methodical questioning, he became convinced that 9.5 percent was' the more appropriate rate. As the presenter slowly dug himself a deeper grave, Love persisted. Sensing the growing tension, an experienced member of the loan committee broke in to ask, "Did you promise the customer the loan at 9 percent?" When the presenter sheepishly admitted that he had, then the course was clear. Love agreed that the loan be approved at 9 percent because it had been promised to the customer, even though the more appropriate rate should have been 9.5 percent. This example helps illustrate that TCB loan policy was a means to good business and not an end in itself—the real business of good banking in Texas was keeping promises with valued customers and building profitable long-term relationships.

The socialization of new members into the organization also reveals some interesting aspects of the culture. Texas Commerce recruits top-notch talent claiming, "We recruit only from the top 10 percent from the best business schools in the country" ("Texas Commerce: Master of Controls" 1984, 41). One of the first Texas banks to recruit strongly outside the Southwest, TCB provided these new recruits with thorough training regarding the loan policies and procedures of the bank. Many of those who were interviewed, however, point out that the real lessons about how the bank is actually managed came after they had begun working. Several former managers described a scene in which the new recruit met with his or her boss and the boss's boss. In this setting, the new recruit's boss received a thorough "chewing out" from his or her boss, much to the surprise of the recruit. This lesson helped underscore the importance of always being prepared to be challenged and ready to defend one's position.

Although many of the characteristics of the TCB culture initially present the picture of a highly centralized system directed and controlled by a great leader, the reality is a little more complex. As an example, take the typical structure of the TCB loan committee meeting, which by design is similar throughout the bank. Top officers of the bank sit around a large conference table along with those who will be presenting the loans. The loan decisions will be made during the meeting by this committee of officers, in itself a practice somewhat unusual in the banking industry. In addition, around the perimeter of the room are seated a number of interested observers, trainees, and executives. Altogether, as many as 25 to 30 people may be in the room.

This public setting is one of the prime training grounds in the bank as well as the stage on which up-and-coming loan officers "make their mark." Successes and failures are very public, and this creates a fertile ground for stories about personal careers. If Ben Love's decisions were made behind closed doors, or in a more private setting as in most banks, there would be far fewer stories to foster the image of a hard-driving analytic style, or to underscore the importance of knowing a loan inside out before bringing it to the committee. Ironically, if the style of these meetings were not so open, the perception of strong central control might not be so great.

The topics of leadership, management systems, and culture are not unfamiliar to Ben Love. He once wrote a paper entitled "People and Profits" (Love 1967), which was an analysis of the bank's history and leadership. After being chosen Texas Business Executive of the Year in 1983, he gave an acceptance speech titled "Productive Leadership." In this speech, he described the culture of his own bank as having four components: (1) a lean staff, which contributed to productivity by providing the necessary autonomy to "let the bankers bank"; (2) systems, or established policies and procedures, which were administered by committees and provided a public forum in which views were made known and socialization of junior members of the organization could occur; (3) goals, which in TCB's case were restricted to a limited number of simple and clear objectives, that told people what to do, but not how to do it; and finally, (4) the reward of high salary, promotion, and opportunities for ownership. These principles provide a highly accurate account of the TCB culture, but they neglect the importance of Ben Love's smooth but forceful means to enforce this system.

Management Practices

The key values and principles that structure TCB's management system are reflected in unique management practices, which seem closely related to the organization's success. One of the most intriguing practices was that all loans of more than $50,000 must be unanimously approved by the members of the loan committee. A single dissenting vote is enough to veto any application that appears risky. As Love puts it, "If significant lending problems develop at Texas Commerce, we will not have to go looking for the people responsible." This system forces thorough discussion of the issues involved in each and every loan and requires a high level of responsibility on the part of each member for the committee's decisions.

The composition of the bank's board of directors also reflects its integration with the Houston business community. The board, numbering around 45, includes many of the bank's best customers, as well as such dignitaries as Lady Bird Johnson, former President Gerald Ford, and Barbara Jordan, former congresswoman and the first black woman to serve on the board of directors of a major Texas bank. The board members work hard on behalf of the bank, and sometimes themselves serve as a "loan production office," by bringing business directly into the bank through their own contacts and connections.

This close connection with the board members has not, however, been without some difficulties. Recently, because of the downturn in the oil business and real estate, a few board members have themselves been involved in bad loans. Four recent resignations can be directly traced to problem loans made to board members.

Another practice that distinguishes TCB from other banks is its program of calling on customers. The "call program" was one of Ben Love's first innovations after taking control of TCB. He divided up business sectors based on SIC codes and then instituted a system that required frequent contact ("calls") with current and prospective customers as well as the careful documentation of those contacts by the callers. The philosophy seemed to be, "We stir up enough lending opportunities in the marketplace so we don't have to grab at every opportunity we uncover. If we see a potential problem with a prospect, we will let some other bank make that loan." This program was a valuable tool that allowed the bank to be both aggressive and conservative at the same time.

Since the call program divided prospective customers by business sector and required callers to specialize in one market segment, particular callers got to know their customers and the dynamics of a particular business, rather than the less systematic methods of earlier bankers. The expectation that the bank would come to know its customers and its customers' businesses better enabled TCB to anticipate the risks present in any loan.

Although statistical objectives defined the goals of the bank, they did not define the means. The blue books showed the performance of each bank on a monthly basis, and strong performers were recognized at the officers' meetings, which occurred each Friday morning. Those who had been successful were encouraged to talk about how they did it, and every effort was made to transfer successful practices to the not-so-successful banks. Like the loan committee, this practice combined, in a public setting, elements of strong central control as well as teamwork and consensus management.

As noted earlier, another interesting characteristic of the bank was the rate of turnover among high-level officers. In fact, it also appears that this rapid turnover was common throughout the organization and throughout the industry. The turnover presumably resulted from the bank's high standards and the severe consequences for those who did not meet them. The bank, not unlike Procter & Gamble, has served as a training ground for many of its competitors. Bright young managerial talent gained training and experience at TCB, and were either forced out or left of their own accord to take other attractive positions in the banking industry.

Effectiveness

By nearly any measure of effectiveness, TCB must be considered a very successful organization. The definition of effectiveness, in the bank's terms, is also very close to the financial measures of effectiveness used in the quantitative study presented in Chapter 4. Surviving both boom and bust periods, TCB has performed very well in comparison to its direct competitors.

The bank's effectiveness in dealing with human resources, however, is somewhat more controversial. High turnover was cited several times as a problem, but on closer inspection TCB does not appear to have abnormally high turnover for the banking industry. Much like Procter & Gamble, TCB has served as a training ground for many Texas bankers, and has generated a number of competitors who know TCB's systems and strategies. In return, TCB usually has its pick of the best new recruits in the Texas banking industry, and over the years selects those who will lead the bank in the future.

The problem of leadership succession is also a significant issue that has not yet been dealt with effectively. Ben Love will be a hard act to follow. Much of the discussion about the future of the bank, in fact, focuses on what will happen when he retires. On the one hand, there are few managers within the TCB system who have the broad range of internal control and external marketing skills that Love has. On the other hand, the current leadership team is quite young; many of the key executives are not yet 50 years old. This young team actually operates the bank, and, if left intact, it could conceivably function effectively for the next decade.

This is only true, however, if the bank continues to operate the same as it has in the past. Traditionally, TCB has concentrated on the "middle market"—commercial banking with midsized firms. The system described in this chapter is extremely well adapted to that business, and that has been reflected in the bank's performance.

The more difficult question to answer is how the bank may adapt as it expands into new areas such as consumer banking, small business, or investment banking. The well-oiled machine has the potential problem of being a highly efficient single-purpose organization, whose adaptability has not yet been tested in other areas. The synergy of the merger with Chemical Bank depends on the ability of the two banks to execute *jointly* a strategy, but the past tells us little about the adaptability of TCB to this new set of circumstances.

Despite these criticisms, TCB has done very well at protecting and enhancing the assets of its stakeholders and the jobs of employees. Although many were surprised by the speed with which TCB merged with Chemical Bank after the change in the interstate banking laws, in retrospect this may have been the best way to protect its customers, stakeholders, and employees. For example, two other large Texas banks, InterFirst and Republic of Dallas, merged to pool their assets shortly after the TCB merger. This venture failed, and the newly formed bank sought relief from the Federal Deposit Insurance Corporation. Thus, TCB's merger is hard to criticize. Although the merger may not represent the peak of Ben Love's career, it is nonetheless another example of strong and effective leadership in a time of crisis.

The Culture and Effectiveness Model

Texas Commerce Bancshares provided a challenge to the findings of this study as they were presented in Chapter 4. From the quantitative findings, the bank appeared to have an autocratic management system and a tight system of internal control. Most of the organizations with these internal characteristics were low performers, but TCB was a consistently high performer. To some degree, this unusual finding can perhaps be discounted because TCB was operating in a region with a booming economy during the time the bank was studied, but it still appears quite clear that TCB was a high performer even in comparison with other Texas banks.

Because of this anomaly, TCB has a particularly important contribution to make to the development of the culture and effectiveness model presented in this book. As a beginning, a qualitative assessment of the bank's culture in terms of the four dimensions of the model is presented below.

Involvement. To the degree that high involvement exists within TCB it resembles Procter & Gamble. Involvement is based on competition against a standard and against each other. Consensus is required at the loan committee level of TCB, but in general this is an organization that works because of clearly defined goals and highly specialized tasks, not because of the spontaneous and autonomous involvement of executives, managers, and employees. One exception to this, which is quite likely not captured by the survey measures, is the distinction TCB makes between means and ends. Ends are predetermined, and individuals have little or no say in those decisions. How they meet these goals, however, is an area where most managers have a high degree of autonomy. The example of how successful practices were transferred from one bank to another shows how a strong sense of teamwork can be built in an organization that has clearly defined goals as well as rewards that are oriented toward reinforcing the strong individual performers.

Consistency. In its consistency in the implementation of loan policies, TCB is remarkable. This is true both with respect to internal controls and in terms of the aggressive and systematic behavior that TCB has shown in the marketplace. At each step, methods are well designed, clearly described, and unquestioningly enforced. Perhaps more important, the industrial management approach created a system that ensured quality control during a time of rapid expansion. Because it is both the quality and the quantity of loans that ultimately determine a bank's fate, the only way to jointly optimize growth and stability is to uncover more potential loans than the competition, and then systematically go deeper into each loan to make a "better" decision (one that minimizes risk but maintains customer relations). TCB's systematic approach to this problem is clearly at the heart of its competitive advantage and success.

Adaptability. The pressure created by the blue books, monthly goals, and internal control systems required an obsession with the marketplace. When the market changed, practices changed, and some of TCB's greatest successes were in finding new ways to loan money in real estate, energy, or the international arena. Specialization by market segment was high and allowed for different strategies in different industries. Specialization may have created some internal rigidity and bureaucratic red tape, but, for the most part, it appears that the organization's systems responded to the demands of the market. The combination of consistent standards and a high degree of flexibility is a good illustration of an organization with simultaneously loose and tight structures.

The real challenge to the adaptability of the organization, however, will be to grow beyond the middle-market orientation, which has been its hallmark for years, and devise a system that will be equally effective in exploiting new markets. Ironically, the success of the existing system may make this process more rather than less difficult.

Mission. The bank's mission has undergone an important transition over the past 20 years. It continues to be an elite institution, with a high degree of dedication to the service of Houston and Texas. Nonetheless, the transition from the Jesse Jones era, with a quasi-public function to serve, to an era characterized by a continual obsession with 15 percent annual growth represents a change from a mission based on community to a mission based on a number. Sensitivity to populist values in Texas has waned, partially as a result of the growth and prominence of the region in the national economy and partially as a result of the enormous increase in size of the Texas banks themselves. The culmination of this trend was in the swift and noncontroversial approval of interstate banking by the Texas legislature, and TCB was quick to merge with Chemical Bank in the interest of survival and stability for customers' assets.

Despite this radical change in the fundamental mission of the organization, in both cases the mission was a compelling one. One might argue over the degree to which there was intrinsic or extrinsic acceptance of the community mission or the return on assets mission, but they have nonetheless been powerful sources of direction. The most precarious periods in the bank's history, by contrast, appear to be the periods of leadership transition, when there was no compelling shared mission.

Lessons Learned from the Texas Commerce Bancshares Culture

As in each of the other case studies, most members of TCB saw a close connection between the internal culture of the organization and the bank's performance over time. Most attributed this to clear and simple goals, a consistent and systematic approach to both internal functioning and to customers, and an adaptive and competitive orientation toward the marketplace. Few attributed the success to a spontaneous participation and involvement like members of People Express or Medtronic did about their organizations, but instead emphasized the motivational qualities of a clear set of goals and rewards. As such, it seems that the culture and effectiveness model was helpful in describing the reasons why TCB was successful, even though the bank itself does not fit very well with the findings presented in Chapter 4.

Texas Commerce Bancshares also provides an intriguing study in leadership. In all the cases in this book, there has been some tendency to attribute to top leadership the forces that influenced the organization's course. But at TCB, Ben Love was more often pointed to as the cause, and the organization as the effect, than in any other case study. There are perhaps several ways to explain this.

First, maybe it is true and should be taken at face value. A dominant leader provided direction, control, and legitimacy during a period of enormous growth and transition. Second, perhaps the creation of a system of tight control, stark objectivity, and little emotion needed a symbolic leader, who served to enforce compliance and provide the system with character and identity. Third, the regional culture of Texas and the Southwest has produced many great heroes, and holds an ideology that tends to emphasize proactive free will rather than determinism. One can never, of course, decide which of these three interpretations is right and which is wrong, but must instead settle for the compromise that there is probably some truth in all of them. All these interpretations also explain in part why this case study in particular became more of a character study of top leadership than did some of the others.

This case study also provides an important lesson about the manner in which culture change occurs. Cultures can be transformed, but those transformations are unlikely to occur voluntarily or spontaneously through participation. Culture change occurs through the shaping of an organization's systems in response to a shifting environment. If environmental shifts do not occur, cultural change is unlikely. Cultures carry tremendous amounts of inertia, which is only overcome by introducing new and successful ways of adapting and then waiting for those values to become internalized. Slowly the mission becomes reinterpreted. Involvement and participation may be critical to the implementation and reinterpretation process, but they do not often serve as the impetus for cultural change.

For mangers and executives, there are two major lessons about corporate culture to be gained from this case. The first is the importance of "symbolic" management. Ben Love was larger than life. When asked how he felt about Love's influence, one recently appointed loan officer replied, "I'm proud to walk in Ben Love's shadow." From his capacity to remember the details of a new recruit's resume to his ability to directly supervise the CEOs of *all* member banks and communicate with them regularly, Love seemed to be *pervasive*. This allowed him to create a powerful culture and meaningful system and use it to leverage his leadership. As a result, the power of the system now extends *far* beyond his own active control.

The second lesson is in the management of goal-directed behavior. The TCB philosophy holds that individual responsibility for obtaining objectively measurable goals is the foundation of an effective organization. Organizations that rely on·these principles alone, however, do not always provide coordination, consensus, or socialization. In TCB, this system of goal-directed behavior was frequently played out in public settings. These settings, such as loan committees and officers' meetings, provided a forum in which the efforts of these goal-driven individuals could be integrated into a system. In these settings consensus was developed, new recruits were trained and socialized, the less successful learned from the more successful, and the culture was transmitted. This rare balance between a goal-oriented and an organization-oriented focus served to diminish internal competition and direct it toward objective organizational goals.

CHAPTER ELEVEN

Summary and Conclusions

This book has presented a theory of corporate culture and organizational effectiveness, based on quantitative and qualitative research findings, and rooted in the literature of organizational studies. Such a theory can perhaps never be conclusively "proven," but can stand as a framework for integrating, interpreting, and applying findings about organizational culture and effectiveness.

The theory has argued that an organization's culture has a direct impact on its effectiveness and performance. Strategies, structures, and their implementation are rooted in the basic beliefs and values of an organization and present both limits and opportunities for what may be accomplished. In addition, the theory also implicitly argues that the effectiveness of an organization must be studied as a cultural phenomenon linking assumptions and shared values with management practices and strategies in order to understand a firm's adaptation over time.

Rather than simply argue that culture "causes" effectiveness, however, the qualitative case studies in this book have also described the way in which an organization's culture is shaped through past successes and failures. The nature of a particular culture is, therefore, a reflection of the original strategies of the founders of a firm, as well as the learning and retention that have occurred over time.

Thus, an organization's culture may be seen as a code, a logic, and a system of structured behaviors and meaning that have stood the test of time and serve as a collective guide to future adaptation and survival. This definition helps to explain why cultures can be abstract and mystical, yet concrete and immediate; impossible to change, yet rapidly changing; complex and intricate, yet grounded in very basic values; and occasionally irrelevant to business issues, yet always central to an organization's strategy and effectiveness. This definition also explains why culture must be studied as both a cause and an effect.

A serious attempt has been made in this book to address both an academic audience and a business and professional audience. The academic necessities of models, literature reviews, and evidence inevitably entails slower reading than a more popular book. Nevertheless, the academic literature has been dealt with as a reference point, rather than an end in itself, and the concepts have been illustrated wherever possible in the language of business. The goal is to address the issues of culture and effectiveness with a breadth and generality that permits organizational action without losing the academic audience, while doing justice to the complex conceptual issues without appearing tedious to a manager, executive, or human resource professional.

The hoped-for benefit of trying to address both of these audiences has been to combine the strengths of each point of view and to address the linkages between the abstract and concrete elements of culture. Academics have been content to address primarily the deeply seated assumptions, values, and language of a culture without considering the more practical and overt manifestations that appear as the structures and strategies of a business organization. More popular authors, in contrast, have explicitly regarded culture as functional, but have made little progress in seriously considering the evidence about whether culture actually has a direct impact on organizational functioning. This book has attempted to provide a model of how these two perspectives can be combined, and the productive learning that can occur when they are.

Four central concepts are used to summarize and organize the book's findings about culture and effectiveness and to relate them to the organizational studies literature. These concepts are an attempt to generalize about the characteristics of an organization's culture associated with effectiveness and performance, and to build them into a theory. The four elements of the theory—involvement, consistency, adaptability, and mission—often make contradictory demands on an organization. High consistency may mean limited adaptability, and a clear mission can only be realized through the involvement of the organization's members. Yet some organizations appear to meet these contradictory demands and have developed cultures with all four of these characteristics. These organizations, the theory argues, are likely to be the most effective.

This final chapter addresses four main topics in an attempt to summarize the many questions that have been raised by this book. The first topic concerns the culture and effectiveness model itself: How does the evidence presented throughout this book bear on the model? What has been learned about each of the four components of the framework and the interaction among them? This summary statement also attempts to raise issues regarding the model and its application and to point the way for future research.

The second major topic addressed in this concluding chapter is organizational change. Both the quantitative and the qualitative data are intertwined with the processes of organizational change, but the model itself is not a theory of change. How does cultural change occur in organizations? Can the culture and effectiveness model be used to describe change processes? What can be learned about planning and managing organizational change from the five case studies that examined how cultural change occurred naturally? This section also deals with the concept of cultural inertia and its implications for managing a changing organizational culture.

This chapter also comments on the issue of studying organizational cultures. The research in this book has relied on several different methodologies, with implications for both organizational research and management application. This section draws together this experience and raises some key issues that should be addressed by any study of organizational culture, and also describes future directions for research on organizational culture and effectiveness.

The chapter ends by focusing on the implications of the ideas and findings in this book for managers and executives. Using the model as a guide, this final section summarizes the skills a manager should have, the questions they should ask, and the actions they should take to effectively manage organizational culture.

The Culture and Effectiveness Model

The evidence presented in this book has been integrated around the four central concepts of involvement, consistency, adaptability, and mission. The first step in summarizing the results of this research is to review the quantitative and qualitative evidence that has been presented in support of each of these four elements of the model. This section begins with a summary of the evidence and a discussion of key issues and concludes with an elaborated version of the culture and effectiveness model.

The Quantitative Evidence

As noted at the end of Chapter 4, the quantitative evidence makes a strong case for the impact that involvement and adaptability have on organizational effectiveness. Using measures of both informal involvement in decision making and more formal participation through organizational design and governance, these results present convincing evidence that there are positive short- and long-term impacts of high-involvement systems. The evidence for adaptability is less direct, but the responsiveness to input and the ability to adapt work systems to changing conditions also appear to be useful predictors of organizational performance. Less clear from these quantitative analyses are the sources and causes of involvement and the implications of voluntary or involuntary strategies for involving organizational members. As the summary of the case studies below will show, there are many different strategies for creating high-involvement systems, even though the impacts may be similar.

The quantitative analyses also give only a partial picture of the impacts of adaptability. In particular, the quantitative analyses fail to address those aspects of adaptability which center around the organization's response to external forces. The results give some evidence of an organization's capacity to restructure internally, but do not capture the degree to which the organization senses and reacts to its external environment. These omissions primarily reflect the theoretical focus of the *Survey of Organizations* and the limitations of that data base. These are problems that can be readily resolved in future quantitative culture research.

The quantitative evidence speaks less directly to the issues of consistency and mission, but still provides some intriguing results. For example, organizations with highly consistent management systems and little variability in the survey data appear to be better performers than less consistent ones. However, high consistency does not appear to predict high performance in the future. Instead, the evidence seems to suggest the opposite: organizations with a good measure of *inconsistency* appear to be higher performers in the longer run. These results seem to indicate that a static consistency can be a liability over time if it impedes the organization's capacity to adapt to its environment. As contingency theory has shown, internal variety within an organization is needed to adapt to a complex and changing organizational environment.

The quantitative data also speak to the mission concept in several small but significant ways. First, the survey items measuring leadership ideals, or the type of leadership respondents would ideally like to have, are slightly *better* predictors of organizational performance than respondents' perceptions of actual leadership behaviors. This seems to indicate that high ideals, which are a significant element of mission, may be an important cultural characteristic of an effective organization. The leadership data also support the idea that the actual amount of goal emphasis present in an organization is one aspect of leadership that is a potent predictor of future performance, and point to the importance of a sense of direction to effective organizations. In these two ways, the quantitative data at least suggest the impact a sense of mission may have on effectiveness. Stretching the comparative data base to address these questions at this point requires a considerable leap of faith, but the evidence is intriguing and can be explored further in future research.

The Qualitative Research

The qualitative research expands on each of these four concepts, and helps to add to the generalizations derived from the quantitative data. There are not enough case studies to generalize based on the qualitative data alone, but, in combination with the quantitative data, they provide a useful way of both developing and testing the theory at the same time.

Involvement. The case studies help to distinguish between two different types of *involvement*, one spontaneous and informal and the other more formalized and planned. Both appear to have a positive impact on effectiveness. This distinction helps explain some of the many different approaches that may be taken in creating a high-involvement system. The formality of the approach taken seems to be determined more by the context in which the high-involvement system exists rather than by any given set of techniques. For example, People Express and Medtronic both provide examples of informal involvement, spontaneity, and autonomy. Both were highly effective during an early, entrepreneurial stage of growth, but neither of the original systems lasted because they did not make the transition to a more formal system of involvement as they grew in size. Procter & Gamble (P&G) and Texas Commerce Bancshares (TCB), in contrast, represent large organizations with highly formalized systems of involvement. Involvement in these organizations appears to be based on elements of both voluntary cooperation and internal competition against a standard. Nonetheless, the P&G approach appears to have created a system with a high level of involvement within the context of a large hierarchical bureaucracy. This also appears to be true in the TCB case even though involvement per se does not receive high scores on the survey measures.

These examples suggest that the distinction between formal and informal, or voluntary and involuntary, involvement is important and that a transition from one to the other occurs as an organization grows. Although some attention to this distinction appears in the organizational literature, much of it (e.g., Dachler and Wilpert 1978) has concentrated on labor-management relations and contrasted European-style formal representation systems with informal participation. The more fruitful approach may be to examine the use of formal structures that require task-oriented informal interaction and coordination. Ad hoc task teams, cross-functional product teams, and quality circles are but a few examples of the structural approaches that have developed to encourage responsible autonomy and involvement.

This approach also implies that involvement in large organizations need not be voluntary to be effective. The more effective approach may well be to build structures that require participation and involvement, rather than to rely on spontaneous *bottom-up* involvement.

Consistency. The case studies also help to elaborate the concept of *consistency*. Rather than being a unitary concept, several different forms of consistency were evident in the case studies, all of which are rooted in the concept of normative integration, or the level of strength and ' agreement regarding an organization's normative system. The first of these forms is the consistency between ideology, or the stated foundations of a system, and actual practices. One of the best illustrations of this aspect of consistency comes from the early days of People Express Airlines, and the deliberations over the first restructuring (see Chapter 7). At that time, the fundamental issue of concern in the organization was how to continue to grow in a way that remained true to the original ideology. Medtronic also provides an example of the ongoing dilemma of carrying out the founding ideology and mission in actual business practice. It is interesting to note that in both these examples, the needed consistency between ideology and practice was achieved through both changes in practice and in reinterpretation of the ideology.

A related phenomenon is the concept of a "strong" culture with an internalized system of control, rooted in shared values and norms. The early phases of People Express and Medtronic give a good illustration of this principle. In both these cases there were very few rules—just a few meaningful principles to which the members of the organization were strongly committed. These cases help to show how shared values, rather than administrative control, are the true source of coordinated behavior and social control. This internalized type of system appears to be a far more efficient and flexible method than any system of external social control, but requires the creation of meaningful roles and the commitment of individuals to them.

Another form of consistency, appearing in the case studies, is the highly controlled, efficient, machinelike bureaucracy that characterized P&G and TCB. In these two cases, their methodical systems were also well attuned to the market and the external environment, and, for the most part, avoided being concerned with process for process sake. Both organizations had well-defined ways in which work was done and highly efficient repetitive processes. Contingency theory may emphasize that a controlled machine bureaucracy is only effective in a highly stable environment, but both these organizations were successful over a period of decades when the business environment went through continual and fundamental change. This suggests that a high degree of consistency and predictability may be at least a partial means of adapting to change.

An important feature in the effectiveness of these highly consistent systems appears to be their capacity to distinguish between the "expected" and the "unexpected" case. From the case studies in this book, probably the best illustration of this principle is the TCB example (see Chapter 10) in which an interest rate decision at the loan committee was spared further scrutiny because the loan officer had *promised* a customer the loan at a lower rate. This showed that the "process" is not immutable and that it exists for a larger purpose—to serve the customer. A more general illustration of the same principle was P&G's admiration for a manager who knows how (and when) to go around the system and how (and when) to use it. Systems that standardize and follow the logic of high-volume, standardized mass production, but still allow for special treatment of the unexpected case, appear to be the most effective.

James Thompson (1967) dealt at a structural level with a very similar phenomenon—that of "buffering" a technical core so that it could operate at a high economy of scale and at high levels of standardization, free from the turbulence of the organization's environment. The "treatment of the unexpected case," however, often takes place at the individual level rather than at the structural level. Individuals make decisions about the use or nonuse of routine processes. The important point for culture research is that the norms regarding these decisions are specified by the organization's culture, and appear to be key to the effective application of highly standardized systems.

A fourth aspect of consistency in the case studies appears as conformity. As many have noted before, corporations create conformity and breed a consistency of style and appearance. Conformity is a separate phenomenon from the other two types of consistency discussed above, because there is little that is ideological about it, and it often becomes disconnected from the functionality of a system.

As Halberstam writes about Ford financial executive Ed Lundy in *The Reckoning* (1986):

He had elaborate rules for financial presentations. Some of them were his, and some had been handed down by his predecessor, Ted Yntema, and embellished by him. The word "employee," for example, must always be written with only one "e" at the end. Ford must always be referred to in a presentation as "The Company." No infinitives could be split. As long as Ed

Lundy was with the Ford Motor Company, it was never "under these circumstances," it was always "in these circumstances." Something would be "compared with," not "compared to." The phrase "due to" was not to be used, since "due" he liked to say, was a word used in connection with library books; similarly, the word "current" as a synonym for "present" was barred, for a current was a river. Sentences were not to start with the word "however." He kept a Webster's dictionary on his desk, the classic Second edition, not the Third, for he thought the editors had corrupted the Third. Once during a critical meeting to consider an expenditure of more than $100 million, a young staff member was startled to find that the principal issue between Lundy and one of his top deputies, Will Caldwell, also a grammarian, was not the topic at hand but the proper use of "which" and "that". (p. 252)

A bureaucratic system usually requires some measure of conformity and compliance to operate, but conformity and compliance can often extend well beyond function. At this point they quickly become counterproductive barriers rather than a source of common ground and integration.

When all of these forms of consistency are considered, the case studies suggest that a well-integrated structure, coupled with a tight system of feedback and control, can often be a precondition for motivation in a large bureaucracy. Autonomy and ambiguity, in contrast, can sap motivation unless they take place within a structure that has the capacity to coordinate and direct. When structure, feedback, and control become ends in their own right, however, the resulting conformity can become a barrier of bureaucratization.

Adaptability. As noted in the discussion of the quantitative results, the case studies help to distinguish two broad types of *adaptability*. One is the internal capacity to transform, reorganize, and redirect—the opposite of rigid bureaucratization. The second form of adaptability is the capacity to respond to external forces such as markets and stakeholders. Ideally, these two characteristics are coupled—the forces that drive internal change are external, and internal systems remain highly instrumental with respect to external objectives.

Effective organizations are usually obsessed with customers and vigilant in their analysis of competition. This characteristic is true not only at the top but throughout the organization. When an organization's culture tends to support an orientation of insularity, tradition and reverence for the past quickly become obstacles.

All the cases give examples of the central importance of adaptability to effectiveness, and the ways in which tradition can become a barrier rather than a source of meaning and direction. Medtronic's early stages are a classic example: its close linkages to patients and surgeons and the risks shared with them drove the company's internal processes and systems. Difficulties occurred when the organization's successful growth led to a heightened sense of entitlement and a concern with internal processes as an end in themselves. These emergent internal processes eventually grew to be a barrier between the company and its customers. People Express stuck to their once-valid assumption that it had "created a product, the demand for which could not be satisfied" long after its reputation for chaotic service began chasing away business travelers. The airline's concern with its principles of internal organization during the first restructuring also limited its ability to recruit, train, and socialize the new organizational members, who were needed to ensure that the airline continued to deliver good service. Concentration on internal organization may also have directed the airline's attention away from the competition's computer technology—an oversight that eventually had severe consequences.

Procter & Gamble and Texas Commerce Bancshares provide generally positive examples of how adaptability can be achieved in a mature and efficient system, where adaptation must be accomplished through a large bureaucracy. The key cultural value in this setting may well be a thorough understanding of the existing system, coupled with a keen knowledge of when *not* to use it. The critical issue in adaptability may be the decision about what is "standard" and what is not.

Finally, Detroit Edison, like many other utilities, suffered major trauma as a function of rapid and complex changes beginning during the early 1970s. Without minimizing the magnitude of these changes or the barriers to change posed by the capital-intensive nature of the industry, a significant part of the problem can be traced to a world view and accompanying bureaucratization born of years of plenty, stability, and steady growth. In response to the crises of the 1970s, linkages to important constituencies, such as the state legislature, local labor leaders, and the black community, were engrafted, and slowly took hold. Core values and the system they created, however, were much slower to change.

Mission. The case studies strongly reinforce the importance of a sense of mission in the effectiveness of all these organizations. In each case, mission links a relatively abstract definition of meaning and purpose with a far more concrete sense of direction as a business. This link is perhaps the strongest argument for the cultural perspective on organizational effectiveness: Values underlie the systems that support the organization's direction as a business. These must be studied as an integrated set in order to understand change and adaptation.

The biggest crises revealed in each of the five case studies occurred when the organization's basic mission came into question. In Medtronic, the reliance on humanism and the application of technology did not solve the emerging problems posed by increasing government scrutiny, the growing competition in the pacemaker industry, or the increasing competitiveness of the health care industry at large. These changes required Medtronic to reconsider its basic mission and conclude that since they had now become a larger, more mature organization, a tighter system of internal control and a greater concern with competition were necessary to evolve beyond the era when Medtronic had a monopoly in an industry it had created.

Some of the most uncertain periods in the history of People Express can also be traced to a loss of confidence regarding the basic mission of the organization. Two events stand out. First, the decision to buy Frontier raised the possibility that the organization would not continue to grow internally. Was Don Burr poised to become the next big corporate raider? This raised the question of how central the innovative management practices, which had been doctrine up to that point, would be to the future of the organization. A later event, the May 1986 announcement that People Express was moving upscale with higher fares and a higher level of service, called into question one of the most basic tenets of the organization: its commitment to expanding the travel market by introducing "flying that was cheaper than driving" and drawing customers who had never flown before. This event, along with the steadily worsening Frontier financial situation, was widely interpreted by financial analysts and the industry as a clear sign of loss of direction and confidence. The People Express way was no longer working.

The crisis of mission for Detroit Edison took a different form, but nonetheless appeared to have a fundamental impact on the effectiveness of the organization. The turbulence of the 1970s and 1980s slowly and painfully led to the reexamination of a fundamental question, What does it mean to be a public utility? As noted in Chapter 8, being a public utility for five decades meant applying steadily advancing technology to build larger and larger power plants to support a growing industry, a growing population, and a steadily rising per capita consumption of electricity. In a few short years, the definition changed drastically. Public opposition to nuclear power, concern with conservation of energy and decentralization of power generation, and government intervention in the production of power and the hiring and advancement of the people who produced it all became priorities. The mission, in an abstract sense, had perhaps remained the same. Translating that mission into operational terms, however, involved a thorough transformation of the organization, its stakeholders, and their linkages. Through this transformation, a sense of meaning and direction was lost and has not been entirely regained.

The message that the case studies seem to hold for the mission concept is that meaning, direction, and the structures linking the two must be continually recreated in reaction to a fluid and turbulent environment. The meaning and direction that once served as a source of integration can quickly outlive their usefulness. The late Nobel Laureate physicist Richard Feynman was fond of telling the following story:

> Certain Pacific islanders . . . wanted the cargo planes to keep returning after World War II was over. So they made runways, stationed a man with wooden headphones and bamboo for antennas, lighted some fires, and waited for the planes to land. "They follow all the [right steps], but they're missing something essential because the planes don't land." (Gleick 1988, 1)

In order to escape the islanders' dilemma, meaning and direction must be continually recreated and constantly redefined.

The Outliers

As described at the beginning of Chapter 5, the quantitative findings, which showed a close relationship between involvement and participation at one point in time and financial performance several years in the future, were used as a point of reference for selecting the case studies. Three of the case studies, Medtronic, People Express, and Detroit Edison, were selected because they fit that statistical pattern quite well, and two others, Procter & Gamble (P&G) and Texas Commerce Bancshares (TCB), were deliberately selected because they did not fit the pattern. Special attention needs to be paid to these two outliers and the implications that they have for the culture and effectiveness model. In addition, on closer inspection, People Express may also need special consideration since the survey data on involvement and participation bear so little resemblance to the actual system portrayed in the case study.

The first possible explanation for the two outliers, P&G and TCB, might be the financial measures of effectiveness used in the quantitative study. If, for example, the criteria for effectiveness had included growth over a long period of time, rather than profitability, P&G would have been judged one of the most effective organizations of all. The effectiveness of TCB was better represented by the financial performance criterion, but would be somewhat less outstanding if the bank were compared only to other banks in the same geographic region. If the criteria of effectiveness were more oriented toward growth, TCB would also have fared well.

A second measurement issue that may have led P&G and TCB to appear as outliers is the sample of respondents drawn from each of the organizations. Medtronic, People Express, and Detroit Edison all had

100 percent samples. In contrast, P&G had a sample that overrepresented the manufacturing organization (and perhaps overestimated the level of involvement overall); and TCB had a sample that was drawn from its lead bank in Houston, which was the stable core rather than the most dynamic area of expansion (and perhaps may have underestimated the level of involvement overall). Thus, there is at least the possibility that a more accurate survey sample would have resulted in P&G's and TCB's being less extreme outliers.

In addition to examining these measurement issues, however, it is also necessary to ask a more basic question, Do these outliers exhibit cultural characteristics not included in the original quantitative analysis? Examining the two outliers from this perspective presents a surprizingly clear picture: Both of the outliers were highly consistent, methodical machine bureaucracies, which, with continual adjustments and refinements, for the most part have remained highly responsive to their external environments. They were also two of the three largest organizations among the case studies.

A more detailed example of the similarity between these two organizations comes from comparing the P&G brand management system and the TCB call program. Both innovations gained competitive advantage by creating a narrow area of responsibility, managed by a relatively small and responsive suborganization with substantial autonomy. Performance could be evaluated by the numbers. This tended, in both cases, to create a complementary rather than a competitive system, where peers performed against a standard rather than against each other.

The finding that both of the outliers from the involvement-performance axis are characterized by highly consistent cultures also fits the logic of the model quite nicely, since consistency was posed as an opposite cultural characteristic from involvement. The puzzle, however, is that both positive and negative outliers from the involvement axis would be *highly* consistent. One might expect, instead, that one outlier would be high on consistency and one would be low. The resolution of this puzzle will clearly require further research.

Another difficult measurement problem uncovered by this study is posed by the People Express case. From the quantitative data, the organization appears to be strictly average on both the survey and the performance data. The performance data give an accurate representation of the airline, so this part of the problem can be easily understood; at the time this study was conducted, People Express was a break-even company in a break-even industry. The survey data, however, are considerably more difficult to explain. The data portray the company as about average in participation and involvement, but the case study shows that involvement at that time was incredibly high—most employees put in voluntary 16-hour days, made a major investment in company stock, and had extensive authority and autonomy.

There are several possible explanations for this situation. First, the survey items used to measure involvement are better suited to a bureaucratic setting. They ask questions about decisions being made at appropriate levels and about individuals having input into decisions that affect them, so the phrasing may make more sense in the context of a large hierarchical firm. The early stage in the life cycle of the organization and the rapid pace at which it grew serve to make these bureaucratic points of reference less appropriate. This problem could perhaps have been addressed through the classic "behavior anchoring" strategy of specifying the actual behaviors that constitute high and low involvement. But even this strategy falls short when one recognizes that the behavioral anchors would still not allow for comparison with other organizations or even among employee populations within the airline. In addition, the actual behaviors that constituted "involvement" changed quite rapidly over the short history of the airline.

The resolution of this question lies only in an understanding of the meaning given to different forms of involvement and the *expectations* that all organizational members had regarding their own involvement. One of the most distinctive features of People Express at this time was the enormous expectations that organizational members had regarding what their level of involvement would be. The most plausible explanation of these results may be that the sky-high expectations of new members of the airline made their actual level of involvement appear about average.

Summary of the Model

Examining the quantitative and qualitative results of this study has raised several important questions about each of the elements in the model. These questions suggest several ways to elaborate the original framework presented earlier in this book. Figure 11.1 presents a brief summary of the model listing several characteristics for each of the four elements. This version of the model also includes a plus or minus sign, linking each of the four elements and indicating whether the relationship between the two elements is generally positive or negative.

As emphasized in the discussion in this chapter, the model shows that involvement has an impact on effectiveness through both informal processes and formal structures. Consistency acts through normative integration reflected in both the match between ideology and practice and in the level of predictability in an organization's systems. Adaptability influences effectiveness through both internal flexibility and external focus, and mission impacts effectiveness by providing both meaning

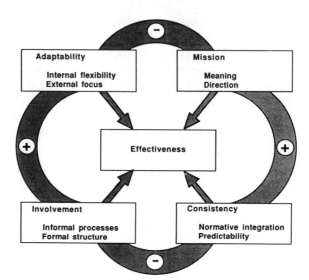

Figure 11.1 The culture and effectiveness model

and direction. Adaptability and involvement are likely to occur at the same time, but are in some ways incompatible with mission and consistency. At the same time, however, the fundamental assumption of this model is that the most successful organizations display all four cultural characteristics at once.

For the academic researcher, this model spells out a research agenda and a framework for integrating findings about culture and effectiveness. For the manager or executive, this same model identifies a set of cultural characteristics, associated with effectiveness, that can serve as a standard for comparison. The cases studies provide examples and details that help to draw the link between the abstract concepts and the actual structure and systems, pointing the way for application. The goal for managers, as defined by this model, is to develop an awareness of the culture-making process and use that to increase simultaneously these four cultural characteristics of their organizations.

How Does Cultural Change Occur in Organizations?

Although the culture and effectiveness model is not itself a framework for studying organizational change, each of the case studies presented here describes fundamental change and transformation. This section of the chapter examines those changes in an attempt to build a better theory of organizational change and to shed light on the debate about whether culture can be purposively managed or changed (Martin, Sitkin, and Boehm 1985; Trice and Beyer 1984).

A quick review of the case studies shows quite convincingly that fundamental transformation and reorientation occurred in almost all the organizations. Medtronic developed from a humanistic, paternalistic, and monopolistic producer of pacemakers to a cost-effective industry leader in a broad array of electro-medical technology. People Express grew from a revolutionary upstart, driven by empowerment and spontaneous enthusiasm, to one of the five biggest airlines in the United States, and struggled to gain control of its growing organizational structure. Detroit Edison, reacting to external changes, slowly evolved from an engineering-driven operating and construction company and master of its own destiny, to an operating company struggling to protect the public's investment while responding to the diverse needs of a broad new set of stakeholders.

Procter & Gamble grew from being the original mass market consumer products firm, focusing on a limited number of products, to a widely diversified corporation competing in hundreds of markets worldwide. In more recent years, the P&G brand management system, a model of consumer marketing, has been criticized for its rigidity and obsessive reliance on due process, thorough research and written communication. The P&G formula has been questioned and substantial changes have occurred. Texas Commerce Bancshares has also made several fundamental transitions in growing from a community institution, modeled on the vision of Jesse Jones, to a masterpiece of industrial management and a national leader in banking performance. Since merging with Chemical Bank in 1986, TCB is now involved in another transition.

Furthermore, each of these changes, with the possible exception of People Express, was generally successful: they increased the organization's ability to adapt and led to a new internal form that supported the adaptation process. As such, these changes seem to contradict some of the conventional academic wisdom about organizational and cultural change, and are, therefore, worthy of comment.

First, it seems clear that in each case study, cultural change occurred in response to the demands of the business environment. The changes were typically instrumental and adaptive. They were most often driven by a crisis of mission and strategy and the need to adapt, rather than by any intention to change the internal organization itself. The cultures changed only as a belief in the instrumentality of a new direction became widely accepted within the organization. In contrast, much of the literature on organizational change has emphasized or advocated internally driven organizational change. There is little support for that version of change in the case studies presented here. As Beer, Eisenstat, and Spector note in *The Critical Path* (1989), programmatic change is far less likely to have an enduring impact on an organization than change that comes as a result of being instrumental and adaptive.

Second, change is often described in the organizational literature as a conversion process of a top leader or leadership which is then transmitted throughout the organization (e.g., Argyris 1964). This model of change implies that an enlightened leader changes his or her mind, and change in the organization follows. The case studies present quite a different model. Change in these organizations meant a change in the leadership—at least at the top. The common scenario is that an enlightened leader and supporting team come into power and recast the organization in their own image. As Thomas Kuhn observed, with respect to scientific revolutions, no one ever really changes sides, the advocates of the older position just die off sooner. Cultural change in each organization meant new players, not the conversion of old players.

Third, the planned organizational change approach (e.g., team building, process consultation, feedback) where change is controlled by a top executive, management team, or staff function does not seem to fit these cases. Existing cultures have enormous inertia, and the causes of change are often indirect, incremental, and unplanned. Change in the case studies was more like diverting a river (with some anticipation of where it would go) rather than damming and rerouting it. Organizational change technology can be a powerful aid, but does not drive the cultural change process in the same way that instrumental adaptation does.

Fourth, the capacity of organizations for change is formidable, even if not absolute. Over a period of decades, fundamental adaptive change occurred in each of the organizations studied. Even People Express, one could argue, "adapted" by merging rather than simply withering away.

Academic researchers, led by the paradigm of population ecology, have recently argued that organizations have little if any capacity to adapt, and, instead, they die and are replaced by new forms. The case studies suggest that this viewpoint may be partly right, but is mostly wrong (Young 1988). All the organizations, when viewed over time, made fundamental adaptive change.

The issue of an organization's capacity to adapt and change is complicated because cultures have tremendous inertia and change very slowly. Culture is by definition a collectively internalized normative system that outlives any one individual. The larger the organization, the greater the inertia. Environmental change, leadership change, and high turnover of people all increase the rate at which culture change can occur, but the process is nonetheless a slow one. As shown by the case studies, a decade is a short period of time in which to expect to institutionalize cultural change within a large organization.

Finally, it is clear from these case studies that culture change *can* be managed, and in fact it is very difficult to *prevent* culture from changing because of the close linkages among underlying values, organizational systems, and the adaptation process. Instrumental behavior that allows the organization to adapt is constantly being incorporated into the culture. The challenge to a manager is to understand the process by which learning is translated into increased organizational capacity and to couple that with an understanding of the utility of that capacity for future adaptation. Thus, managing culture is a process of shaping the learning that occurs as an organization adapts.

On Studying Organizational Culture

Perhaps the most powerful lesson learned from these case studies is the usefulness of applying two research approaches. Taken alone, both the quantitative and qualitative research have substantial limitations. But taken together, they provide substantial support for the culture and effectiveness model and valuable elaboration as to what organizational culture actually is, and how it influences organizational effectiveness.

Each of the two methods applied in this book has significant flaws. The quantitative study suffers from a limited definition of culture and effectiveness and limited experimental control in the research design. It can (and has) been criticized on these points (Locke, Schweiger, and Latham 1986; Siehl and Martin 1988). A quantitative study with a broader collection of measures of culture and effectiveness taken at multiple points in time from a larger number of organizations would be a major improvement.

The qualitative part of the study also has considerable limitations. The pages allocated for each case, although adequate for a narrowly focused teaching case, only allows a general overview of each organization's culture and effectiveness. The combination of library research and approximately 25 personal interviews conducted with members of each of the organizations gives a good picture of the dominant cultural characteristics of each firm, but plainly neglects a thorough analysis of the subcultures that exist in each firm. Finally, the case studies could have been improved by taking a more consistent approach to each organization and building a stronger basis for comparison, rather than by using a clinical analysis that placed more emphasis on understanding and description.[1] Still, like the quantitative study, the qualitative research goes well beyond many other empirical studies of culture and effectiveness in the level of detail and understanding.

---

[1]For the interested reader, the methods used for each case study are discussed in detail in Appendix E.

Combining the two methods, however, seems to result in more than the sum of two partially flawed studies. Several insights from this process bear comment. First, it quickly becomes apparent that both methods are partial and quite limited by themselves. Even a superbly designed quantitative study, which allows for reliable and statistically significant generalizations, does not always allow a researcher to "know what they know." Statistical inference alone does not mean knowledge or understanding, nor does it necessarily imply a new-found ability to control the phenomenon. As Larry Mohr (1982) and others have noted, just because the outcome has been predicted, does not mean that the process has been understood. With only a quantitative study, a researcher must often "guess" (through operationalization) at the processes that accounted for the results. Furthermore, since contextual features of a quantitative study are defined as unwanted influences, there are few opportunities to learn about their probable impact.

On the other hand, qualitative research on culture inevitably results in telling stories and describing the perceptions and reaction of organizational members. Such data can be highly persuasive, but relies largely on the author's insight and intuition for judging which stories and perceptions are most representative of the organization as a whole. Reliance on intuition is a useful shortcut when one is right, but a significant detour when one is not because there are so few rules for deciding when to turn back.

Second, there is a strong urge to criticize each of these methods in the terms of their own logic. So, in a quantitative study, if statistical significance is not high enough, the proposed solution is likely to be to add more cases or develop more precise measures. If the correlations are not strong enough, the recommendation may be to search for moderator variables. Above all, locating the most statistically significant findings and building a theoretical argument to support them is the safest course of action, even if it means ignoring cases or examples that may disconfirm the theory. A contrary form of logic suggests that insignificant results might instead be followed by a series of case studies, designed to give more detailed understanding of the phenomenon.

In contrast, in a qualitative study, the opposite logic prevails. The goal of in-depth understanding typically pushes the researcher deeper into a single phenomenon, with the goal of better understanding the specific case. Seldom, if ever, does the logic of qualitative research lead one to go and gather a smaller amount of comparative data about a larger number of organizations.

This approach of combining methods also makes very different assumptions about what to do with error variance. The approach taken here allows one to build on a point of reference such as a theory, or experimental design, but to treat the "error variance" as potentially the greatest finding. Examining several of the cases carefully allows a researcher to make certain that they fit the theory for the correct reasons (People Express is an excellent example of why this is necessary), and to develop concepts that explain the dynamics of cases that do not fit the theory. This sequence places a researcher in a good position to revise the original theory. Repeating this cycle several times with respect to a particular phenomenon helps to build and test a reliable theory.

Using such contrary logic may seem counterintuitive until one realizes that all research represents a compromise. As Weick (1979) and Thorngate (1976) have noted, it is impossible for social research to be simultaneously general, accurate, and simple. The trade-offs are inevitable. As Figure 11.2 shows, increasing generality means decreasing accuracy and simplicity, and increasing accuracy means decreasing simplicity and generality. Thus, the only possible solution to this dilemma is when multiple studies, diverse in methodology, all reach a similar conclusion. When findings converge across methods, then the theory or hypothesis under consideration is likely to be quite resilient.

Viewing the research in this book with reference to Weick's clock shows that one part of the study, the quantitative study, falls somewhere between twelve and two o'clock. It is highly general and reasonably accurate, but quite complex. This is coupled with a second piece of four to six o'clock research (the case studies), which are highly accurate, reasonably simple, but, by themselves, not very general. Finally, the framework for this study, derived from the literature and fleshed out through the research, is a ten o'clock framework. Only by reaching some consistent explanation of each of these three sources can a theory advance beyond the limitations of any one methodology.

Thus, quantitative and qualitative studies can be highly complementary and can lead to the development of theories and concepts that are

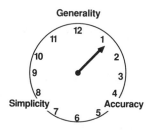

Figure 11.2   Weick's clock

high in both generality and in specificity. Generality does not rule out the ability to tell descriptive and insightful stories, and understanding does not rule out broad statistical generalizations. The goal, at least in culture research, might be to begin by listening to stories, switch to a comparative perspective to tell which stories are most representative, and end by expressing both comparative and intuitive insights through stories that are worth telling and retelling.

Applying the Culture and Effectiveness Model

The findings of this research imply that one of the most important contributions a manager or executive can make is the culture they create. Even though most managers do not see themselves as "culture-makers," the role is unavoidable because leadership and managerial action inevitably create or reinforce key values. Thus, the first step in becoming an effective culture manager is to view building a culture as an explicit role with a set of objectives, rather than simply a by-product of business. Culture management is a long-term strategy and a difficult asset to cultivate. The results of this research suggest that it is well worth the effort.

The payoff comes because culture is a consensual system of regulation that reaches far beyond any system of bureaucratic or administrative control. Does a cardinal need to remind a bishop of the need for religious piety? No, because the value has been internalized. Does an investment banker need to reassure a client that he or she is in business to make money? Of course not, because it is a given. Does a patient on the operating table ever need to worry if a doctor really wants to save his or her life? Never, because it is assumed. Because these examples are special cases, when these bonds of commitment are violated, everyone recognizes that something has gone wrong. The successful culture manager creates a setting in which these types of expectations are applied to every member of the organization. People act because of internalized values, not because of external control.

When managers or executives have created an implicit system of social control built on internalized values, it can free them from some of the demands of constant oversight and administrative control of their organization. When the system begins to regulate itself, the manager or executive no longer needs to devote as much time to monitoring and controlling to ensure that the work gets done. This freedom gives a manager or executive the time to work on the most important leadership task of all: *planning what happens next.* Creating such a culture requires an understanding that social control can be based on consensus and commitment rather than administrative control. This approach to control goes far beyond the typical management skills of moving boxes and arrows on an organization chart. It requires thorough understanding of the dynamics of meaning and commitment for each member of the organization.

Managing culture in this way requires a significant portfolio of skills. The four concepts in the model each suggest a broad area in which concrete skills are necessary.

Involvement. Unused human knowledge and skill within an organization has become a clear competitive disadvantage. The question today is how to capture as much involvement as possible from organizational members and use it to improve both organizational processes and the individuals themselves. Can every member of your organization develop to world-class competitive levels under your current system? Are there barriers to their personal development or the application of their ideas? Do they offer frequent suggestions to improve the processes with which they are most familiar? There are many specific strategies for increasing involvement that are well known and should be an integral part of any manager's portfolio of skills (Lawler 1986; Walton 1986). Effective organizations require a high level of involvement and these strategies should be a part of the methods used by a manager to shape the culture.

Consistency. The most basic implication of the findings on consistency is the need to develop a thorough understanding of the shared values and norms that make up the core of any organization. Several factors are important. First, what are the key values of the organization? What are the ways in which they help or hinder the organization's effectiveness? Second, to what degree are the values actually shared? Is there agreement and consensus? Who supports each specific value and who does not? Depending on the answers to these questions, very different actions may be required. Consider the following possibilities. In one highly individualistic organization, the culture lacked shared values and this made it difficult to achieve coordination or "move as one." In this case, defining and reinforcing key values and expectations was the necessary step to managing consistency. In a second organization, two competing subcultures carried conflicting values and expectations. In this case, defining the positive aspects of both cultures pointed the way to a synthesis that helped reconcile the differences. Both of these are examples of how consistency can be managed and shaped over time.

Socialization of new members of an organization is also a powerful force for managing consistency. One of the most highly consistent cultures among the case studies, Procter & Gamble, relies heavily on socialization and promotion from within to achieve a strong set of shared values and expectations within the firm (Pascale 1984; Weick 1987). This is another example of concrete practices that can be applied to manage the culture of a firm.

Adaptability. Maintaining a competitive advantage implies that the organization's "intelligence" system is not only quite open to new ideas but also actively seeks out sources of competitive advantage, and quickly and successfully incorporates them into its own repertoire. How many new ideas has your own organization recently considered that came from sources of which you were unaware a few years ago? How many of those innovations were adopted? Is insularity a competitive problem? The challenge and complexity for the effective culture manager is not only to adapt successfully today, but to attend to the organizational learning that occurs during adaptation and is incorporated into the organization's culture. Whether or not the learning occurs is likely to determine the organization's ability to adapt in the future. Creating this link between internal and external innovation is a critical part of building an effective organization (Kanter 1983; Tichy 1983).

Mission. In many organizations, mission and vision do not extend far beyond merely repeating what has been successful in the past until it is proven wrong. An effective firm must have a strategic plan and a clear direction, but it must also express the plan in a way that is meaningful to members of the organization. If not, then the vision is unlikely to be successfully implemented. The vision must be translated into goal-directed behavior on the part of each member of the firm. Doing so can help channel competitive behavior towards external goals rather than internal competitors. Having a strong mission changes behavior by forcing people to monitor their current behavior against a preferred future state (Weick 1979; Davis 1987).

Perhaps the most profound questions a manager can ask to understand the culture he or she has created are, What would happen if I left the organization? Would the organization I have created continue to function much the same way it did when I was here? What would happen if administrative controls were lifted? Would the organization still continue doing the same things that it has done based on internalized values? The effective manager should be able to point to an adapting system that would continue on course, without his or her hands being directly on the wheel.

Obviously, creating such a culture may have required direct management intervention on many occasions, and without continued direct leadership it will soon begin to decay. The point is not that passive management is the answer but that managers who build a system that will function based on internalized commitment have created a highly valuable asset.

For sake of contrast, consider the situation in which the functioning of an organization is highly dependent on a single leader, and is unable to continue without him or her. The system may collapse without his or her intervening constantly to direct, control, or monitor. Clearly, in this case the manager has not created and developed what the research presented in this book has found to be a highly important asset: an effective organizational culture.

Conclusion

The economic value of collective human contributions to business organizations is a classic paradox. The discovery and application of technology, the development of financial instruments and strategies, and the design and structuring of complex organizations are all the creation of collective human action. Machines cannot yet invent themselves. Nonetheless, the objects created are often attributed more value in a business organization than the people and processes that created them. The artifact is an asset; the creator a cost.

This study of culture and effectiveness has been a modest attempt to swim against the current by exploring the relationship between the characteristics of a human social system and the effectiveness of the business which it has been designed to manage. The results have, it is hoped, been an encouraging step in the conceptualization and empirical support of that old cliché that people, individually and collectively, are an organization's most important asset.

Measuring Climate
and Culture:
Some Basic Validity Tests

A complete discussion of the validity of the Survey of Organizations (SOO) indexes is beyond the scope of this book and would add little to that already presented elsewhere (Taylor and Bowers 1972). A few validity issues, however, are unique to this book and are addressed at some length in this appendix so as not to detract from the readability of the book itself. The issues are simple ones: (1) Can climate and culture measures, which refer to an organization as a whole (or an organizational unit), be distinguished from group behavior or individual satisfaction variables included in the survey? (2) Do the respondents within an organization agree more about these characteristics of the organization as a whole than they do about leadership or group behavior?

Appendix A addresses the first question by posing it as one of convergent-discriminant validity, and asking if respondents can discriminate between the "climate" indexes and other measures such as leadership, job design, or group behavior.

The second section of the appendix addresses the second question by presenting a test of homogeneity, or level of agreement among respondents. This text examines the validity of the climate indexes by asking if there is higher agreement among the respondents within an organization on the climate measures than on other measures such as leadership, job design, or group behavior. This condition also must be met if climate variables are to be considered as valid measures of characteristics of the organization as a whole.

Convergent-Discriminant Validity

Even though validity is central to the pursuit of knowledge, and the word itself is virtually synonymous with "truth," in practice, validity assessment in organizational research quickly boils down to a few simple observations: "things" (variables, events, items, or characteristics) are (1) alike (similar, associated, or correlated), (2) unalike (dissimilar, unassociated, or uncorrelated), or (3) useful in predicting some future event (actually a special case of 1). Or, as J. Nunnally, eminent psychometrician, put it:

> Call it the "measurement" and "validation" of constructs if you like, but at least as far as science takes us, there are only (1) words denoting constructs, (2) sets of variables specified for such constructs, (3) evidence concerning internal structures of such sets, (4) words concerning relations among constructs (theories), (5) which suggest cross-structures among different sets of observables, (6) evidence regarding such cross-structures, and (7) beyond that, nothing. (1967, 98–99)

This logic is applied to the problem of differentiating organizational climate indexes, which refer to the entire organization, from measures

Table A.1 Correlation Matrix of Survey of Organizational Indexes

1. Organization of Work	.83						
2. Communication Flow	.70	.78					
3. Emphasis on Human Resources	.75	.71	.87				
4. Decision-Making Practices	.68	.67	.70	.81			
5. Influence and Control	.50	.52	.54	.54	.66		
6. Absence of Bureaucracy	.29	.25	.29	.26	.15	.83	
7. Job Challenge	.45	.44	.56	.46	.28	.30	.85
8. Job Reward	.61	.60	.66	.58	.35	.28	.71
9. Job Clarity	.35	.32	.34	.27	.10	.13	.28
10. Supervisory Support	.40	.54	.47	.44	.35	.19	.33
11. Supervisory Team Building	.46	.52	.46	.45	.39	.22	.43
12. Supervisory Goal Emphasis	.46	.52	.45	.45	.38	.16	.37
13. Supervisory Work Facilitation	.46	.56	.50	.51	.38	.24	.43
14. Supervisor Encourages Participation	.36	.44	.47	.50	.28	.21	.45
15. Peer Support	.30	.40	.30	.35	.28	.13	.27
16. Peer Team Building	.39	.45	.39	.42	.33	.19	.37
17. Peer Goal Emphasis	.35	.37	.35	.36	.32	.14	.30
18. Peer Work Facilitation	.38	.44	.38	.43	.34	.17	.35
19. Group Functioning	.61	.64	.70	.60	.52	.28	.64
20. Satisfaction	.49	.50	.46	.46	.37	.23	.44
21. Goal Integration	.60	.59	.69	.57	.34	.25	.58

Note: Alpha coefficients for each of the indexes are presented in the diagonal of this matrix.

of supervisory leadership, peer leadership, job design, or group functioning, which refer to smaller units of analysis. These analyses ask the question, Do the multiple measures of organizational climate in fact converge, while still remaining distinct from the measures of the other constructs? This is a necessary condition for a valid measure of the culture and climate of an organization.

The question is addressed through an analysis of the intercorrelations of the indexes used in the SOO. The analyses use a standard psychometric technique, smallest space analysis (Guttman 1968; Lingoes 1973), which is a form of nonmetric multidimensional scaling. Smallest space analysis (MINISSA) was used to analyze the matrix of intercorrelations among indexes presented in Table A.1. This matrix was based on SOO responses from 36,000 individuals in 5,994 work groups in 130 organizations, and it includes all the indexes used in the quantitative study in this book. A complete listing of the items that make up each of these indexes is presented in Appendix B.

This analysis describes the data through a relatively simple process. Correlations are taken as measures of similarity, and the order of these correlations (strongest first, weakest last) is represented as distances in geometric space. Clusters of variables represent constructs and are easily spotted in the graphic output. The program attempts to display the original set of correlations as distances in the smallest number of dimensions possible.

The results of this analysis are presented in Figure A.1. This solution

.83													
.34	.58												
.37	.36	.91											
.47	.28	.67	.88										
.42	.35	.91	.78	.84									
.47	.32	.72	.76	.77	.89								
.48	.35	.67	.67	.69	.79	.92							
.31	.26	.41	.34	.34	.42	.32	.87						
.42	.26	.41	.51	.48	.56	.45	.67	.89					
.38	.26	.35	.42	.51	.51	.46	.61	.74	.79				
.42	.27	.40	.48	.49	.61	.49	.64	.79	.79	.88			
.73	.40	.54	.56	.58	.58	.56	.37	.47	.43	.47	.90		
.49	.38	.45	.52	.52	.58	.52	.67	.77	.74	.77	.53	.84	
.65	.39	.33	.41	.37	.42	.47	.24	.34	.34	.34	.73	.42	.75

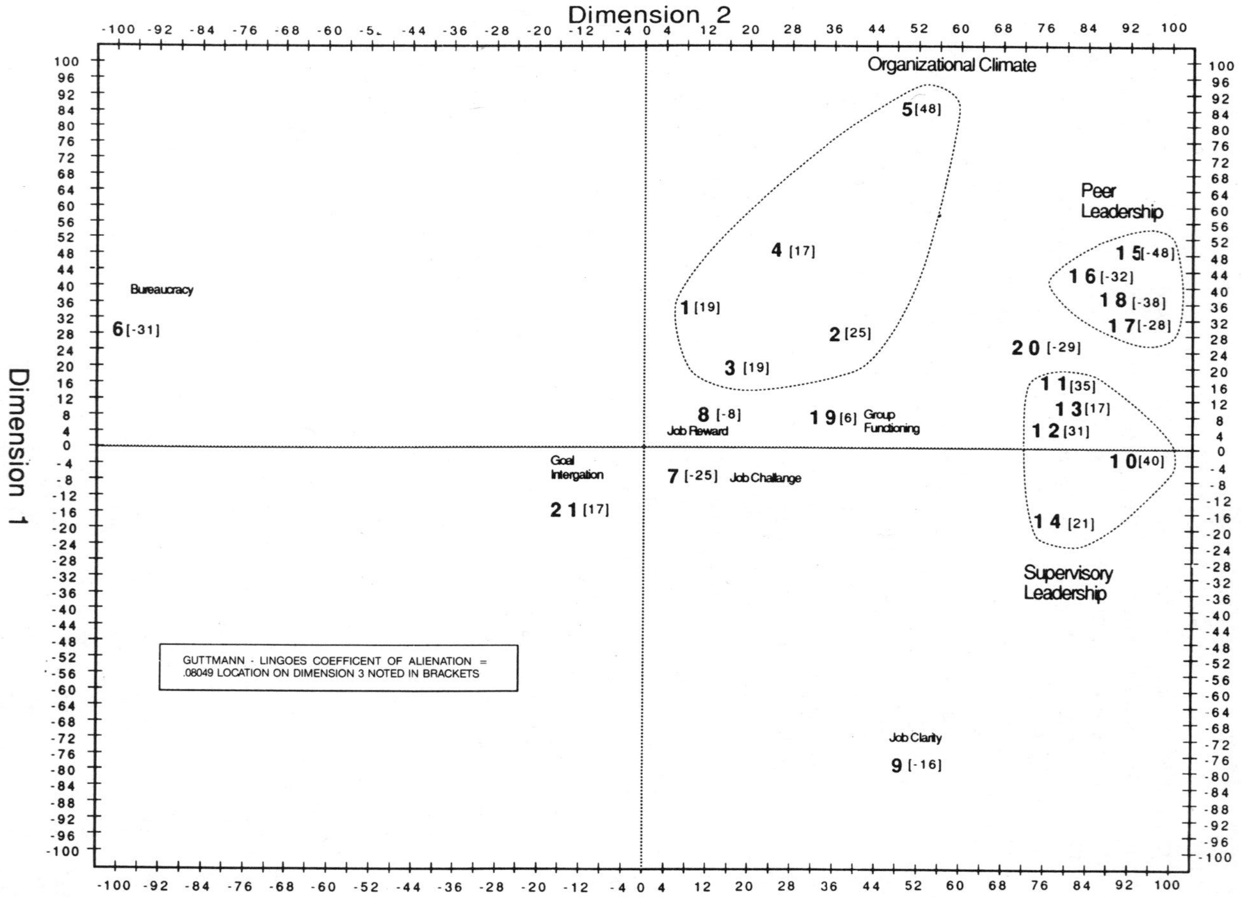

Figure A.1 Convergent-discriminant validity test

shows that the data scale well in three dimensions (K = 0.08) and that the domains of organizational climate, supervisory leadership, and peer leadership form distinct clusters, indicating a high degree of both convergent and discriminant validity. The remaining indexes, absence of bureaucracy, job design, and the outcome measures, do not cluster distinctly.

This diagram demonstrates that respondents can distinguish characteristics of an organization as a whole from characteristics such as leadership, job design, or group behavior. Organizational climate measures, and presumably other measures of an organization's culture, can be distinguished from more "micro" constructs and measured reliably through survey methods.

Also of interest in the diagram are those indexes that do not cluster into the expected domains. The three-job design indexes, and absence of bureaucracy, are all included as components of organizational climate in the 1980 version of the SOO, but they do not appear to cluster distinctly here. These five nonclustering "climate" indexes are relatively recent additions to the survey and have not previously been subject to this sort of analysis. The findings here, along with those presented in the next section, may suggest that the three job design indexes (which themselves do not cluster), interunit coordination, and the absence of bureaucracy may be factors influencing the context of a particular work group rather than a characteristic of the organization as a whole.

The outcome variables included here also do not cluster into a distinct domain, as might be expected. Outcomes are not unitary phenomena; individual satisfaction does not necessarily imply good group functioning or goal integration, for example. It is interesting, nonetheless, to note in this analysis that satisfaction seems to be most closely related to the peer leadership variables and the supervisory leadership indexes, while group functioning and goal integration appear to be more closely related to the characteristics of the organization as a whole.

A Test of Homogeneity

The most basic characteristic of a climate or culture index is its referent—the entire organization. In addition to being distinct from more micro-variables, what other characteristics should a climate measure have?

A consensus exists in the literature on organizational climate that one such characteristic should be a high degree of homogeneity in the responses of the members of an organization (Drexler 1977; James 1982b). If there is not strong agreement among respondents as to a set of conditions in an organization, it becomes very difficult to argue that a particular measure represents the climate or the culture of the organization.

This argument is, in effect, identical to a more general consensus among organizational researchers about the distinction between structural and individual effects, and the methodologies for separating the two when both are assessed through perceptual data. This issue of intraclass homogeneity and structural versus individual effects was first discussed by Blau (1957, 1960) and Davis, Spaeth, and Huson (1961).

Nowhere in the climate literature, however, has the homogeneity issue been posed as a "compared to what?" type of problem. The debate has proceeded without much discussion of the appropriate level of homogeneity for various levels of analysis. Presumably, if measurements have been taken accurately, characteristics of the organization as a whole, such as organizational climate or organizational culture, ought to exhibit the greatest homogeneity—greater homogeneity than individual satisfaction, group functioning, leadership, job design, or any of the measures of more microcharacteristics.

To elaborate on this perspective, it would seem that apart from any "best" estimates of homogeneity or any "absolute value" of a particular estimator that would be necessary to obtain "climate" status, the more important issue for this study is a simple one: Are "climate" measures more homogeneous within site than measures of subunit, group, or individual characteristics?

The analyses presented in this section used a large archive of SOO responses which contained data from 36,000 responses in 5,994 work groups in 130 organizations. The homogeneity test asked the question, How much of the variation in each of the work group's index scores can be explained by knowing the overall mean for the organization to which a work group belonged? If there is more agreement among members of an organization about climate measures than for the other SOO indexes, then that can be taken as evidence of validity.

Table A.2 presents the results of this analysis. Using organization as a predictor in a one-way analysis of variance produced an eta^2 (percent variance explained) for each SOO index. For purposes of comparison, the eta^2 for each SOO index using organizational level as a predictor is also presented in Table A.2.

Table A.2 shows clearly that the initial group of core climate indexes has a much greater degree of homogeneity than nearly all of the other survey indexes. Averaging the proportion of variance (eta^2) by domain also gives a crude estimate of domain homogeneity—core climate measures reflect much higher homogeneity than any other domain.

This table has separated the organizational climate indexes, as formulated in the 1980 SOO index structure, into two sections: organizational climate, comprising those climate indexes that make clear reference to the organization as a whole and have represented the climate domain

Table A.2   Test of Homogeneity by Site

Domain	Index	Eta² Site	Eta² Level
Organizational Climate	Organization of Work	.22	.04
	Communication Flow	.20	.07
	Emphasis on Human Resources	.30	.07
	Decision-Making Practices	.24	.06
	Influence and Control	.16	.03
	$\overline{X}$	.22	.05
Organizational "Context"	Absence of Bureaucracy	.03	.01
	Coordination	.23	.08
	Job Challenge	.04	.06
	Job Reward	.06	.13
	Job Clarity	.00	.02
	$\overline{X}$	.07	.06
Leadership	Supervisory Support	.09	.05
	Supervisory Team Building	.08	.04
	Supervisory Goal Emphasis	.06	.02
	Supervisory Work Facilitation	.06	.02
	Supervisor Encourages Participation	.02	.01
	Peer Support	.10	.04
	Peer Team Building	.10	.02
	Peer Goal Emphasis	.11	.03
	Peer Work Facilitation	.06	.01
	$\overline{X}$	.08	.03
Outcomes	Group Functioning	.11	.02
	Satisfaction	.12	.04
	Goal Integration	.02	.01
	$\overline{X}$	.08	.02

through several revisions, and a second section termed organizational "context," which includes those climate indexes that do not cluster in the climate domain, do not refer to the organization as a whole, and generally have a lower level of homogeneity than the first group of climate indexes.

There are a couple of clear exceptions to this climate-context distinction: interunit coordination seems to be quite consistent within site, indicating greater homogeneity on this measure than might be expected, given that the index does not refer to the organization as as whole. Similarly, the influence and control index, a summary of the ratings of the influence of those at different levels of the organization or the department of which the respondent is a member, is somewhat less homogeneous than the rest of the core climate indexes. With these two exceptions, the results are highly consistent.

Parallel results are also presented for organizational level as a point of comparison. Level, in this case, refers to the hierarchical position of a group within an organization. It is divided into five categories: top management, middle management, second-line supervision, and both blue-collar and white-collar first-line supervision. Some might argue that since conditions are generally better at the top than at the bottom of organizations, a large portion of the variance among group scores should be predicted by knowing their position in the organizational hierarchy.

The results show that organizational level is not a very good predictor of the group index scores (job reward may be a modest exception). Comparing the explanatory power of organizational level across domains shows that there are few differences, and, more important for this analysis, the differences between the homogeneity across domains are much greater when organization is used as a predictor.

These two sets of findings present important evidence that suggests that survey respondents can distinguish characteristics of entire organizations, such as climate or culture, from other factors such as leadership, job design, or group behavior. In addition, respondents do have a higher level of agreement about climate measures than about the more micromeasures. Both these findings help provide support for the idea that climate and culture can be measured with some degree of validity using survey research methods.

APPENDIX B

The Survey
of Organizations

The quantitative sections of this book rely heavily on the Survey of Organizations (Taylor and Bowers 1972). This appendix expands on the brief description of that instrument offered in Chapter 3, and includes a listing of all the items and indexes used in this study.

As noted in Chapter 3, the development of this instrument dates from 1966. The approach taken to the organizational climate concept is consistent with that of Evan (1968), who argued that organizational climate is a "concrete phenomenon reflecting a social psychological reality, shared by people in the organization, and having its impact on organizational behavior". They reject the approach taken by Forehand (1968), who argued that climate should be studied as the interaction of personal and organizational characteristics. It is interesting to note that 20 years later, this same debate is still alive and well (James, Joyce, and Slocum 1988; Glick 1988).

The initial definition of the climate domain that Taylor and Bowers used was largely defined by the original Likert theory (1961, 1967), and led to the development of the following set of indexes:

1. Decision-Making Practices
2. Communication Flow
3. Human Resources Primacy
4. Motivational Conditions

5. Lower Level Influence
6. Technological Readiness

The Survey of Organizations also drew heavily on Bowers and Seashore's four-factor theory of leadership (1966). Items and indexes for both the peer and supervisory leadership domain center on four basic factors:

1. Support
2. Team Building
3. Goal Emphasis
4. Work Facilitation

Bowers and Seashore's formulation can be seen as an integration and extension of the basic dichotomy between consideration, or socioemotional leadership, and initiating structure, or task orientation, within the leadership literature (Bales 1958; Stogdill 1974; Misumi 1985). Support and team building represent the socioemotional side of this dichotomy, while goal emphasis and work facilitation refer to the more task-oriented side of leadership.

Many formulations of organizational climate have included leadership as a part of the climate domain. Some approaches have even equated the two directly. The Taylor and Bowers approach, however, and the approach taken in this study differentiate climate and leadership with respect to unit of analysis. Organizational climate is a characteristic of an organization as a whole, but leadership is an attribute of an individual, and is most relevant to the members of a group led by that individual. This is not to deny that the consistency and character of the leadership style typical to an organization can be a significant element of the organization's climate, but merely to recognize the initial distinction based on referent and level of analysis.

The other domains included in the original instrument were satisfaction, measured through seven items derived from early research on satisfaction (Ash 1954; Baehr 1954; Kahn and Morse 1951), and group process, measured through six items focusing on areas such as group planning, decision making, and information sharing.

The 1969 version of the questionnaire was used by both the Institute for Social Research (ISR) and by Rensis Likert Associates (RLA), a consulting firm formed by Likert on his retirement as director of ISR. Within a few years, both groups made content changes and obtained separate copyright, ISR for the Survey of Organizations, and RLA for the Organization Survey Profile. This book has drawn on data from the common core items of both questionnaires. The content differences in the two instruments have prevented common archiving but do allow for computation of most of the basic Survey of Organization indexes from the Organization Survey Profile items.

In 1980, the two instruments were merged and revised, resulting in an identical instrument, joint copyright, and a common method of processing and archiving. Thus, some of the data used in this study were taken from this fourth data source, the 1980 version of the Survey of Organizations. The current archive includes data from more than 9,000 work groups and more than 200 different organizations, making the SOO and related instruments one of the most widely used organizational surveys of its type.

For the 1980 edition, several different content areas were added and several new indexes were generated in the climate, job design, leadership, and outcome domains. These additions, by domain, include the following:

Organizational Climate

1. Organization of Work
2. Absence of Bureaucracy
3. Coordination
4. Work Interdependence
5. Emphasis on Cooperation

Job Design

1. Job Challenge
2. Job Reward
3. Job Clarity

Leadership

1. Encouragement of Participation
2. Interpersonal Competence
3. Supervisory Involvement
4. Administrative Scope

Outcomes

1. Goal Integration

These additions to the basic core of the questionnaire developed over the period from 1969 to 1980. They came from several sources. First, developments occurred within the field of organizational behavior establishing new domains with a substantial literature and research base. Job design and goal integration are particularly good examples of this type of addition. Second, there was elaboration of the basic model of organizational functioning underlying the instrument. The addition of indexes on interunit coordination, work interdependence, and emphasis on cooperation, for example, reflect the importance of lateral integration to organizational functioning, a point neglected by the original model. Finally, research experience, perceived client needs, and personal research interests all contributed to the continuing development of the instrument.

Items and Indexes

The section below presents a complete listing of the items and indexes used in this study. All items except the satisfaction items begin with the stem "To what extent," and are scaled on a five-point extent scale.

Organization of Work

1. Is this organization generally quick to use improved work methods?
2. Does this organization have goals and objectives that are both clear-cut and reasonable?
3. Are work activities sensibly organized in this organization?
4. Are decisions made at those levels where the most adequate and accurate information is available?

Communication Flow

1. Does your work group get adequate information about what is going on in other departments?
2. Does this organization tell your work group what it needs to know to do the best possible job?
3. Are people above your boss receptive to ideas and suggestions coming from your work group?

Emphasis on Human Resources

1. Does the organization have a real interest in the welfare and overall satisfaction of those who work here?
2. Does this organization try to improve working conditions?
3. Are there things about working here (policies, practices, or conditions) that encourage you to work hard?

Decision-Making Practices

1. Are the persons affected by decisions asked for their ideas?
2. Do employees who make decisions have access to the necessary information from all levels of the organization?

Influence and Control

1. Do supervisors have influence on what goes on in your department?
2. Do nonsupervisory employees have influence on what goes on in your department?
3. Do middle managers have influence on what goes on in your department?

4. Does top management have influence on what goes on in your department?

Absence of Bureaucracy

1. Do you get endlessly referred from person to person when you need help?
2. Do you have to go through a lot of "red tape" to get things done?
3. Do you get hemmed in by long-standing rules and regulations that no one seems to be able to explain?

Coordination

1. Do different departments plan together and coordinate their efforts?
2. Does your department receive cooperation and assistance from other departments?
3. Are problems between departments resolved effectively?

Job Challenge

1. Do you enjoy performing the actual day-to-day activities that make up your job?
2. Does your job let you do a number of different things?
3. Does your job let you learn new things and new skills?
4. Does your job use your skills and abilities—let you do the things you can do best?

Job Reward

1. Does doing your job well lead to things like recognition and respect?
2. Does your job provide good chances for getting ahead?
3. Is your performance adequately recognized and rewarded?

Job Clarity

1. Are you clear about what people expect you to do on your job?
2. Are there times when one person wants you to do one thing and someone else wants you to do something different?
3. Do people expect too much from you on your job?

Supervisory Support

1. Is your boss friendly and easy to approach?
2. Does your boss pay attention to what you are saying when you talk to him or her?
3. Is your boss willing to listen to your work-related problems?

Supervisory Team Building

1. Does your boss encourage persons who work in the group to work as a team?
2. Does your boss encourage people who work in the group to exchange opinions and ideas?

Supervisory Goal Emphasis

1. Does your boss encourage people to give their best effort?
2. Does your boss maintain high standards of performance in the group?

Supervisory Work Facilitation

1. Does your boss provide help, training, and guidance so that you can improve your performance?
2. Does your boss provide the help you need so that you can schedule work ahead of time?
3. Does your boss offer new ideas for solving job-related problems?

Peer Support

1. Are the persons in your work group friendly and easy to approach?
2. Do persons in your group pay attention to what you are saying to them?
3. Are persons in your work group willing to listen to your work-related problems?

Peer Team Building

1. Do persons in your work group encourage each other to work as a team?
2. Do persons in your group emphasize a team goal?
3. Do persons in your work group exchange opinions and ideas?

Peer Goals Emphasis

1. Do persons in your group encourage each other to give their best effort?
2. Do persons in your group maintain high standards of performance?

Peer Work Facilitation

1. Do persons in your work group help you find ways to do a better job?
2. Do persons in your work group provide the information or help you need so that you can plan ahead of time?
3. Do the persons in your work group offer new ideas for solving work-related problems?

Group Functioning

1. Does your work group plan together and coordinate its efforts?
2. Does your work group make good decisions and solve problems well?
3. Is information about important events and situations shared within your work group?
4. Does your work group feel responsible for meeting its objectives successfully?
5. Is your work group able to respond to unusual work demands placed upon it?
6. Do you have confidence and trust in the persons in your work group?

Satisfaction

1. Overall, are you satisfied with the persons in your work group?
2. Overall, are you satisfied with your boss?
3. Overall, are you satisfied with your job?
4. Overall, are you satisfied with this organization?
5. Are you satisfied with the progress you have made in this organization up to now?
6. Are you satisfied with your chances for getting ahead in this organization in the future?

Goal Integration

1. Is this organization effective in getting you to meet its needs and contribute to its effectiveness?
2. Does this organization do a good job of meeting your needs as an individual?

APPENDIX C

ADDITIONAL QUANTITATIVE RESULTS

The quantitative results presented in Chapter 4 are intended to illustrate the findings of this study, without burdening the reader with excessive detail. Nonetheless, a more complete presentation of actual correlations and probabilities may be desirable as background information. This appendix presents the actual results for all of the variables used in this book. For the interested reader, an even more complete set of analyses is also available (Denison 1982).

Each table presents the correlations between one of the Survey of Organization (SOO) indexes and four financial performance measures: return on sales (actual and adjusted) and return on investment (actual and adjusted). As in Chapter 4, the adjusted performance measures reflect performance relative to firms within a given industry in a given year.

Table C.1 Organization of Work and Effectiveness

Ratios		0	+1	+2	+3	+4	+5
				Years			
Return on Sales	r^1	.33	.52	.37	.44	.50	.58
	p^2	.09	.01	.11	.08	.09	.07
Return on Investment	r	.47	.39	.26	.52	.53	.63
	p	.01	.07	.26	.03	.07	.05
Return on Sales	r	.55	.40	.43	.46	.33	.35
(Adjusted)	p	.00	.06	.06	.07	.29	.31
Return on Investment	r	.52	.40	.36	.55	.47	.45
(Adjusted)	p	.00	.07	.11	.02	.11	.18

^{1}r = correlation of SOO index with performance measures
^{2}p = probability

Table C.2 Emphasis on Human Resources and Effectiveness

Ratios		0	+1	+2	+3	+4	+5
				Years			
Return on Sales	r	.22	.35	.20	.32	.33	.40
	p	.26	.09	.37	.18	.23	.19
Return on Investment	r	.54	.35	.18	.49	.44	.48
	p	.00	.09	.42	.03	.10	.11
Return on Sales	r	.36	.21	.20	.23	.15	.20
(Adjusted)	p	.06	.32	.37	.34	.59	.52
Return on Investment	r	.45	.33	.16	.40	.34	.28
(Adjusted)	p	.01	.11	.46	.09	.23	.37

Table C.3 Decision-Making Practices and Effectiveness

Ratios		0	+1	+2	+3	+4	+5
				Years			
Return on Sales	r	−.05	.03	−.19	.30	.31	.42
	p	.77	.89	.39	.23	.29	.19
Return on Investment	r	.12	−.11	−.31	.55	.64	.71
	p	.55	.61	.17	.02	.01	.01
Return on Sales	r	.00	−.12	−.02	.31	.33	.41
(Adjusted)	p	.98	.58	.90	.21	.26	.19
Return on Investment	r	.08	−.04	−.12	.40	.50	.45
(Adjusted)	p	.68	.83	.58	.11	.07	.16

Table C.4 Coordination and Effectiveness

Ratios		0	+1	+2	+3	+4	+5
				Years			
Return on Sales	r	.11	.11	.03	.35	.47	.54
	p	.57	.60	.88	.19	.14	.10
Return on Investment	r	.08	−.10	−.21	.00	.29	.43
	p	.69	.63	.39	.99	.37	.21
Return on Sales	r	−.14	.26	.01	.20	.28	.25
(Adjusted)	p	.48	.25	.94	.46	.40	.47
Return on Investment	r	−.21	−.28	−.06	.14	.52	.43
(Adjusted)	p	.30	.20	.81	.61	.09	.20

Table C.5 Job Reward and Effectiveness

Ratios		0	+1	+2	+3	+4	+5
				Years			
Return on Sales	r	.47	.47	.51	.46	.98	—*
	p	.11	.19	.15	.35	.11	—
Return on Investment	r	.04	−.42	−.20	−.09	.99	—
	p	.88	.25	.59	.86	.07	—
Return on Sales	r	.55	.26	.32	.81	.69	—
(Adjusted)	p	.06	.49	.38	.04	.51	—
Return on Investment	r	.43	−.13	−.05	.50	.65	—
(Adjusted)	p	.16	.72	.89	.30	.54	—

*Insufficient number of cases to compute correlations.

Table C.6 Job Clarity and Effectiveness

Ratios		0	+1	+2	+3	+4	+5
				Years			
Return on Sales	r	.24	.37	.66	.48	.91	—
	p	.44	.31	.05	.33	.26	—
Return on Investment	r	−.33	−.37	.05	−.01	.74	—
	p	.29	.31	.87	.97	.46	—
Return on Sales	r	.47	.73	.83	.92	.16	—
(Adjusted)	p	.11	.02	.00	.00	.89	—
Return on Investment	r	.21	.00	.31	.43	.11	—
(Adjusted)	p	.50	.98	.40	.38	.92	—

Table C.7 Job Challenge and Effectiveness

Ratios		0	+1	+2	+3	+4	+5
					Years		
Return on Sales	r	−.14	.24	.19	−.14	−.70	—
	p	.66	.52	.61	.77	.50	—
Return on Investment	r	.03	−.23	−.23	−.71	−.88	—
	p	.92	.54	.53	.11	.31	—
Return on Sales	r	.02	−.06	−.01	.34	−.98	—
(Adjusted)	p	.93	.87	.95	.49	.12	—
Return on Investment	r	.09	−.24	−.30	−.19	−.97	—
(Adjusted)	p	.77	.51	.42	.71	.15	—

Table C.8 Supervisory Support and Effectivness

Ratios		0	+1	+2	+3	+4	+5
					Years		
				Actual Survey Index			
Return on Sales	r	−.09	.13	.14	.35	.42	.51
	p	.63	.52	.54	.14	.12	.08
Return on Investment	r	.23	.19	.15	.18	.18	.24
	p	.23	.36	.49	.45	.52	.43
Return on Sales	r	.10	.24	.02	.00	.01	.02
(Adjusted)	p	.58	.24	.91	.98	.96	.94
Return on Investment	r	.25	.30	.08	.08	.13	.08
(Adjusted)	p	.19	.14	.71	.74	.64	.78
				Ideal Survey Index			
Return on Sales	r	.19	.43	.79	.29	.40	.41
	p	.31	.03	.00	.23	.15	.18
Return on Investment	r	.47	.57	.85	.02	.02	−.02
	p	.01	.00	.00	.92	.93	.93
Return on Sales	r	.47	.57	.85	.02	.02	−.02
(Adjusted)	p	.01	.00	.02	.75	.94	−.94
Return on Investment	r	.57	.59	.52	−.04	.06	−.02
(Adjusted)	p	.00	.00	.01	.84	.81	.93

Table C.9 Supervisory Team Building and Effectiveness

Ratios		0	+1	+2	+3	+4	+5
				Years			
				Actual Survey Index			
Return on Sales	r	.15	.28	.25	.40	.50	.62
	p	.44	.17	.26	.09	.06	.02
Return on Investment	r	.31	.25	.21	.30	.30	.39
	p	.10	.23	.35	.21	.29	.20
Return on Sales	r	.24	.18	.19	.28	.43	.42
(Adjusted)	p	.21	.38	.40	.24	.11	.16
Return on Investment	r	.29	.19	.17	.30	.44	.41
(Adjusted)	p	.13	.35	.45	.21	.11	.17
				Ideal Survey Index			
Return on Sales	r	.18	.34	.60	−.26	−.29	−.28
	p	.35	.09	.00	.28	.31	.36
Return on Investment	r	.14	.33	.63	.05	−.20	−.20
	p	.47	.10	.00	.82	.47	.52
Return on Sales	r	.18	.16	.36	.01	−.12	−.06
(Adjusted)	p	.34	.44	.10	.95	.65	.85
Return on Investment	r	.11	.12	.43	.15	.01	−.01
(Adjusted)	p	.56	.56	.04	.54	.97	.97

Table C.10 Supervisory Goal Emphasis and Effectiveness

Ratios		0	+1	+2	+3	+4	+5
				Years			
				Actual Survey Index			
Return on Sales	r	.10	.33	.50	.03	.07	.10
	p	.58	.10	.02	.90	.81	.73
Return on Investment	r	.20	.40	.60	.19	−.10	−.03
	p	.29	.05	.00	.44	.71	.91
Return on Sales	r	.26	.33	.41	.22	.17	.18
(Adjusted)	p	.18	.11	.06	.37	.54	.56
Return on Investment	r	.19	.26	.49	.25	.18	.16
(Adjusted)	p	.31	.21	.02	.31	.52	.61
				Ideal Survey Index			
Return on Sales	r	.28	.63	.83	.13	.20	.27
	p	.14	.00	.00	.60	.48	.38
Return on Investment	r	.49	.74	.87	.16	.14	.17
	p	.00	.00	.00	.50	.62	.58
Return on Sales	r	.57	.73	.58	.30	.40	.44
(Adjusted)	p	.00	.00	.00	.21	.15	.14
Return on Investment	r	.59	.67	.63	.18	.33	.34
(Adjusted)	p	.00	.00	.00	.45	.23	.27

Table C.11 Supervisory Work Facilitation and Effectiveness

					Years		
Ratios		0	+1	+2	+3	+4	+5
		Actual Survey Index					
Return on Sales	r	.05	.39	.47	.11	.07	.19
	p	.78	.05	.03	.63	.80	.53
Return on Investment	r	.14	.29	.39	.43	.23	.40
	p	.44	.15	.07	.06	.42	.18
Return on Sales	r	.10	.16	.30	.35	.17	.31
(Adjusted)	p	.61	.42	.17	.14	.55	.31
Return on Investment	r	.10	.18	.40	.54	.36	.45
(Adjusted)	p	.60	.39	.06	.02	.20	.13
		Ideal Survey Index					
Return on Sales	r	.27	.46	.54	−.07	−.10	−.05
	p	.15	.02	.01	.77	.71	.87
Return on Investment	r	.37	.53	.58	.23	.00	.04
	p	.04	.00	.00	.35	.97	.89
Return on Sales	r	.55	.58	.49	.35	.23	.33
(Adjusted)	p	.00	.00	.02	.14	.42	.29
Return on Investment	r	.49	.58	.60	.45	.22	.35
(Adjusted)	p	.00	.00	.00	.05	.44	.25

Table C.12 Peer Support and Effectiveness

					Years		
Ratios		0	+1	+2	+3	+4	+5
		Actual Survey Index					
Return on Sales	r	.22	.35	.37	.16	.25	.21
	p	.25	.09	.09	.52	.37	.49
Return on Investment	r	.42	.39	.42	−.05	−.29	−.31
	p	.02	.05	.05	.82	.29	.31
Return on Sales	r	.36	.32	.32	.07	−.21	−.43
(Adjusted)	p	.05	.11	.15	.77	.46	.15
Return on Investment	r	.32	.18	.14	−.05	−.33	−.60
(Adjusted)	p	.08	.38	.53	.81	.23	.03
		Ideal Survey Index					
Return on Sales	r	.33	.50	.63	.04	.06	.02
	p	.08	.01	.00	.85	.83	.92
Return on Investment	r	.48	.51	.68	−.14	−.33	−.33
	p	.00	.01	.00	.57	.24	.28
Return on Sales	r	.32	.27	.36	−.26	−.45	−.56
(Adjusted)	p	.08	.18	.10	.28	.09	.05
Return on Investment	r	.29	.20	.33	−.15	−.33	−.54
(Adjusted)	p	.12	.34	.14	.54	.24	.06

Table C.13 Peer Team Building and Effectiveness

Ratios		0	+1	+2	+3	+4	+5
				Years			
				Actual Survey Index			
Return on Sales	r	.37	.24	.16	.34	.40	.42
	p	.05	.25	.47	.15	.15	.17
Return on Investment	r	.34	.11	.00	−.25	−.02	−.00
	p	.07	.60	.99	.31	.93	.99
Return on Sales	r	.35	.03	.02	.03	.05	−.08
(Adjusted)	p	.06	.88	.92	.88	.85	.78
Return on Investment	r	.29	−.02	−.14	−.07	.04	−.09
(Adjusted)	p	.12	.91	.53	.75	.89	.77
				Ideal Survey Index			
Return on Sales	r	.28	.53	.63	−.37	−.46	−.48
	p	.14	.00	.00	.12	.09	.10
Return on Investment	r	.51	.59	.66	.07	−.20	−.15
	p	.00	.00	.00	.77	.48	.61
Return on Sales	r	.57	.54	.35	−.07	−.12	−.12
(Adjusted)	p	.00	.00	.11	.76	.67	.69
Return on Investment	r	.60	.52	.40	.17	.09	−.05
(Adjusted)	p	.00	.00	.06	.49	.74	.86

Table C.14 Peer Goal Emphasis and Effectiveness

Ratios		0	+1	+2	+3	+4	+5
				Years			
				Actual Survey Index			
Return on Sales	r	.22	.37	.39	.08	.18	.26
	p	.24	.06	.07	.72	.53	.40
Return on Investment	r	.46	.34	.30	−.04	.12	.17
	p	.01	.10	.17	.94	.66	.58
Return on Sales	r	.45	.40	.27	.14	−.03	−.07
(Adjusted)	p	.01	.05	.23	.55	.91	.82
Return on Investment	r	.49	.33	.18	.07	.17	.05
(Adjusted)	p	.00	.11	.41	.76	.54	.87
				Ideal Survey Index			
Return on Sales	r	.20	.51	.72	.04	.08	.17
	p	.28	.01	.00	.87	.76	.58
Return on Investment	r	.48	.53	.69	.08	.11	.18
	p	.00	.00	.00	.72	.68	.57
Return on Sales	r	.51	.57	.45	.12	.10	.15
(Adjusted)	p	.00	.00	.03	.61	.71	.62
Return on Investment	r	.57	.55	.52	.18	.33	.27
(Adjusted)	p	.00	.00	.01	.45	.24	.39

Table C.15 Peer Work Facilitation and Effectiveness

Ratios		Years					
		0	+1	+2	+3	+4	+5
		Actual Survey Index					
Return on Sales	r	.27	.25	.25	.18	.20	.23
	p	.16	.22	.26	.47	.48	.45
Return on Investment	r	.13	.07	.04	−.09	.11	.18
	p	.50	.72	.84	.70	.68	.56
Return on Sales	r	.16	−.05	.10	.24	.26	.20
(Adjusted)	p	.41	.80	.64	.33	.35	.52
Return on Investment	r	.09	−.09	.04	.21	.33	.35
(Adjusted)	p	.64	.67	.83	.39	.23	.26
		Ideal Survey Index					
Return on Sales	r	.21	.39	.49	−.24	−.32	−.32
	p	.26	.05	.02	.32	.26	.30
Return on Investment	r	.47	.45	.54	.12	−.11	−.06
	p	.01	.02	.01	.61	.70	.83
Return on Sales	r	.56	.54	.31	.04	.08	.15
(Adjusted)	p	.00	.00	.16	.84	.77	.63
Return on Investment	r	.55	.56	.51	.28	.23	.29
(Adjusted)	p	.00	.00	.01	.25	.42	.34

Double-Checking
the Results:
An Analysis
of Sample Quality

All of the results presented in Chapter 4 were based on a single sample of 34 organizations. In some ways this is a very large sample. Very few comparative studies of organizational behavior have used this large a sample, and relatively few data bases could conceivably yield such a sample. But in many ways, this sample is very small. Computing and interpreting statistics with 34 cases is sometimes risky because of the chance of making generalizations that have been influenced by a small number of atypical cases. This appendix presents a summary of two types of tests that were performed to double-check the results and make certain that the results presented are not, in fact, a "false positive," which has been determined by a few odd cases.

The section is divided into two parts. The first addresses several issues centering around what might be called "match quality." As mentioned earlier, the survey data do not include the responses of all members of all the organizations studied. Some organizations surveyed everyone, but others surveyed only those at the top, the bottom, or within particular divisions. Organizations in which everyone was surveyed can be said to have a better "match" between the survey measures of behavior and the financial measures of performance and effectiveness. This raises important questions: How does the quality of the match between the survey and the financial data influence the findings of the study? Do the results improve if the worst matches are excluded from the analysis? Or do they get worse or even disappear altogether? If the underlying relationship actually exists, then one might expect that the results would improve when the lowest quality matches were excluded. If the relationship diminishes or disappears when these lower quality cases are excluded, then the overall findings of the study would become more suspect.

The second way in which the quality of the study sample was examined consisted of a search for outliers. As it turns out, only one of the firms in the sample was losing money during the period of the study. This firm had a number of the behavioral characteristics that would suggest it might perform poorly, but its presence in the sample sometimes appears to have an effect on the statistical generalizations. This required a reanalysis of the data with the outlier excluded, and a comparison of the results with and without the outlier. Interpreting data with an outlier can be risky business: excluding it entirely denies the importance of an actual case, but ignoring its influence on statistical analyses can lead to questionable generalizations.

Each of these tests is somewhat complicated, even though an effort has been made to keep them simple. The tests should nonetheless be of interest to many readers, and should at least provide the less specialized reader with an example of the attempts that were made to double-check the findings.

Testing the Effects of Match Quality

Out of the 34 firms in the study sample, only a small number (5) include data from all members of the organization. All the other cases in the study have less-than-perfect samples. Twenty-three of the firms have samples that were judged adequate, with hundreds or thousands of responses from the organization and a good representation of the structural divisions of the firm. The remaining six firms (noted with minus signs in Table 3.1) have a small enough number of respondents, or represent a small enough proportion of the firm, that the quality of the match between the survey data and the financial data becomes a question.

In order to avoid reaching false positive conclusions, the data were reanalyzed with the six poorest matches excluded. The results with these six firms excluded were then compared with the results for the entire sample. The logic used here was that if the correlation found in the original results was accurate (a ''true'' measure of the underlying relationship), the correlation in the smaller sample should be stronger, since the cases that were being excluded were actually a source of error. For example, if the "true" relationship between involvement and effectiveness was 0.50, the inclusion of a number of cases with "error" (such as a limited sample of survey respondents from the organization) might reduce the observed correlations to 0.40.

If, in contrast, no "true" relationship existed, but a small number of cases with errors coincidentally "fit" the expected pattern, then the strong correlations that appeared when the entire sample was analyzed should disappear, or at least get smaller, when those cases with errors are excluded. So, the test for the effects of match quality boils down to a simple question: Does the correlation between the behavioral measures and performance indicators increase or decrease when the cases with the poorest match between the survey data and performance data are excluded? If the correlations are stronger, this tends to support the initial conclusions. If the correlations are weaker, this would call those findings into question.

Table D.1 addresses this question by systematically comparing the two sets of results, and looking at the number of differences, and whether those differences resulted in stronger or weaker correlations. An explanation of each of the columns in the table follows.

The first column of the table divides all of the Survey of Organization indexes into five domains and lists the individual indexes within each of these domains. The first, most macrodomain, is organizational climate, and the indexes refer to management practices within the organization as a whole. The second domain, context, refers to organizational conditions as they impact the work group from which the data were gathered. The next two domains, supervisory and peer leadership, refer to the leadership behavior of both formal supervisors and peers at the work group level. The final domain, the outcome variables—group functioning, satisfaction, and goal integration—once again refers to the outcomes at the work group level.

The second column presents the number of differences that appeared when the two sets of correlations were compared. For example, the first row of column two says "2/36." This means that out of the 36 correlations between the organization of work index and the three performance measures, return on investment, return on sales, and return on equity, for years 0 through +5, two of those correlations were substantially different when the reduced sample was compared to the overall sample. The definition used for "substantially different" was that the difference in the two correlations was greater than 0.10.

The third column simply presents these ratios as proportions: thus, 6 percent (0.06) of the correlations were "different" when the the overall

Table D.1 Testing of Effects of Match Quality

Indexes by Domain	Number of Differences	Percentage Differences	Stronger	Weaker
Climate				
Organization of Work	2/36	.06	1	0
Communication Flow	0/36	.00	0	0
Emphasis on People	1/36	.03	1	0
Decision-Making Practices	0/36	.00	0	0
Influence and Control	1/36	.03	0	0
		$\overline{X}$ .02	Totals 2	0
Context				
Absence of Bureaucracy	10/18*	.56	4	0
Coordination	4/18	.22	0	0
Job Challenge	15/18	.83	9	0
Job Reward	13/18	.72	7	0
Job Clarity	2/18	.11	1	0
		$\overline{X}$ .47	Totals 21	0
Supervisory Leadership				
Supervisory Support	3/36	.08	0	0
Supervisory Team Building	17/36	.47	17	0
Supervisory Goal Emphasis	11/36	.30	11	0
Supervisory Work Facilitation	15/36	.42	15	0
		$\overline{X}$ .32	Totals 43	0
Peer Leadership				
Peer Support	15/36	.42	14	0
Peer Team Building	12/36	.33	4	0
Peer Goal Emphasis	1/36	.03	1	0
Peer Work Facilitation	13/16	.36	7	0
		$\overline{X}$ .28	Totals 26	0
Outcomes				
Group Functioning	7/36	.19	5†	0
Satisfaction	10/36	.28	12	0
Goal Integration	4/18	.22	1	0
		$\overline{X}$ .23	Totals 18	0

*This set of indexes only had performance measures available for years 0 through 2 of the study. Thus, the total number of correlations which could be compared was 18.
†Also includes differences where a correlation not significant at the 0.25 level in the overall sample became significant in the reduced sample.

sample and the reduced sample were compared. By the same token, 2 percent (0.02) of the correlations for the climate domain as a whole were substantially different when the two samples were compared.

The final two columns make a further distinction among the "differences" noted in columns two and three. These two columns only include those correlations that were statistically significant at the 0.25 level to begin with, and had differences between the two samples that were greater than 0.10. This distinction was made in order to exclude those instances where the differences between the correlations from the two samples was greater than 0.10, but the correlations themselves were very small. Columns four and five divide these differences into those where the reduced sample correlation was stronger than the correlation in the overall sample, and those where the reduced sample correlation was weaker than the correlation in the overall sample.

The results of this analysis are quite clear: all differences are in the expected direction. The correlations that change when the poorest matches are excluded *increase*. This makes it quite clear that the poorest matches in the sample have not created a false positive result. In fact, the overall sample probably resulted in an *underestimation* of the "true relationship." Thus, if the data quality were better, the results would probably be somewhat stronger.

A second interesting result of these analyses is that the estimates of the impact of the climate variables on performance are distorted far less by the inclusion of poor matches than are the estimates for the other domains. Sampling theory (Kish 1965, 88) also makes this an expected outcome: fewer responses are needed to obtain an accurate estimate of a population characteristic when the phenomenon of interest is more homogeneous. Climate measures, since they refer to the entire organization, should elicit a more homogeneous response than leadership measures, which refer only to the immediate work group. This is true because all members of an organization share the same set of overall conditions, but may have quite different sets of supervisory or peer relations. Thus, when poorer quality samples from individual organizations are included in the analysis, the estimates of the impact of the climate variables, being the most homogeneous, deteriorate far less than do the estimates of less homogeneous characteristics such as context, leadership, or outcomes.

This brief test helps to provide a useful perspective on the findings presented in Chapter 4. The correlational findings do not seem to be strongly influenced by the quality of the survey data. In those cases where the quality of the data does appear to have an influence on the findings, the impact is to *reduce* the significance of the findings and underestimate the actual impact of culture on effectiveness. This finding suggests that the overall quantitative results of this study are, if anything, a bit conservative in their assertions. If the data were better, the findings would probably be stronger.

Analyzing the Effects of an Outlier

The analyses presented in Chapter 4 were also double-checked to make certain that the results could not be accounted for by outliers—a small number of extreme cases that have a strong influence on the summary statistics. The purpose for checking for outliers was the same as the checks for the effects of match quality—to avoid drawing premature conclusions from the results that were presented in Chapter 4. Several different types of analyses were done to assess the stability of the results. These tests pointed out that there was a clear outlier in the data: only one of the firms lost large amounts of money during the period of the study. As it turns out, this firm also had several other characteristics that do tend to have an influence on the overall results of the study.

The outlier's potential influence on the overall results can be clearly seen in the example in Figure D.1. This example shows one of the situations where an extreme score on a behavioral measure, in this case variance on the organization of work index, and an extreme score on the performance measure, return on investment, combine to give a result that strongly influences the observed correlation.

When the outlier case is removed and the data are reanalyzed, the negative correlation between variance and performance that was presented in Chapter 4 still appears, but the relationship is much weaker. With the total sample, the correlation between variance on the organization of work index and financial performance in years 0, $+1$, and $+2$ ranges between -0.50 and -0.80. When the outlier is removed, this correlation drops to -0.15 to -0.30.

This type of finding poses a dilemma. Throwing the outlier out of the analysis denies that it exists, but including it risks making some inaccurate generalizations. This section of Appendix D addresses this problem by asking three different questions.

1. What would the results look like without the outlier? Which findings are influenced by the outlier? Which findings are relatively unaffected?
2. What does the outlier itself tell us about the relationships among organizational culture, organizational behavior, and organizational effectiveness? What can be learned from looking at the outlier alone?

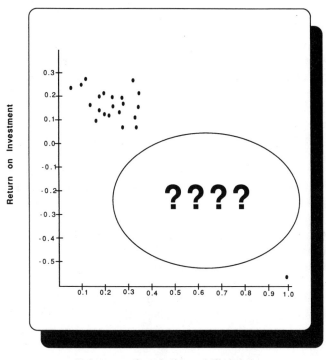

Figure D.1   Scatterplot with outlier

3. How representative is the sample? Are they a "typical" collection of firms with respect to the survey measures? Are they typical with respect to performance?

What Would the Results Look Like without the Outlier?   Answering this question involved redoing all the analyses, in an effort to isolate the statistical effects of the outlier. Both sets of results, with and without the outlier, are presented by Denison (1982), for those who wish to examine the differences in detail. The overall picture, however, is quite clear. The only findings presented in Chapter 4 that are altered significantly are the findings about the relationship between variance on the climate measures and performance. When the outlier is included, there is a strong negative correlation between variance and performance, but when the outlier is excluded it becomes a modest negative correlation.

This tempers the relationship and its interpretation somewhat, but does not remove it altogether.

Correlations between mean scores and performance are occasionally altered when the outlier is excluded, but these relationships are not affected to the same degree that the variance-performance correlations are. In most instances, the correlation may be reduced somewhat, but the basic form of the relationship does not change. One interesting influence that removing the outlier has is to change the slightly negative correlations that were reported for the relationship between decision-making practices and performance in years +1 and +2 to moderately positive correlations. This is because the worst year for performance for this outlier was year +2, and the firm then dropped out of the panel for years +3 through +5. This change also helps to temper some of the rather substantial changes in correlations between year +2 and +3 that are observed throughout the results in Chapter 4. In general, removing the outlier tends to smooth these relationships in a way that often makes the results more rather than less interpretable.

What Can Be Learned from Looking at the Outlier Itself? The outlier has three characteristics that should be noted. First, its performance over the period of time of the study is very low. Year 0 performance is low, but the company is still marginally profitable. In year +1, the firm loses money, and in year +2 it loses a lot of money. In years +3 to +5, the firm is no longer in the sample. In year +2, the firm's performance is in the lowest 2 percent of the sample of 556 firms used to standardize the data for analysis.

Second, although the mean scores for the survey indexes are often low, they are usually not extremely low. The one exception is that the members of this organization appear to have low ideals. When respondents are asked questions about their ideal preferences for leadership behaviors, they appear largely indifferent. Their responses vary a great deal across the organization, and the average of the group scores in this organization is mediocre at best. This is in contrast to a situation where most respondents readily endorse the ideals associated with the supervisory and peer leadership scales.

Third, as noted above in Figure D.1, the perceptions of organizational members about management practices and organizational conditions vary widely from group to group throughout the organization. There is little agreement as to how decisions are made, how work is organized, leadership styles, and so on. There is low consensus and, arguably, a weak organizational culture within this firm. The central values, beliefs, and principles of the organization, if they exist, do little to help guide and direct the actions and behaviors of the organization's members.

There is much that can be learned from firms that fail, and the results of this study would be all the more interesting if there were more firms that were losing money. The individual characteristics of the outlier firm help to inform the general theory of the relationship between organizational culture and effectiveness in a way that the more successful firms do not. A study where there was an even distribution of firms across the entire range of profitability would begin to help resolve this problem.

How Representative Is the Study Sample? The final check for the quality of the sample used in this study focuses on the *representativeness* of the study sample. This question was addressed in three separate ways. First, how does the study sample compare on the average scores for the survey indexes? Is the sample about average? Better than average? Since there is no "yardstick" by which the study sample could be compared with "all" organizations, or a representative cross section of organizations, this question was addressed by comparing the study sample with 114 firms in the Survey of Organizations archive.

Second, Figure D.1 shows that the outlier firm had a very high level of variance across groups within the company. How much of an outlier is it? Is this the least consistent firm ever studied using the survey? Only slightly abnormal? The second part of this section addresses this question by again comparing the study sample to the Survey of Organizations (SOO) archive.

Third, Figure D.1 also raises the question as to how unusual the outlier firm is with respect to performance, and how representative the sample is of typical performance patterns of a large sample of firms. This question is addressed by comparing the performance of the sample of firms used in this study with the much larger sample of firms used to standardize each of the study firms with respect to industry performance.

The results of the first step, comparing the study sample to the SOO archive as a whole, are presented in Figure D.2. This figure plots the grand mean for all of the firms in the study sample, plus the outlier firm, against the SOO norm for second-level supervisors. Plus or minus one standard deviation is also noted on the figure. This particular norm was chosen because it is the best approximation of the average norm for data from all hierarchical levels. Hierarchical norms are available for top management, middle management, second-line supervisors, and blue- and white-collar first-line supervisors. Choosing any particular norm for comparison with an entire organization (or a sample of organizations) is always somewhat problematic given that responses from higher levels are usually more positive and that any organization is usually a fairly unique mix of people from different levels.

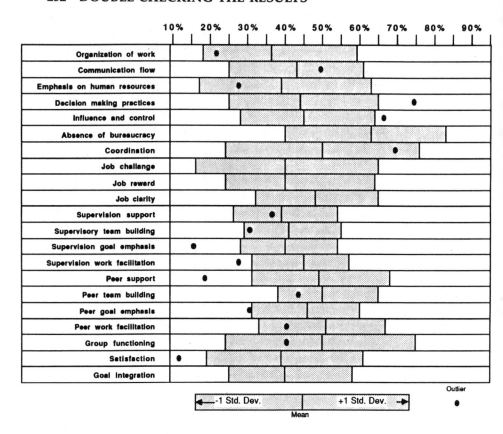

Figure D.2 Comparing the outlier to Survey of Organizations norms

This figure makes two points about the representativeness of the study sample. When compared to the archive as a whole, the study sample is average, or very slightly below. Nearly all of the percentile scores are between 40 and 60, with a couple of minor exceptions. Second, the outlier, while ranging widely in comparison with the norms, is not "off the scale." The outlier has a very interesting pattern of responses, showing both positive and negative features, but can hardly be said to be an "outlier" with respect to the archive as a whole.

The second step in this section compares the variance for firms in the study sample to the variance in the set of firms in the SOO archive. One hundred fourteen firms were used for comparison purposes, and the results, presented in Table D.2, compare the study sample, excluding the outlier, to the archive sample with respect to variance on one of the key indexes, organization of work.

Table D.2 Comparison of Within-Site Variance of Study Sample and Archive Sample (Outlier Excluded)

		<.05	.05–.10	.10–.15	.15–.20	.20–.25	.25–.30	.30–.35	.35–.40	.40–.45	.45–.50	.50–.55
							Site Variance					
Study Sample N = 17	%*	6	0	17	39	17	6	17	0	0	0	0
	N	1		3	6	3	1	3				
Archive Sample N = 114	%*	4	10	24	20	18	7	6	7	3	2	1
	N	4	11	27	23	20	8	7	8	3	2	1

*Percent of cases for each sample falling within specified variance range.

This table shows clearly that the study sample as a whole is quite representative of the archive with respect to variance. Variance on other indexes follows a similar pattern. What this table does not show, however, is the extreme variance of the outlier case with respect to the archive as well as the study sample. The variance of the outlier on the organization of work index is 1.02, which means that the variance is nearly twice as high as any other firm in the archive. This confirms that the outlier is an extremely inconsistent case, and that research that tried to locate firms which had extremely high variance in the archive and then match them with performance data would be unlikely to shed much light on the relationship between consistency and performance.

The final comparison in this section contrasts the study sample with the 556 firms that were originally used to standardize the performance data by industry. Performance data from all 20 years available from COMPUSTAT were used to provide a point of comparison for the study sample. These results are presented in Table D.3.

Table D.3 Comparison of Income/Investment Ratio for Study Sample and Industry Sample

Income/Investment	Study Sample		Industry Sample	
	N	%	N	%
1.00–2.00			3	.0
.75–1.00			1	.0
.50–.75			5	.0
.40–.50			15	.2
.35–.40			19	.2
.30–.35			46	.5
.25–.30	1	4.8	93	1.0
.20–.25	1	4.8	232	2.6
.15–.20	1	4.8	576	6.3
.10–.15	8	38.4	1,839	20.2
.05–.10	7	33.3	3,657	40.3
.00–.05	2	9.5	2,145	23.6
−.05–.00			192	2.1
−.10–.05			97	1.1
−.15–.10			55	.6
−.20–.15			23	.3
−.30–.20			31	.3
−.40–.30			15	.2
−.50–.40			11	.1
−.75–.50	1	4.8	15	.2
−1.00–.75			4	.0
−2.00–1.00			6	.0
−3.00–2.00			2	.0
< −5.00	—		1	.0
	21		9,083	

This shows that the study sample is quite similar to the larger comparison sample. In both samples, 60–70 percent of the firms had income/investment ratios that ranged between 5 percent and 15 percent. The point of difference for this comparison, once again, is the outlier firm; only 0.003 of the firms in the comparison sample had return ratios that were as low or lower than the outlier.

Even though the set of tests presented in this appendix have not "proven" that the results in Chapter 4 are correct, the additional tests have ruled out a large number of factors that might have led to spurious results and unwarranted conclusions. In an arena where proof and causality are extremely hard to come by, this type of support is a welcome and necessary backstop to the types of conclusions and interpretations presented in Chapter 4.

APPENDIX E

Case Methodology and Procedures

This appendix describes *how* the case studies presented in Chapter 6 through 10 were conducted. The appendix outlines a general approach which was common across each of the organizations and, perhaps more interesting, identifies the variations and different approaches that occurred with each of the firms. This section will be of primary interest to researchers who share a concern with conducting culture research and gaining access to interesting research sites.

As mentioned in Chapter 5, several research models have guided these case studies. These might be described as the ethnographic model (Rohlen 1974), the phenomenological model (Geertz 1973), the clinical model (Schein 1985), and the teaching case model. A brief discussion of these research traditions will help highlight the rationale for the approach taken in this book.

The *ethnographic* model typically attempts a complete understanding of a social organization. History, perspectives of various subgroupings, patterns of structure and interaction, functional adaptation to the natural environment, and symbolic meaning must all be incorporated. Months or even years of intimate contact and thorough description are prerequisites for good ethnography. The case studies in this book aspire to such a standard, but inevitably fall short. The fact that these cases stem from a comparative framework, are based on relatively short periods of contact, and were intended to be presented in a relatively short space placed limitations on these cases when viewed from the ethnographic perspective. Nonetheless, the attempt to provide a broad picture and to deal simultaneously with both functionalist and interpretive perspectives on social organization were clear guidelines derived from the ethnographic model.

The *phenomenological* model places greater emphasis on the understanding of meaning from the perspective of the individual social actor and an understanding of the symbolic expression and transmission of that meaning. It shares with the ethnographic method a concern with description, but is more likely to apply that description to an understanding of symbolic meaning, rather than an understanding of function, structure, and social roles. The cases in this book draw from the phenomenological approach in that the underlying assumptions and values are presumed to be the central structure that provides integration to the social organization. The underlying structure and its symbolic transmission is, in the end, a parsimonious way to understand the organization.

The *clinical* model shares some similarities with the previous two models, but takes a far more diagnostic perspective. This model is closest to the approach taken in this book, in that the case studies are often compared to a normative theoretical model. The clinical perspective has also influenced the approach taken in this study in another way. Rather than treat the interviews as "cases," on which parallel data were collected (a logic which is much closer to the use of the data in the quantitative part of the study), the clinical approach continually poses new questions as the process unfolds, and expands the picture accordingly. Asking parallel questions of each respondent and then adding up the responses might in some ways be more "efficient," but the clinical method allows a far greater flexibility of investigation and interpretation. The application of this approach is described in more detail below.

The last model that guided this research is the teaching case model. The teaching case model differs from the other approaches in that cases are written with a focus on a specific situation. In general, this model was probably the least influential of the four, but is relevant in that these cases attempt to highlight the specific issue of culture and effectiveness, albeit with a much broader background than in a teaching case.

These four perspectives have helped to place the approach used in these case studies in a broader context. Now the issues of case selection, organizational entry, and the common methodology are addressed.

Selection and Entry

The selection of organizations for case study is discussed at some length in Chapter 5. Since there were a relatively small number of firms that represented some of the categories in Figure 5.1, selecting a firm virtually required successful entry; there were very few backup firms that would fit the framework as well as the original five.

Thus, entry was not nearly as "neutral" a process as it is usually described in textbooks and training on organizational research. Because of this, formal training on organizational entry was of little help, and I eventually began contrasting the "classic" approach to organizational entry with the way things actually happened.

First, the classic approach. Most organizational researchers are trained that the "proper" way to gain organizational entry is to contact a manager, executive, or professional counterpart in the organization who may have an interest in the research and may be willing to help gain access. Then the researcher writes a proposal describing the research activities and rationale, usually in the language of scientific research and scholarship. The professional counterpart then passes this request up the organizational hierarchy to the appropriate levels for a decision.

Some form of this approach was taken with each organization. It usually failed. A story best describes some of the learning that occurred.

A colleague I had met in a professional association was a member of one of the organizations I had targeted for a case study. He agreed to have lunch and talk about ways in which he could help me with this research. After describing the research to him, I started asking questions about the organization. His response was that he could not be interviewed until the project was approved and so the best thing for me to do was to write a proposal and return it to him for review.

The brief proposal I wrote was quickly rejected. Good idea, but too much time, and they were too busy. Since I was reluctant to give up on this organization as a case study, I thought of two other approaches. I knew a manager who was retired, and found that groups of recent retirees met regularly on a social basis. By going to one of these meetings, I was able to find 25 willing interviewees who were able to tell lots of stories and provide background information.

I told this story to a friend who once worked for a regulatory agency that had dealt with the organization. He suggested I call someone he had once worked for in the agency but who now worked for the organization. This person suggested several executives in the company whom I should call. All responded quite openly to my calls and requests for interviews and information, and saw value in the work I was doing.

Two lessons in particular stand out from this story and others like it. First, there are as many ways to gain access to an organization as there are people in it, and probably more. Trying several at once with a description of the research designed to interest the company will usually work.

The second lesson is that the "models" that corporations have for dealing with journalists and consultants are generally quite a bit stronger than the "models" that they have for dealing with academic researchers. Firms have far more elaborate and frequent "transactions" with journalists and consultants than they do with academic researchers. Learning some of these norms can be a useful addition to classical research training. For example, having a completed draft of a case study, with a clear intention to publish it, helped me gain increased access to the top executives of four of the five firms. They did not question my right to publish what I had written about their organizations (even though I frequently reiterated my commitment to publish the cases disguising the organizations' names if that was their preference) and were quite willing to invest the time to ensure accuracy and to explain their side of the story. Nor did they necessarily expect more favorable treatment in return, and they greatly respected that each chapter would reflect my interpretations and conclusions. At times I felt that I was being dealt with like a journalist, but it was very effective in improving the quality of several of the cases.

Methods

Despite many differences in the case studies, a number of factors were the same for each case. Each entailed extensive background reading, including the popular press, annual reports, and other public records. There was a tremendous volume of material available on all of the companies, and for three of the companies (Texas Commerce Bancshares, Detroit Edison, and Procter & Gamble) one or more books had been written on their history, which provided invaluable insight and background.

The core of each case study relied on at least 25 personal interviews with a variety of managers from different levels and functions of each organization. Special attention was paid to interviewing both new and long-term members of each organization, and special effort was made to locate the "storytellers" who understood the history and liked to talk about their companies. The CEO or president as well as other top officers were interviewed in four of the five organizations. Attempts were also made to interview knowledgable outsiders: jounalists, consultants, and fellow academics who knew the organization well. Former employees were also an important source of perspective on all of the organizations.

As noted above, the approach taken within each firm derived from the clinical model in the sense that the questions and line of inquiry evolved as the case study progressed. Through this process, I developed some strong guidelines about how to "use" the redundancy that occurred as interviews were conducted. Although a core of basic questions were frequently asked,[1] a specific decision was made not to follow the survey research model in which *parallel* questions were asked of each individual, with summarization by counting and aggregation. Instead, interviews were used to test and develop an emerging picture of the organization with each successive interview. For example, some clear areas of overlap and redundancy (or conflict and inconsistency) usually began to emerge after interviewing five or six individuals in a firm. At this point, these results were summarized, and then served as a basis for the development of a new set of questions that were both broader and deeper. This process of summarizing and refocusing usually happened four or five times as common themes were probed more deeply and differences about the interpretation of these themes were explored. This approach also helped to uncover new, less common themes and perspectives.

Description of the Methods in Each Organization

Despite these general similarities, there were significant differences in each of the case studies. These differences often stemmed from my initial process of entry, the depth of my involvement with each organization, and the nature of the cooperation and interest within each firm. This section describes how I did research in each organization and the ways in which it may have influenced the case studies.

Medtronic. I first contacted Medtronic in late 1984 through a manager whom I met at a conference. He suggested that I contact the communications manager, who was receptive to the idea of a case study, and saw considerable overlap between the issues I wanted to pursue in my case study and Medtronic's needs to assess the vision that top leadership held of its future following a recent reorganization. After some discussion, Medtronic hired me as a consultant to interview essentially all the top managers, plus several of the board members. Nearly all these interviews were conducted jointly with the communications manager, who was extremely useful in interpreting and adding to each of the individ-

---

[1]Examples of frequently asked questions include queries regarding the core values of the organization, the "rites and rungs" of a career there, the differences between groups in power and prestige, the unique characteristics that distinguished the organization from others, the impact of the firm's history on its culture, and the perceived relationship between the organization's culture and its effectiveness.

ual interviews. In addition to top management, a number of other individuals were interviewed. In total, the perceptions of 30 to 35 individuals closely associated with the company, plus the considerable background material available on the company, formed the basis for the case study.

Two years later, after the case study had been written and the book was ready to be published, I asked Medtronic for a final review on the chapter. At that time, since significant changes had taken place in the organization, I was invited to return for a set of 5 to 10 interviews to make the case as current as possible. These interviews included several individuals whom I had previously interviewed as well as the new CEO and chairman.

People Express Airlines. My relationship with People Express Airlines was different from the other four companies. The airline was not a part of the quantitative study as originally formulated, but was added later after the quantitative measures necessary to compare it to the sample as a whole had been obtained. I did research at People Express from June 1981 until early 1986, mostly in collaboration with Richard Hackman of Yale and now Harvard University. The research was in two main areas: studies of groups and team development, and an annual organizational survey tracking the reactions of members of the organization to the innovative practices and current issues. Other writings on People Express include Cohen and Denison (1989) and Denison (1989a, 1989b).

Interviews at People Express were not specifically focused on culture and effectiveness, although given the ideological character of the organization the topic was generally unavoidable. The case study for People Express was written from project reports, field notes, earlier papers, and memory of the hundreds of vivid conversations on the topic of organizational culture. After this case was drafted and the book was nearing publication, the draft was reviewed by the past chairman and several others who knew the organization very well.

Detroit Edison. Two book-length descriptions of Detroit Edison (Miller 1957, 1971), public records, and local press coverage gave me a wealth of background material on the company. After several false starts, interviews were eventually conducted with approximately 25 past or current members of the organization, including the current president and a number of top executives. Several knowledgeable outsiders were also interviewed, including consultants and members of the Public Service Commission. The mix of interviews also helped in the understanding of what I found to be three different perspectives on the organization: Edison as a technical organization; Edison as a political organization; and Edison as a work environment amidst change in the turbulent 1970s. A different set of interviews could have perhaps led me in a different direction, but the continually recurring themes and the review of the completed drafts by members of the organization all helped to ensure an accurate portrayal.

Procter & Gamble. Only one of the five organizations, P&G, was not interested in being a case study for this book. After a few initial attempts at "formal" entry, I became aware of the large number of P&G alumni, nearly all of whom had strong bonds and strong opinions about the organization.

Two approaches were taken in order to develop this case using interviews with past members of the organization. The first of these techniques was a snowball sample. Once I began interviewing past members of the organization, whenever we focused on a topic that I wanted to know more about, I would ask if there was someone else that the interviewee would recommend I talk to about that topic. At the end of each interview, I would also ask for the names of other individuals whom I might interview. This approach generated an ever-expanding list of interviewees. The second approach to the problem of gaining interviews involved the use of a published directory of P&G alumni (Thomas 1987). In part this strategy developed because the quantitative data on P&G dated from the 1960s: I needed to get a retrospective picture of the culture during that period. From this list, a sample of 100 individuals, who were in the organization during the time of the quantitative study, were selected. A survey with a series of open-ended questions about P&G culture was mailed to each individual. Twenty-two were returned with detailed comments, and telephone interviews were conducted with five or six.

This combination of approaches helped produce a highly consistent picture of P&G, and one that was supported by the wealth of published information on the company. In addition, later research done for a case study at the University of Michigan (McLeod and Denison 1988) confirmed many of the themes that were most relevant to an understanding of the P&G of the sixties to early eighties.

The approach taken in the P&G case study had one major limitation, however, in that it focused heavily on the marketing and advertising organization. Since the quantitative data were drawn primarily from the manufacturing side, this created a less-than-desirable match between the case study and the quantitative data.

Texas Commerce Bancshares. Research for the case study on TCB began with a series of five interviews with former members of the organization, as well as with several academic researchers who had studied TCB. Several of these people suggested that I talk with Marshall Tyndall, executive vice-president of marketing, who might be willing to help arrange this research. When I did this, his reaction was generally positive, but approval was slow in coming. While waiting, I began writing a draft of the case based on background materials and interviews with past members of the organization.

Once this case was completed, it helped serve as a focus for my request and raised considerable interest both at TCB and at Chemical Bank of New York, TCB's partner in a recent merger. Before long, a meeting was arranged with the TCB chairman and the executive vice-presidents of marketing and human resources to review the draft chapter and to discuss the further interviewing that I wanted to do to complete the case. In total, approximately 25 personal interviews were conducted, including several individuals from Chemical Bank who had been involved in the merger. When coupled with the substantial background information available on TCB, this provided a solid basis for the case.

Conclusions

As should be apparent from this description, the case studies were conducted eclectically and opportunistically. Parallel sampling schemes and interviews perhaps could have improved the quality of the data, but would seem unlikely to have changed the cases greatly, since all of the material which appears in the cases is based on convergence from multiple sources. But it also seems quite likely that if the firms had been approached with a plan for parallel data collection, which included all the "trappings of rigor," much of the interviewing that I did do might have been precluded.

This observation leads to several suggestions. First, access and rigor may involve a trade-off. Requiring immediate rigor may lead to a quick rejection. Perhaps the best approach, even when rigor is required, is to move slowly. Do background research in detail first, so that any request for further access comes from a thorough understanding of the organization. Initial interviews should be exploratory and informal for two reasons: first, to build trust and legitimacy, and, second, to gain enough knowledge of the organization to begin asking more specific, parallel questions of a number of respondents. At this point, if desired, additional "rigor" may be designed into the research, as a part of the continual process of "summarization and refocusing" described above.

References

Abegglen, J. C., and Stalk, G., Jr. 1986. *Kaisha: The Japanese corporation.* New York: Basic Books.

Abernathy, W., and Hayes, R. 1980. Managing our way to economic decline. *Harvard Business Review* 58(4):67–77.

Aldrich, H. E. 1979. *Organizations and environments.* Englewood Cliffs, NJ: Prentice-Hall.

Argyris, C. 1964. *Integrating the individual and the organization.* New York: John Wiley & Sons.

Argyris, C. 1965. *Organization and innovation.* Homewood, IL: R. D. Irwin.

Argyris, C. 1980. *The inner contradictions of rigorous research.* New York: Academic Press.

Ash, P. 1954. The SRA employee inventory: A statistical analysis. *Personnel Psychology* 7:337–364.

Ashby, W. R. 1952. *Design for a brain.* New York: John Wiley & Sons.

Baehr, M. E. 1954. A factorial study of the SRA employee inventory. *Personnel Psychology* 7:319–336.

Bales, R. F. 1958. Task roles and social roles in problem-solving groups. In E. E. Maccoby, T. M. Newcomb, and E. L. Hartley, *Readings in Social Psychology.* New York: Holt, Rinehart and Winston.

Barley, S., Meyer, G. W., and Gash, D. 1988. Cultures of culture: Academics, practitioners, and the pragmatics of normative control. *Administrative Science Quarterly* 33:24–60.

Barney, J. B., and Ouchi, W. G., eds. 1986. *Organizational economics.* San Francisco: Jossey-Bass.

Becker, G. 1964. *Human capital: A theoretical and empirical analysis, with special reference to education.* New York: Columbia University Press.

Beer, M., Eisenstat, R., and Spector, B. 1989. *The critical path: Developing the competitive organization.* Unpublished manuscript. Harvard Business School. Boston, MA.

Bennis, W. G., and Nanus, B. 1985. *Leaders: The strategies for taking charge.* New York: Harper and Row.

Berger, P., and Luckmann, T. 1966. *The social construction of reality: A treatise in the sociology of knowledge.* Garden City, NY: Doubleday.

Black, J. S., and Stephens, G. K. 1988. Two paradigms of organizational culture: A review of definitions, methods, and findings. Working paper, Graduate School of Management, University of California, Irvine.

Blau, P. M. 1957. Formal organization: Dimensions of analysis. *American Journal of Sociology* 63:58–69.

Blau, P. M. 1960. Structural effects. *American Sociological Review* 25:178–93.

Blumer, H. 1969. *Symbolic interactionism: Perspective and method.* Englewood Cliffs, NJ: Prentice-Hall.

Bowers, D. G. 1973. OD techniques and their results in 23 organizations: The Michigan ICL study. *Journal of Applied Behavioral Science* 9:21–43.

Bowers, D. G. 1975. *Navy manpower: Values, practices, and human resources requirements.* Ann Arbor: Institute for Social Research, University of Michigan.

Bowers, D. G. 1983. What would make 11,500 people quit their jobs? *Organizational Dynamics* 11(3):4–19.

Bowers, D. G., and Hausser, D. L. 1977. Work group types and intervention effects in organizational development. *Administrative Science Quarterly* 22:76–94.

Bowers, D. G., and Seashore, S. 1966. Predicting organizational effectiveness with a four-factor theory of leadership. *Administrative Science Quarterly* 11:238–63.

Brogden, H. E., and Taylor, E. 1950. The dollar criterion: Applying the cost accounting concept to criterion construction. *Personnel Psychology* 3:133–54.

Brummet, R. L., Flamholtz, E., and Pyle, W. C. 1968. Human resource management: A challenge for accountants. *The Accounting Review* 43:217–24.

Buckley, W. F. 1967. *Sociology and modern systems theory.* Englewood Cliffs, NJ: Prentice-Hall.

Buckley, W. F. 1968. Society as a complex adaptive system. In *Modern systems research for the behavioral scientist*, edited by W. F. Buckley, 490–513, Chicago: Aldine.

Buenger, W. L., and Pratt, J. A. 1986. *But also good business.* College Station: Texas A & M University Press.

Burke, W. (ed.), 1983. Organizational culture. *Organizational Dynamics.* 12(2):4–80.

Cameron, K., and Freeman, S. 1989. Cultural congruence, strength, and type: Relationships to effectiveness. Presentation to the Academy of Management annual convention, August 1989, Washington, DC.

Cameron, K. S. 1986a. A study of organizational effectiveness and its predictors. *Management Science* 32(1):87–112.

Cameron, K. S. 1986b. Effectiveness as paradox: Consensus and conflict in conceptions of organizational effectiveness. *Management Science* 32(5):539–53.

Cameron, K. S., and Whetten, D. A. 1983. *Organizational effectiveness. A comparison of multiple models.* New York: Academic Press.

Campbell, J., Dunnette, M. D., Lawler, E. E., and Weick, K. E. 1970. *Managerial behavior, performance, and effectiveness.* New York: McGraw-Hill.

Carroll, D. T. 1983. A disappointing search for excellence. *Harvard Business Review* 61(6) (Nov.-Dec.):78–88.

Cascio, W. 1982. *Costing human resources: The financial impact of behavior in organizations.* New York: Van Nostrand Reinhold.

Cascio, W. 1987. *Costing human resources: The financial impact of behavior in organizations.* Boston: PWS–Kent.

Cohen, S., and Denison, D. R. 1989. Flight attendant teams. In *Groups that work*, edited by J. R. Hackman. San Francisco: Jossey-Bass.

Cooley, C. H. 1922. *Human nature and the social order.* New York: Scribner.

Dachler, H. P., and Wilpert, B. 1978. Conceptual dimensions and boundaries of participation in organizations: A critical evaluation. *Administrative Science Quarterly* 23:1–39.

Daft, R. L. 1984. Symbols in organizations: A dual-content framework of analysis. In *Organizational symbolism*, edited by L. R. Pondy, P. J. Frost, G. Morgan, and T. Dandridge, 199–206. Greenwich, CT: JAI Press.

Davis, S. M. 1987. *Future perfect.* Reading, MA: Addison-Wesley.

Davis, J. A., Spaeth, J. L., and Huson, C. A. 1961. A technique for analyzing the effects of group composition. *American Sociological Review* 26:215–25.

Deal, T. A., and Kennedy, A. A. 1982. *Corporate culture.* Reading, MA: Addison-Wesley.

Denison, D. R. 1982. The climate, culture, and effectiveness of work organizations: A study of organizational behavior and financial performance. Ph.D. diss., University of Michigan.

Denison, D. R. 1984. Bringing corporate culture to the bottom line. *Organizational Dynamics* 13:5–22.

Denison, D. R. 1989a. The rise and fall of People Express Airlines: A case study in organizational culture and effectiveness. Working paper, University of Michigan.

Denison, D. R. 1989b. Airline maintenance control. In *Groups that work,* edited by J. R. Hackman. San Francisco: Jossey-Bass.

Drexler, J. A. 1977. Organizational climate: Its homogeneity within organizations. *Journal of Applied Psychology* 62:38–42.

Dyer, W. G., Jr. 1982. Patterns and assumptions: The keys to understanding organizational culture TR-ONR-7. *Office of Naval Research.* Arlington, VA.

Eliade, M. 1959. *Cosmos and history: The myth of the external return.* New York: Harper and Row.

Evan, W. 1968. A systems model of organizational climate. In *Organizational climate,* edited by R. Tagiuri and G. Litwin. Cambridge, MA: Harvard University Press.

Flamholtz, E. 1974. *Human resource accounting.* Encino, CA: Dickenson.

Flamholtz, E. 1985. *Human resource accounting.* 2d ed. San Francisco: Jossey-Bass.

Forehand, G. A. 1968. On the interaction of persons and organizations. In *Organizational climate,* edited by R. Tagiuri and G. Litwin. Cambridge, MA: Harvard University Press.

Forum Corporation. 1974. *Organizational climate and practices questionnaire.* Boston.

Franklin, J. L. 1973. *A path analytic approach to describing causal relationships among social-psychological factors in multi-level organizations.* Ph. D. diss., University of Michigan.

Franklin, J. L. 1975a. Down the organization: Influence processes across levels of hierarchy. *Administrative Science Quarterly* 20:153–64.

Franklin, J. L. 1975b. Relationships among four social-psychological aspects of organizations. *Administrative Science Quarterly* 20:422–33.

Frederickson, N. 1966. Some effects of organizational climates on administrative performance. *RM-66-21.* Princeton, NJ: Educational Testing Service.

Frost, P. J., Moore, L. F., Louis, M. L., Lundberg, C. C., and Martin, J., eds. 1985. *Organizational culture.* Beverly Hills, CA: Sage.

Garfinkel, H. 1967. *Studies in ethnomethodolgy.* Englewood Cliffs, NJ: Prentice-Hall.

Geertz, C. 1973. *The interpretation of cultures.* New York: Basic Books.

Georgopoulos, B. S. 1972. The hospital as an organization and problem solving system. In *Organizational research in health institutions,* edited by B. S. Georgopoulos. Ann Arbor, MI: Institute for Social Research.

Georgopoulos, B. S. 1986. *Organizational structure, problem solving, and effectiveness.* San Francisco, CA: Jossey-Bass.

Gibson, J. L., Ivancevich, J. M., and Donnelly, J. H. 1973. *Organizations: Structure, processes, behavior.* Dallas: Dallas Business Publications.

Giddens, A. 1979. *Central problems in social theory: Action, structure, and contradiction in social analysis.* Berkeley: University of California Press.

Gleick, J. 1988. Richard Feynman dead at 69; Leading theoretical physicist. *New York Times,* Feb. 17, p. 1.

Glick, W. H. 1988. Response: Organizations are not central tendencies: Shadowboxing in the dark, Round 2. *Academy of Management Review* 13(1):133–137.

Goodman, P. S., Pennings, J., and associates. 1977. *New perspectives on organizational effectiveness.* San Francisco: Jossey-Bass.

Gordon, G. G. 1985. The relationship of corporate culture to industry sector and corporate performance. In *Gaining control of the corporate culture,* edited by R. H. Kilman, M. J. Saxton, R. Serpa & Associates, 103–25. San Francisco: Jossey-Bass.

Guion, R. M. 1973. A note on organizational climate. *Organizational Behavior and Human Performance* 9:120–25.

Guttman, L. 1968. A general non-metric technique for finding the smallest coordinate spaces for a configuration of points. *Psychometrika* 33:469–506.

Hackman, J. R. 1984. The transition that never happened. In J. Kimberly and R. Quinn (eds.), *Managing Organizational Transitions.* Homewood, IL: Richard D. Irwin.

Halberstam, D. 1986. *The reckoning.* New York: William Morrow.

Halpin, A. W., and Croft, D. B. 1962. *The organizational climate of schools.* St. Louis: Washington University Press.

Hannan, M., and Freeman, J. 1977. The population ecology of organizations. *American Journal of Sociology* 82:929–64.

Hellriegel, D., and Slocum, J. W., Jr. 1974. Organizational climate: Measures, research and contingencies. *Academy of Management Journal* 17:255–80.

James, L. R. 1982a. Organizational climate: Another look at a potentially important construct. TR-ONR-IBR82-4. Washington; *Office of Naval Research*, Arlington, VA.

James, L. R. 1982b. Aggregation bias in estimates of perceptual agreement. *Journal of Applied Psychology* 76:214–24.

James, L. R., and Jones, A. P. 1974. Organizational climate: A review of theory and research. *Psychological Bulletin* 81:1096–1112.

James, L. R., Joyce, W. F., and Slocum, J. W. 1988. Comments: Organizations do not cognize. *Academy of Management Review* 13(1):129–132.

Jaques, E. 1951. *The changing culture of a factory.* New York: Dryden Press.

Jelinek, M., Smircich, L., and Hirsch, P. (eds.) Organizational culture. *Administrative Science Quarterly* 28(3):331–502.

Johanneson, R. F. 1976. Some problems in the measurement of organizational climate. *Organizational Behavior and Human Performance* 10:95–103.

Jones, M. O. 1988. How does folklore fit in? Paper, presented to the Academy of Management, August, Anaheim, CA.

Joyce, W. F., and Slocum, J. W. 1982. Climate discrepancy: Refining the concept of psychological and organizational climate. *Human Relations* 35:951–72.

Joyce, W. F., and Slocum, J. W. 1984. Collective climate: Agreement as a basis for defining aggregate climates in organizations. *Academy of Management Journal* 27(4):721–42.

Kahn, R. L., and Morse, N. C. 1951. The relationship of productivity to morale. *Journal of Social Issues* 7:8–17.

Kanter, R. M. 1983. *The change masters: Innovations for productivity in the American corporation.* New York: Simon and Schuster.

Katona, G. 1975. Why consumer attitudes matter more than economics. *Nation's Business* 63:34–36.

Katz, D., and Kahn, R. L. (1966, 1978). *The social psychology of organizations.* New York: John Wiley & Sons.

Kish, L. 1965. *Survey sampling.* New York: John Wiley & Sons.

Kluckhohn, C. 1951. The concept of culture. In *The policy sciences,* edited by D. Lerner and H. Lassell. Palo Alto, CA: Stanford University Press.

Knorr-Cetina, K., and Cicourel, A. V., eds. 1981. *Advances in social theory and methodology: Toward an integration of micro- and macro- sociologies.* London: Routledge and Kegan Paul.

Kuhn, T. S. 1970. *The structure of scientific revolutions.* Chicago: University of Chicago Press.

Lafollette, W. R., and Sims, H. P. 1975. Is satisfaction redundant with organizational climate? *Organizational Behavior and Human Performance* 13:257–78.

Lawler, E. E. 1977. The new plant revolution. *Organization Dynamics* 6(3):2–12.

Lawler, E. E. 1986. *High involvement management: Participative strategies for improving organizational performances.* San Francisco: Jossey-Bass.

Lawler, E. E., Hall, D. T., and Oldham, G. R. 1974. Organizational climate: Relationship to organizational structure, process, and performance. *Organizational Behavior and Human Performance* 11:139–55.

Lawrence, P. R., and Lorsch, J. W. 1967. *Organization and environment.* Cambridge, MA: Harvard Business School.

Levi-Strauss, C. 1963. *Structural anthropology.* Translated by C. Jacobson and B. Schoepf. New York: Basic Books.

Lewin, K. 1951. *Field theory in social science.* New York: Harper and Row.

Likert, R. L. 1961. *New patterns of management.* New York: McGraw-Hill.

Likert, R. L. 1967. *The human organization.* New York: McGraw-Hill.

Likert, R. L. 1973. Human resource accounting: Building and assessing productive organizations. *Personnel* 50:8–24.

Likert, R. L., and Bowers, D. G. 1969. Organizational theory and human resource accounting. *American Psychologist* 24:585–92.

Likert, R. L., and Bowers, D. G. 1973. Improving the accuracy of p/l reports by estimating the change in dollar value of the human organization. *Michigan Business Review* 25(2):15–24.

Likert, R. L., Bowers, D. G., and Norman, R. 1969. How to increase a firm's lead time in recognizing and dealing with problems of managing its human organization. *Michigan Business Review* 21(1):12–17.

Lingoes, J. C. 1973. *The Guttman-Lingoes non-metric program series.* Ann Arbor, MI: Mathesis Press.

Litwin, G. H., and Stringer, R. A., Jr. 1968. *Motivation and organizational climate.* Cambridge, MA: Harvard University Press.

Locke, E. 1968. Toward a theory of task performance and incentives. *Organizational Behavior and Human Performance:* 3:157–89.

Locke, E. A., and Schweiger, D. M. 1979. Participation in decision-making: One more look. *Research in Organizational Behavior* 1:265–339.

Locke, E. A., Schweiger, D. M., and Latham, G. P. 1986. Participation in decision making: When should it be used? *Organizational Dynamics* 14(3):65–79.

Louis, M. R. 1980. Surprise and sense making: What newcomers experience in entering unfamiliar organizational settings. *Administrative Science Quarterly* 25:226–50.

Louis, M. R. 1981. A cultural perspective in organizations: The need for and consequences of viewing organizations as culture-bearing milieux. *Human Systems Management* 2:246–58.

Love, B. 1967. People and profits: A bank case study. Master's thesis, Southwest School of Banking, Dallas.

Lundberg, C. 1985. On the feasibility of cultural intervention in organizations. In *Organizational culture,* edited by P. J. Frost, L. Moore, M. Louis, C. Lundberg, and J. Martin. Beverly Hills, CA: Sage.

McLeod, P. M., and Denison, D. R. 1988. Socialization and recruitment in brand management at Procter & Gamble. Case study. University of Michigan Business School.

McGregor, D. 1960. *The human side of enterprise.* New York: McGraw-Hill.

McKelvey, B. 1979. Comment on the biological analog in organizational science, on the occasion of Van de Ven's review of Aldrich. *Administrative Science Quarterly* 24:488–93.

Macy, B. A., and Mirvis, P. H. 1976. A methodology for assessment of quality of work life and organizational effectiveness in behavioral-economic times. *Administrative Science Quarterly* 21:212–26.

March, J. G., and Simon, H. A. 1958. *Organizations.* New York: John Wiley & Sons.

Marks, M., and Mirvis, P. H. 1986. The merger syndrome: When Corporate Cultures Clash. *Psychology Today,* Oct., 36–42.

Martin, J. 1981. A garbage can model of the psychological-research process. *American Behavioral Scientist* 25(2):131–51.

Martin, J. 1982a. Breaking up the mono-method monopolies in organizational research. Working paper, Stanford University Graduate School of Business Administration.

Martin, J. 1982b. Stories and scripts in organizational settings. In *Cognitive social psychology,* edited by A. Hastorf and A. Isen, 155–305. NY: Elsevier-North Holland.

Martin, J, and Powers, M. E. 1983. Truth or propaganda: The value of a good war story. In *Organizational symbolism,* edited by L. R. Pondy, P. J. Frost, G. Morgan, and T. C. Dandridge, 93–107. Greenwich, CT: JAI Press.

Martin, J., and Siehl, C. 1983. Organizational culture and counterculture: An uneasy symbiosis. *Organizational Dynamics* 12(2):52–64.

Martin, J., Feldman, M. S., Hatch, M. J., and Sitkin, S. B. 1983. The uniqueness paradox in organizational stories. *Administrative Science Quarterly* 28:438–53.

Martin, J., Sitkin, S. M., and Boehm, M. 1985. Founders and the elusiveness of cultural legacy. In *Organizational culture* edited by P. J. Frost, L. Moore, M. Louis, C. Lundberg, and J. Martin, 99–104. Beverly Hills, CA: Sage.

Mead, G. H. 1934. *Mind, self, and society.* Chicago: University of Chicago Press.

Miller, J. 1978. *Living systems.* New York: McGraw-Hill.

Miller, K. I., and Monge, P. R. 1986. Participation, satisfaction, and productivity: A meta-analytic review. *Academy of Management Review* 29:727–53.

Miller, R. C. 1957. *Kilowatts at work: A history of the Detroit Edison Company.* Detroit: Wayne State University Press.

Miller, R. C. 1971. *The force of energy: A business history of the Detroit Edison Company.* East Lansing: Michigan State University Press.

Mirvis, P. H., and Lawler, E. E. 1977. Measuring the financial impact of employee attitudes. *Journal of Applied Psychology* 62:1–8.

Mirvis, P. H., and Macy, B. 1976. Human resource accounting: A measurement perspective. *Academy of Management Review* 1:74–83.

Mirvis, P. H., and Marks, M., 1985. Merger syndrome: Stress and uncertainty. Part 1. *Mergers and Acquisitions* 20(2):50–55.

Mirvis, P. H., and Marks, M 1985. Merger syndrome: Management by crisis. Part 2. *Mergers and Acquisitions* 20(3):70–76.

Misumi, J. 1985. The behavioral science of leadership. English edition edited by Mark F. Peterson. Ann Arbor, MI: University of Michigan Press.

Mitroff, I. I. 1984. *Shareholders of the organizational mind.* San Francisco: Jossey-Bass.

Moch, M., and Seashore, S. 1981. How norms affect behaviors in and of corporations. In *Handbook of organizational design, Vol. 1.,* edited by P. Nystrom and W. Starbuck, 210–37. New York: Oxford University Press.

Mohr, L. B. 1982. *Explaining organizational behavior.* San Francisco: Jossey-Bass.

Morgan, G. 1986. *Images of organization.* Beverly Hills, CA: Sage.

Myers, M. S. and Flowers, V. S. A framework for measuring human assets. *California Management Review* 16(4):5–16.

O'Toole, J. J. 1985. *Vanguard management: Redesigning the corporate future.* Garden City, NY: Doubleday.

Ouchi, W. G. 1980. Markets, bureaucracies, and clans. *Administrative Science Quarterly* 25:129–41.

Ouchi, W. G. 1981. *Theory Z.* Reading, MA: Addison-Wesley.

Ouchi, W. G. 1983. Competitive advantage. Paper presented at the Michigan Business School.

Parsons, T. 1951. *The social system.* Glencoe, IL: Free Press.

Parsons, T., Bales, R. F., and Shils, E. A. 1953. *Working papers in the theory of action.* Glencoe, IL: Free Press.

Pascale, R. T. 1984. Fitting New Employees into the Company Culture. *Fortune,* May 28, 28–40.

Pascale, R. T. 1985. The paradox of "corporate culture": Reconciling ourselves to socialization. *California Management Review* 13(4):546–558.

Pascale, R. T., and Athos, A. G. 1981. *The art of Japanese management: Applications for American executives.* New York: Simon and Schuster.

Pascale, R. T., and Kaible, N. 1982. Recruitment and socialization at Procter & Gamble. Case study. Stanford University Business School.

Payne, R. L., and Pugh, D. S. 1976. Organizational structure and climate. In *Handbook of industrial and organizational psychology,* edited by M. D. Dunnette. Chicago: Rand McNally.

Payne, R. L., Fineman, S., and Wall, T. D. 1976. Organizational climate and job satisfaction: A conceptual synthesis. *Organizational Behavior and Human Performance* 16:45–62.

Pecorella, P. A., Bowers, D. G., Davenport, A. S., and Lapointe, J. B. 1978. *Forecasting performance in organizations: An application of current value human resource accounting.* Ann Arbor, MI: Institute for Social Research.

Pennings, J. M. 1982. *Organizational climate: Second generation research.* Presentation to the Academy of Management annual convention, August. New York, NY.

Peters, T. J., and Austin, N. 1985. *A passion for excellence.* New York: Random House.

Peters, T. J., and Waterman, R. H. 1982. *In search of excellence.* New York: Harper and Row.

Pettigrew, A. M. 1979. On studying organizational cultures. *Administrative Science Quarterly* 24:570–81.

Pfeffer, J. 1982. *Organizations and organization theory.* Marshfield, MA: Pitman.

Pfeffer, J., and Salancik, G. R. 1978. *The external control of organizations: A resource dependence perspective.* New York: Harper and Row.

Phillips, J. R., and Kennedy, A. A. 1980. *Shaping and managing shared values.* Staff paper, McKinsey and Co., New York, NY.

Pondy, L. R. 1983. Union of rationality and intuition in managerial action. In *The executive mind,* edited by S. Srvivastva, 169–91. San Francisco: Jossey-Bass.

Pondy, L. R., Frost, P. J., Morgan, G., and Dandridge, T. C. (eds.) 1983. *Organizational Symbolism.* Greenwich, CT: JAI Press.

Pritchett, P. 1987. *Making mergers work: A guide to managing mergers and acquisitions.* Homewood, IL: Dow Jones-Irwin.

Pritchard, R. D., and Karasick, B. W. 1973. The effects of organizational climate on managerial job performance and job satisfaction. *Organizational Behavior and Human Performance,* 9:126–46.

Quinn, R. E. 1988. *Beyond rational management.* San Francisco: Jossey-Bass.

Quinn, R. E., and Cameron, K. S. 1988. Paradox and transformation. In *Paradox and transformation,* edited by R. E. Quinn and K. S. Cameron. Cambridge, MA: Ballinger.

Quinn, R. E., and Rohrbaugh, J. 1983. A spatial model of effectiveness criteria: Towards a competing values approach to organization analysis. *Management Science* 29:363–77.

Reich, R. 1982. Industrial policy. *New Republic* 187:32–34.

Rohlen, T. 1974. *For harmony and strength: Japanese white-collar organization in anthropological perspective.* Berkeley: University of California Press.

Ross, G. H. B. 1980. Constituents, environmental turbulence and organizational effectiveness. Technical report, Institute for Social Research, Ann Arbor, MI.

Sathe, V. 1983. Implications of corporate culture: A manager's guide to action. *Organizational Dynamics* 12(2):4–23.

Schein, E. H. 1981. Does Japanese management style have a message for American managers? *Sloan Management Review* 23:55–68.

Schein, E. H. 1985. *Organizational culture and leadership.* San Francisco: Jossey-Bass.

Schisgall, O. 1981. *Eyes on tomorrow: The evolution of Procter & Gamble.* New York: Doubleday.

Schneider, B. 1972. Organizational climate: Individual preferences and organizational realities. *Journal of Applied Psychology* 56:211–17.

Schneider, B. 1975. Organizational climate: Individual preferences and organizational realities revisited. *Journal of Applied Psychology* 66:459–65.

Schneider, B. 1985. Organizational behavior. *Annual Review of Psychology* 36:573–611.

Schneider, B., and Snyder, R. A. 1975. Some relationships between job satisfaction and organizational climate. *Journal of Applied Psychology* 60:318–28.

Schwartz, H., and Davis, S. M. 1981. Matching corporate culture and business strategy. *Organizational Dynamics* 10:30–48.

Scott, R. W. 1977. Effectiveness of organizational effectiveness studies. In *New perspectives on organizational effectiveness,* edited by P. Goodman and J. M. Pennings. San Francisco: Jossey-Bass.

Seashore, S. E. 1954. *Cohesiveness in the industrial work group.* Ann Arbor, MI: Institute for Social Research.

Seashore, S. E. 1983. A framework for an integrated model of organizational effectiveness. In *Organizational effectiveness,* edited by K. S. Cameron and D. A. Whetten. New York: Academic Press.

Selznick, P., 1957. *Leadership in administration.* Evanston, IL.: Row, Peterson.

Siehl, C., and Martin, J. 1981. Learning organizational culture. Working paper, Stanford University Graduate School of Business.

Siehl, C., and Martin, J. 1982. The management of culture: The need for consistency and redundancy among cultural components. Paper presented at the annual meeting of the Academy of Management, Boston.

Siehl, C., and Martin, J. 1988. Organizational culture: A key to financial performance. In *Organizational culture and climate,* edited by B. Schneider forthcoming. San Francisco: Jossey-Bass.

Soloman, J. 1987. Investors' link at tight-lipped P&G, Ray Colton, plans to retire this month. *Wall Street Journal,* 10, 28.

Starbuck, W. H. 1971. *Organizational growth and development.* Baltimore: Penguin Books.

Starbuck, W. H. 1982. Congealing oil: Inventing ideologies to justify acting ideologies out. *Journal of Management Studies* 19:3–27.

Stogdill, R., 1974. *Handbook of Leadership.* New York: NY: The Free Press.

Stuart, A. 1979. Ben Love conquers all in Houston. *Fortune* 100(10):122–32.

Sutton, R. I., and Rafaeli, A. 1988. Untangling the relationship between displayed emotions and organizational sales: The case of convenience stores. *Academy of Management Journal* 31(3):461–87.

Tagiuri, R., and Litwin, G., eds. 1968. *Organizational climate: Explorations of a concept.* Boston: Division of Research, Harvard Business School.

Taylor, J. C., and Bowers, D. G. 1972. *Survey of organizations.* Ann Arbor: The University of Michigan.

Terkel, S., 1970. *Working.* New York: Pantheon Books.

Texas Commerce: Master of controls. 1984. *Dun's Business Monthly*, Dec., 40–41.

"They didn't listen to anybody," 1986. *Forbes:* December 15, 168–69.

Thomas, J. T. 1987. *The fifth annual Procter & Gamble marketing alumni directory.* Chicago: Wilkins and Thomas.

Thompson, J. D. 1967. *Organizations in action.* New York: McGraw-Hill.

Thorngate, W. 1976. "In general" vs. "it depends": Some comments on the Gergen-Schlenker debate. *Personality and Social Psychology Bulletin* 2:404–10.

Thurow, L. C. 1980. *The zero-sum society: Distribution and the possibilities for economic change.* New York: Basic Books.

Tichy, N. 1983. *Managing strategic change: Technical, political, and cultural dynamics.* New York: John Wiley & Sons.

Tichy, N. 1987. *The transformational leader.* New York: John Wiley & Sons.

Torbert, W. R. 1987. *Managing the corporate dream: Restructuring for long-term success.* Homewood, IL: Dow Jones-Irwin.

Trice, H. M., and Beyer, J. M. 1984. Studying organizational cultures through rites and ceremonials. *Academy of Management Review* 9:653–69.

Uttal, B. 1983. The corporate culture vultures. *Fortune* 108(7):66–77.

Van de Ven, A. H., and Ferry, D. L. 1980. *Measuring and assessing organizations.* New York: Wiley-Interscience.

Van de Ven, A. H., and Astley, W. G. 1981. Mapping the field to create a dynamic perspective on organization design and behavior. In *Perspectives on organization design and behavior*, edited by A. Van de Ven and W. F. Joyce, 427–68. New York: Wiley-Interscience.

Van Maanen, J. 1977. Experiencing organizations: Notes on the meaning of careers and socialization. In *Organizational careers: some new perspectives*, edited by J. Van Maanen. New York: John Wiley & Sons.

Vroom, V., and Yetton, P. 1973. *Leadership and decision making.* Pittsburgh: University of Pittsburgh Press.

Walton, R. E. 1972. How to counter alienation in the plant. *Harvard Business Review:* Nov.-Dec., 70–81.

Walton, R. E. 1977. Successful strategies for diffusing work innovations. *Journal of Contemporary Business:* Spring issue, 1–22.

Walton, R. E. 1980. Establishing and maintaining high commitment work systems. In *The organizational life cycle: Issues in the creation, transformation, and decline of organizations*, edited by R. J. Kimberly and R. H. Miles, 208–90. San Francisco: Jossey-Bass.

Walton, R. E. 1986. From control to commitment in the workplace. *Harvard Business Review* 63:76–84.

Walton, R. E. 1987. *Innovating to compete.* San Francisco: Jossey-Bass.

Weick, K. E. 1979. *The social psychology of organizing.* 2d ed. Reading, MA: Addison-Wesley.

Weick, K. E. 1985. Cosmos vs. chaos: Sense and nonsense in electronic contexts. *Organizational Dynamics* 14:51–64.

Weick, K. E. 1987. Organizational culture as a source of high reliability. *California Management Review* 29:112–27.

Welles, N. 1983. Is Love enough? *Banking,* March 115–16.

White, B. J. 1988. Accelerating quality improvement. Presentation to The Conference Board, Total Quality Performance Conference, New York, NY.

White, L. 1949. *The science of culture.* New York: Grove Press.

Whyte, W. H. 1951. *The organization man.* New York: Simon and Schuster.

Who's excellent now? 1984. *Business Week,* Nov. 5, 76–78.

Wilkins, A. 1978. Organizational stories as an expression of management philosophy: Implications for social control in organizations. Ph.D diss., Stanford University.

Wilkins, A., and Ouchi, W. G. 1983. Efficient cultures: Exploring the relationship between culture and organizational performance. *Administrative Science Quarterly* 28:468–81.

Williamson, O. 1975. *Markets and hierarchies: Analysis and antitrust implications: A study in the economics of internal organization.* New York: Free Press.

Williamson, O. E. and Ouchi, W. G. 1981. The markets and hierarchies perspective: Origins, implications, prospects. In A. Van de Ven and W. F. Joyce (eds.), *Perspectives on Organization Design and Behavior.* New York: John Wiley and Sons.

Woodman, R. W., and King, D. C. 1978. Organizational climate: Science or folklore? *Academy of Management Review* 3:816–26.

Young, R. 1988. Is population ecology a useful paradigm for the study of organizations? *American Journal of Sociology* 94(1):1–24.

Yuchtman, E., and Seashore, S. E. 1967. A system resource approach to organizational effectiveness. *American Sociological Review,* 32:891–903.

Zald, M. V., and Ash, R. 1966. Social movements in organizations: Growth, decay, and changes. *Social Forces* 77:327–41.

Index